From Cuenca to Queens

From Cuenca to Queens
An Anthropological Story of Transnational Migration

ANN MILES

 University of Texas Press, Austin

Requests for permission to reproduce material from this work
should be sent to Permissions, University of Texas Press, P.O. Box
7819, Austin, TX 78713-7819.

∞ The paper used in this book meets the minimum requirements
of ANSI/NISO Z39.48-1992 (R1997) (Permanence of Paper).

Library of Congress Cataloging-in-Publication Data

Miles, Ann (Ann M.)
From Cuenca to Queens : an anthropological story of transnational
migration / Ann Miles.
        p.   cm.
Includes bibliographical references and index.
ISBN 0-292-70205-1 (cloth : alk. paper)
ISBN 0-292-70171-3 (pbk. : alk. paper)
   1. Ecuadorian Americans—New York (State)—New York—
Social conditions.   2. Immigrants—New York (State)—
New York—Social conditions.   3. Ecuadorians—Migrations.
4. Transnationalism—Case studies.   5. Ethnology—Case studies.
6. Ecuador—Emigration and immigration—Case studies.
7. United States—Emigration and immigration—Case studies.
8. Queens (New York, N.Y.)—Social conditions.   9. Queens
(New York, N.Y.)—Biography.   10. Cuenca (Ecuador)—
Biography.   I. Title.
F128.9E28M55 2004
974.7'230046886—dc21   2003007700

Por Charo, para siempre

Contents

Illustrations

Acknowledgments

I met the Quitasacas in 1989, a time when we all seemed, at least to me, a good deal more innocent and naive. I was new to Ecuador and to doing fieldwork, and they were a young family just trying to make it in the big city. We all had such high hopes for the future. Over the years we have faced the joys and hardships that come with being human in a modern world. The Quitasacas have had (relatively speaking) far more hardship than joy. To them I owe more than I can ever repay and more than any acknowledgment can possibly convey. Good friends enrich your life, making you a better person than you might otherwise be. The Quitasacas are the very best of friends.

This book was a long time coming, and many others have helped me along the way. Among those whom I would like to thank are my teachers and mentors at Syracuse University. First and foremost I must thank Hans C. Buechler for his long-standing support, encouragement, and dedication. Hans is one of the most prolific anthropologists I know, and he is truly what a mentor ought to be. From the first paper I delivered at a professional meeting to the last one I gave a few months ago, I could count on Hans to be in the audience. From him I learned about the Andes, but also about the writing process and the ins and outs of being a professional anthropologist. Hans is an example to me, both personally and professionally, of how to do it right. I must also thank his wife, Judith-Maria Buechler, who is always free with advice, encouragement, and guidance. In the Department of Anthropology at Syracuse I also worked with and owe a debt of gratitude to Deborah Pellow, Susan Wadley, William Mangin, and Michael Freedman. Rebecca New and Alice Honig in the Early Childhood Development Program gave freely of their time and expertise. To all those kids in Toddler Room B in 1988, thanks for the lessons.

There are many people in Ecuador to whom I am indebted. Al Eyde of the Colegio Americano of Guayaquil helped me get settled in Guayaquil and provided me with access to the squatter settlements. In Cuenca I would like to thank the visionaries of Consulcentro, including Fernando Cordero (now the mayor of Cuenca) and most especially Jaime Astudillo Romero (now the rector of the Universidad de Cuenca), for their support and interest in my early work on migration. Indeed, it was Jaime who first encouraged me to study transnational migration in Cuenca, in part because he knew I interpreted things differently than he did. Our conversations were always exceedingly stimulating. Thanks also to my fellow anthropology students Patricio Carpio Benalcázar and Marco Freire for those long conversations about migration and Marxism. I am eternally grateful to Ana Luz Borrero Vega of the Universidad de Cuenca. Ana Luz is a remarkably kind woman and a dedicated scholar; although her academic training is in geography, she has the soul of an anthropologist. Her knowledge of local culture and scholarship is unequaled. Esha Clearfield, whom I met in 1999, generously shared her data and thoughts with me; Debbie Truhan was there when I needed her; and the door and the heart of Blanca Mendoza, that wonderful *conversona,* are always wide open. Finally, I owe a great deal to the intrepid Lynn Hirschkind, who has read and improved so much of my work over the years. Through her scholarly contributions and her assistance to others, Lynn has laid the cornerstone for anthropological work in Cuenca.

Many others have given me moral support or intellectual guidance — and a few have done both. Lauris McKee has helped me at several crucial junctures in my career, providing advice, support, and even emotional buttressing. Among those who have read my work on migration and families at various times and offered invaluable commentary are Janet Fitchen and Barbara Johnson. Many thanks are due to my dear friends and colleagues Kathleen Skoczen and Christina Harrison. Kathleen has long been my most constant reader, bravely wading through multiple drafts of countless papers over the years, and Christina and I shared exhilarating conversations about transnational migration as we drove around the Michigan countryside talking with Mexican farmworkers. Christina's optimism does me a world of good. In terms of this book, I am especially indebted and grateful to Susan Hamilton and Jason Pribilsky. Both Susan and Jason read very early drafts of the manuscript and provided me with sage advice and much-appreciated encouragement. I have relied on Jason for a second opinion on Ecuador and on Susan for her unfailing sense of what rings true. I would also like to acknowledge Art Desjardins, who, along with Rich McMullen, graciously took on the task of creating a map for the book. The reviewers for the University of Texas Press gave me much to think about, and the book is greatly improved because of their careful reading. Many, many thanks to Theresa May, the editor-in-chief at the University of Texas Press, who never wavered in her support for this project.

Western Michigan University has provided financial assistance over the past seven years and the time and space to complete this project. While the initial fieldwork was supported by a Shell Foundation Dissertation Research Award, two of the four subsequent trips were funded wholly or in part by Western Michigan University. In 1995 I received a Faculty Research Award and in 1997 a Presidential Award. The two chairs of the Department of Anthropology, first Robert Sundick and then Robert Ulin, encouraged my career progress and saw to it that I got the time to write. I also owe a great deal to the countless students I have had over the years. They have helped me learn how to explain things clearly and encouraged my writing with their curiosity.

Finally, I must thank my own families. My parents, Frank and Rose-Marie Miles, instilled in me a curiosity about the world and encouraged me to question everything, appreciate humility, find a profession I love, and work hard—a good set of lessons for an anthropologist or anyone else, for that matter. Thanks, Mom, for the countless letters you sent during those lean years when mail was all there was—some days it was just good to know that my mother loved me. During my first stay in Ecuador my sister Renie visited me, providing me with a beautiful collection of slides and photographs (some of which appear in this book); my other sister, Kitty, sweetened my life in Cuenca by sending care packages laced with licorice drops. Since 1993 my husband, Rich, has been my steady companion, unfailing supporter, and greatest champion. Rich has read every page of the manuscript several times, listened while I tried to work out problems, and held my hand when the going got rough. His generous spirit seems to know no limits. I am also grateful to my daughter, Isabel, whose cheerful playing brightened our time in Ecuador. Children's play can highlight "cultural difference" and then, in the blink of an eye, make it disappear.

Time Line of Important Events

Circa 1983 — Rosa and Lucho move permanently to Cuenca from Cumbe

Late 1987 — Rosa's brother Carlos migrates to New York

December 1988 — Ann arrives in Cuenca from Guayaquil

February 1989 — Ann meets Rosa and her family

September 1989 — Rosa and Lucho baptize their four youngest children; Ann becomes Alexandra's godmother

December 1989 — Ann leaves Cuenca

Circa January 1991 — Rosa's brother Miguel migrates to New York

Circa December 1992 — Rosa and Lucho purchase a taxi

June 1993 — Rosa and Lucho's youngest son, Billy, is born

June 1993 — Ann returns to Cuenca for two months to study ethnomedicine

June 1995 — Ann (with Rich and Isabel) returns to Cuenca for two months to study natural medicine stores

June 1995 — Billy is baptized; Rich and Ann become his godparents

October 1995 — Vicente migrates to New York

July 1997 — Ann visits Cuenca for two weeks

May 1999 — Ann and Rich visit Vicente on Staten Island before going to Ecuador for two months to interview the family about transnational migration

August 2000 — Ann visits Vicente in New York

October 2000 — Lucho arrives in New York

From Cuenca to Queens

1.1. *Vicente, the author, and her daughter, Isabel, in New York in August 2000. We are leaning against Vicente's car. Note the Ecuadorian flag in his hands.*

1 | *From Cuenca to Queens*
Transnational Lives

It had been a beautiful summer day in New York, so we decided to take one last picture outside in the sunshine. The photo was surely going to be sent to the family in Ecuador, so Vicente suggested that we pose in front of his new car. In the photograph Vicente is leaning against his car, looking relaxed and casual. He is wearing the Western Michigan University polo shirt that I had just brought him and a pair of baggy blue jeans. His lips show just a glimmer of a smile, but his eyes are completely obscured by his mirrored sunglasses. Nothing is revealed in the reflected glass — nothing at all. He has let the Ecuadorian flag in his hands slip down so that it is there to be noticed but is not central to the photograph. Even though it was Vicente's idea to hold the flag, its presence now looks like an afterthought. On the other side of me, with the irreverence that no Ecuadorian child can show, my daughter, Isabel, squints at the camera, sticking her tongue out.

When I looked at that photograph a month later back in Michigan, I imagined just what the family in Ecuador would notice and say about it: they'll mention, I thought, that Vicente is heavier but looks healthy and well. His siblings will all admire his sunglasses. Everyone will notice how nice his car is, and they'll comment on how big all the cars on that Brooklyn street are. They'll be surprised at the lush greenery of the park across the street — that's not part of their image of New York or of their experiences in Andean Ecuador. They'll probably call my Isabel a *majadera* — a smart aleck. Her pose in that picture surely confirms their impressions from last summer's visit that she is a little whipper-snapper. Someone — maybe Alexandra, the eldest daughter — will mention that she has never seen me wearing shorts before. No doubt the picture will be examined closely for several days and then finally placed in an important spot somewhere in the family's living room.

This book, much like that photograph, is about the construction of images, impressions, imaginings, and stories of transnational migration as it is experienced and understood by one Ecuadorian family. Vicente, the eldest son in this family, migrated to the United States in 1995 to look for work, leaving behind a country stagnating under the weight of political and economic turmoil and an unsure and saddened family. Among other concerns, they mourn Vicente's absence almost as they would a death, worry about him because he is undocumented in a foreign land, and wonder if he has changed in some deeply undesirable way. Even though his migration is a very singular and noteworthy event in that family's history, however, individual family members do not understand it in exactly the same way. While they all miss Vicente and are affected by his emigration, their personal experiences vary considerably. This book attempts to capture these different points of view.

I have known the Quitasaca family for about twelve years, and I first met Vicente when he was a boy of fourteen. Although I knew back then that he was interested in all things North American, I could not predict where this interest would take him or his family. Over the years immigration to the United States from Ecuador has become increasingly common; but because of the distances that it entails and the expense and danger of the journey, it is never taken lightly. Ecuadorians do not move back and forth across the U.S. border in the same way that Mexicans often do. Once an Ecuadorian arrives in the United States, it frequently takes years to summon the courage and save the money to make a visit back to Ecuador. Many come to the United States *andando por la pampa* (literally, walking across the plains), which means taking an airplane as far as Panama and seeking overland transportation from there, usually with the help of *coyotes* (guides). It takes plenty of motivation to take that arduous, months-long journey more than once. Transnational migration to the United States from Ecuador often means, as it has for the Quitasacas, years of separation.

I explore here the global and local issues that provoke emigration from Ecuador and one family's ambivalent feelings toward the circumstances that make emigration appear to be the most sensible option. In the 1980s, the Quitasacas moved from a rural town to Cuenca, the third largest city in Ecuador, for economic advancement; yet they never seem to get ahead. Sometimes it seems to them that transnational migration is the only choice. Moreover, loss of their favored son and brother under these circumstances has set in motion a series of shifts in family relationships and brought to the fore emotions that have provoked them to think about their lives in new and sometimes troubling ways. The emotional responses to transnational migration move freely and fluidly between feelings of desire, fear, anger, sadness, elation, loss, regret, and resignation. Often what the family members imagine for Vicente is far better or far worse than the reality of his life; yet these visions are often most prominent in their thoughts and therefore become the basis for actions and responses.

Most migrants, like Vicente, leave for reasons that are both individual and familial. Vicente always wanted to live in the United States, in part because it signaled a shift in social identity and status that he so badly sought. U.S. migrants have money and cosmopolitan experiences that make them people of substance — at least among their peers. The United States is associated with modernity and money, powerful currencies in a country like Ecuador, where "tradition" has long been a means for perpetuating largely uncontested social and economic differentiation. When people are relegated to the margins of society, as Vicente and his family are, the seemingly endless opportunities for employment in the United States are very alluring. Vicente left to improve not only his own prospects but also those of his family. As the eldest son, he felt a responsibility to help his siblings finish school, to ease his parents' worries about their old age, and to save enough to start a business so that sometime in the future he could support a wife and children. Yet Vicente's conflicting roles as an individual seeking his fortune and as a responsible member of the family are a source of constant tension for all. His family worries that Vicente has fundamentally changed because of the unbridled consumerism and lax morality of the United States. Perhaps, as in the case of so many others, his character has been temporarily or even permanently "ruined" by so much exposure to North American ways. Perhaps, they think, he has forgotten his family.

Another transnational narrative is embedded in this book, however: the story of an anthropological relationship and the unfolding ethnographic process. The core chapters of this book are named for different individuals in the Quitasaca family, and each chapter highlights one person's story of Vicente's transnational experience. But this is also my story of how I came to know the members of the family and how I interpreted what I heard, saw, and experienced with them over twelve years. It is a narrative of multiple journeys across both physical and conceptual space. As an anthropologist and as a person, I grew during this period, and so

ɛnte and Alexandra (the eldest daughter
ιildren to young adults during this time.
ittle different because of the experience
ιcludes knowing one another. In the end
re of our connection to one another, but
ɔns of that connection more fully.
ɔns evolve through time; in an effort to
. ..–p ᴜ.ᴜɪ process to the reader, each of the core chapters is orga-
ɴɪᴢᴇ ᴅ ᴄʜ ᴏɴᴏʟᴏɢɪᴄᴀʟʟy. Εvery chapter begins with a description of the
individual and events taken from my field notes and diaries from my
first stay in Ecuador in 1988–1989 through my return visits in 1993, 1995,
1997, and 1999. Most of my visits with the family were extremely informal; while I occasionally had some specific questions I wanted to explore
with them, more often than not my "fieldwork" with them consisted of
hanging out and chatting about whatever came up. Contrary to the Quitasacas' suggestion, I have used pseudonyms for many of the individuals
described here.

One of my goals in the fieldwork sections is to highlight the process of ethnographic data collection and to demonstrate how small and
seemingly insignificant comments, everyday activities, and casual observations often form the foundation for cultural analysis. I have edited
these notes and added to them to make them readable, but I have not
altered their substance in any significant way. These notes reveal how
time and life experiences affect the individual, the family, and family
dynamics; how issues emerge and then sometimes fade in the family's
consciousness; and how I, as an occasional participant-observer in their
lives, describe what I learn. They tell how the larger conditions of social
and economic change affect the family, especially as the children mature
and consumer goods become more and more desirable if not accessible.
As I read my notes, I found that a certain process was unfolding within
the notebooks themselves, as descriptions slowly gave way to analysis.
I came to understand the meanings of transnational migration only by
thinking through ideas about family and gender roles, child rearing and
socialization, and social inequalities.

My relationship with each of the family members has been a bit different, which certainly affects what I learned about them. The chapter
on Rosa, Vicente's mother, is by far the longest and most detailed, because she is the family member with whom I have spent the most time
and have the closest relationship. Her chapter clearly reveals the challenges, joys, and ambivalence of anthropological relationships. While

Rosa and I have been good friends almost from the first, my relationship with her husband, Lucho, has changed considerably over time. When we first met, he joked continually with me — mostly, I imagined, out of sheer discomfort. There is little precedent in his world for male/female friendships; while I was his wife's "friend," I was unlike any of her other female companions. He had little experience in dealing with someone of my ambiguous social status — single, female, and foreign. As time passed and I became godmother first to Alexandra (their eldest daughter) then years later to Billy (their youngest child), Lucho began to treat me with considerably more respect, honesty, and even real affection.

While the first part of each chapter presents the family member through my eyes as I came to understand him or her over the years, these chapters end with the family members speaking directly about Vicente's migration and their own lives. These sections show how each individual responds to his migration and, more centrally, how it becomes a lens through which larger social processes are brought into focus. Alexandra, for example, is now the eldest child at home; but as a girl she will never have a position in the family equal to Vicente's. Her narrative not only reveals her feelings about her brother's absence but teaches us about the ways in which gender roles and expectations have made her life distinctly different from her brother's. Vicente's migration has made Beto (his sixteen-year-old brother) think about his own sense of identity. Reflecting on his understanding of what it means to be Ecuadorian with me brought forth tears of anger at the racism he faces in school and even at home. When he says, "I am a *moreno* [dark skinned person] with an Indian name," it is both an embittered explanation of his life circumstances and a powerful cry of resistance against a social system that generally excludes him.

The Quitasacas live in a country that has faced a series of crises in the past decade, leaving the nation politically unstable and economically crippled. Over the years I have watched the buying power of families diminish to the point where, in 1999, the economy was so depressed that families were making difficult choices over what they could eat and still afford to send their kids to school. Strikes and protests rocked the country that year, as the government suspended or reduced subsidies for rice, gasoline, and even health care. The Quitasacas also live in a city where access to basic opportunities is closely linked to family name and inherited connections. Their rural heritage and "Indian" name place them near the bottom of the social hierarchy, and there is very little there from which to make a living. Yet, while a certain easily understandable hopelessness pervaded many of their conversations with me, the family (especially the younger generation) also expressed a remarkable degree of resiliency. Both Alexandra and Beto offer stinging critiques of the social, political, and economic conditions facing them; but they also discuss the importance of having personal goals and working to achieve something meaningful in their lives. Their parents, calloused by a lifetime of dashed expectations, are somewhat less optimistic.

My Anthropological Story

Most significant journeys—whether physical or intellectual—stretch across space and time and weave them together in unique and interesting ways. While writing a multisited ethnography obviously involves moving through physical space, what may be less obvious are the intellectual influences that subtly affect what an ethnographer "sees" and how it is interpreted. One of the intellectual influences on this work comes from an anthropologist, Oscar Lewis, who wrote primarily in the 1950s and 1960s. His most renowned work is *The Children of Sánchez: Autobiography of a Mexican Family*. This poignant family study was one of the first anthropological works to explore the notion that culture is experienced differently by different individuals in the same family. *The Children of Sánchez* is rich in ethnographic detail and shows us, with little intrusion by the anthropologist, how different members of a family understand, interpret, and enact their culture. Lewis believed that family studies offer rich terrain for anthropological inquiry, because it is through families living the realities of everyday life that larger cultural forms are revealed (Lewis 1959:3). His studies, especially *Children of Sánchez,* were very well received at the time of their publication; the book was even made into a major motion picture starring Anthony Quinn (Melhuus 1997).

While Lewis's work on family life history was generally praised in anthropology, he was also subject to much criticism within academia for his ideas concerning "the culture of poverty" (see Leeds 1971; Melhuus 1997). In *Children of Sánchez* Lewis argued that the poor in fact do have culture (something that was not taken as a given at the time) and that the culture of poverty is rational, persistent, and passed down from generation to generation (Lewis 1961:xxiv). The culture of poverty could be recognized by patterns such as higher death rates, low participation in national institutions (for example, labor unions and political parties), low educational levels, and higher rates of alcoholism and wife beating.

Lewis saw all of these traits as "attempts at local solutions for problems not met by existing institutions" or, in other words, a cultural adaptation to poverty that furthers survival (Lewis 1961 : xxvvi). He was very careful in defining the culture of poverty as existing within modern states, not "primitive" societies, because it is in states that gross and obvious inequalities of wealth are present (Lewis 1961). These theories were ultimately adopted by policymakers who interpreted the "culture" of the poor as something that was largely deviant and had to be eradicated in order to make economic progress (a position not really taken by Lewis himself).

Those who criticized Lewis, however, rightly noted several problems. First, the "culture of poverty" approach focuses too much attention on the behaviors of the poor, while ignoring the institutions and processes that create and maintain poverty. Second, it removes agency from the poor, painting a picture of people who can only react to social conditions, not create or alter them. Third, it focuses too much on finding broad, generalizable patterns across cultural contexts, thus obscuring the importance of subtle differences. In the last two decades the ideas expressed in these critiques have come to represent the foundations on which many modern ethnographies, including this one, are constructed.

Despite these criticisms, Lewis was a "compassionate ethnographer," as a recent reviewer called him, and his book clearly demonstrates a deep respect for those with whom he worked (Melhuus 1997). Because of his technique of juxtaposing narratives from various family members, male and female alike, his manuscript resonates with concerns about multiple voices, gender, class, and identity—issues that have become so important to recent social theory. While there are many differences between what I do here and what Lewis did forty years ago (including my focus on a single issue and concern with making the anthropological process transparent), I do borrow from him the idea that a single family can reveal much about the meanings of culture in individual lives.

While I may acknowledge an intellectual debt to Lewis, who wrote half a century ago, this book is also very much a product of its own intellectual times. Given anthropology's concerns in the past two decades with representation and authority (see Marcus and Cushman 1982; Clifford 1986, among many others), it is not surprising that I place myself much more obviously in this book than Lewis ever did in his. I enter the text not because I think the story is about me (or because I want it to be about me) but in order to highlight the ethnographic process. I do in fact tell the story—there is no way around that. I am the one who watched and listened to the Quitasacas for the last decade or so, who wrote down what I thought mattered, and who translated and edited their words. In the end the Quitasacas come to the reader through me and are reflected in the all too human relationships we formed. The second half of the title, "An Anthropological Story of Transnational Migration," is an acknowledgment of that inescapable anthropological reality (see Bruner 1986; McCarthy Brown 1991; Gelles and Martínez Escobar 1996, among many others).

The word "transnational" has become ubiquitous in the social sciences in the past decade or so, but it is often used without much explanation. One may rightly ask how transnational migration differs from international migration. I use "transnational" throughout this book because I think we need a term that goes beyond simply revealing that migrants are moving across international borders and that captures the dynamic nature of the transformations that occur because of it. Transnationalism, according to Nina Glick Schiller, Linda Basch, and Cristina Blanc-Szanton, is "the processes by which immigrants build social fields that link together their country of origin and their country of settlement" (Glick Schiller et al. 1992:1). In other words, transnational migration implies that migrants do not just leave one social setting to go to another: the very process of crossing borders creates new social and cultural patterns, ideas, and behaviors. Transnational migrants not only grapple with making sense of a different place but can also transform both the place and themselves through their actions. The term "transnationalism" draws attention to the connections between people and places—connections that extend well beyond obvious national borders (Glick Schiller et al. 1992: 1). Therefore, even though the Quitasacas are physically separated by distance, their lives remain deeply intertwined.

In addition to situating the Quitasacas in historical and structural contexts, I am also concerned with describing the changes that have occurred since I began going to Ecuador. We now live in a world with rapid telecommunications; but when I first went "to the field" in 1988, I found it difficult even to make a phone call to the United States. Few people I knew had telephones; sometimes I would be permitted to make a collect call in the central calling facility in the city and then, inexplicably, sometimes I would not. Fax machines were just coming out (although I didn't know what they did); and email, the Internet, and cybercafés did not exist. Mail took at least three weeks to get to me—and that was when the postal workers were not on strike. But don't get me wrong. I am not complaining about the isolation that Ecuador's poor communication system created, because in the long run I think that it made for much better fieldwork. I went to Rosa's house when I was lonely, not to my email. The Quitasacas had their own phone by 1995; when Alexandra needs to communicate with me quickly now, she goes into a downtown cybercafé, pays about one dollar U.S., and sends me an email. Ecuador just doesn't feel as far away as it did before.

Finally, while this book covers a certain period and attempts to tell a coherent if not entirely complete "story," the real story, of course, never really ends. Indeed, as I was writing this book in the late fall of 2000 I received a call from Vicente asking me to call Ecuador, because Rosa was quite ill. His details, as always, were sketchy. When I called, I found out that she had indeed been seriously ill but was on the mend after emergency surgery on her kidneys. I also learned that—after twelve years of thinking about it—Lucho had finally emigrated to New York. He went independently of Vicente, with the help of a friend. I am sure that his absence has altered yet again the emotional, economic, and personal lives of the family. In an ironic twist, with Rosa so ill, the eldest daughter, Alexandra (who was once thought to be a hopeless outcast), is now the de facto head of the family. So, while the family members' interviews end here while Lucho is still contemplating the decision to emigrate— freezing a moment as that photograph did—in the real world the story continues.

2.1. *Vicente at work in a restaurant in New York City, circa 1996.*

Transnational Migration
Economies and Identities

Nothing works out exactly as planned when doing fieldwork. In fact, if I had followed my original research proposal, I would have worked not in Cuenca but in Ecuador's largest city, Guayaquil. Located on the coast, Guayaquil is a muggy, fast-paced, disorganized place with a large and growing population. My plan was to study the problems faced by families from the Andean highlands when they moved to the city's expansive squatter settlements. I had wrongly made the assumption that squatter settlements in Guayaquil would resemble those in Lima, Peru, which I had visited years earlier. Rural-to-urban migrants in Lima often form mutual-aid societies, and migrants from a single rural area live in the same neighborhood and help one another (see Mangin 1974; Skar 1994). Not so in Guayaquil. In the "Guasmo" (as the neighborhood I lived in is called), migrants from the coast and the highlands live intermingled with one another, and finding highland families was difficult. Even when I did find them, they often worked from dawn to dusk in town and were rarely home. I spent countless hours walking the dusty dry-season streets to reach an informant's home, only to find the doors locked and bolted when I got there. Eventually, however, I did become quite friendly with one family from the highlands. They talked to me endlessly of the beauty of the sierra (highlands) and encouraged me to visit Cuenca, where they had lived for many years. They also told me point-blank that they thought I, like most foreigners, would find Cuenca far more congenial than Guayaquil. Frustrated with my lack of progress in Guayaquil after three months, I took an exploratory trip to Cuenca in December. The rest, as they say, is history.

Since then I have made the journey between Guayaquil and Cuenca

innumerable times, and the bus ride always feels to me like a journey between two different worlds. On the first part of the trip the bus travels
inland from the flat coast, stopping at a number of good-sized towns.
Many of these towns, like La Troncal, are vibrant commercial centers
that grew up around the export of bananas. The bus windows are always
open on this portion of the trip, as the restless passengers look for a cooling breeze or try to buy some snack from an itinerant vendor in a noisy
town. The air is muggy and smells like fried food and over-ripe fruit.
Soon after the bus passes La Troncal and begins its ascent into the highlands of Cañar, the landscape changes dramatically. People shut the bus
windows one by one against the cool, musky, damp air and get sweaters and jackets out of their bags. A quiet like the cloudlike fog we are
passing through descends on the passengers, and many people drop off
to sleep. Banana plantations give way to scrubby pastures; and as the bus
travels through the misty fog, we can spot an occasional child or woman
shepherding goats or sheep. Many miles pass between lonely-looking,
isolated hamlets.

Invariably, at least in my memory, the sun shines as the bus makes
its final descent into the countryside surrounding Cuenca. The air is
redolent with the smell of eucalyptus, and the scraggly vegetation of the
plains is replaced by groves of trees, green fields of potatoes and corn,
and flowering ornamental bushes. I often have a visceral reaction of relief, if not joy, when the bus breaks out of the clouds and into this pictur-
esque landscape. I know that the noise, bustle, and hassles of Guayaquil
are safely behind me, as is the lonely *altiplano* (high plains). Although
Cuenca is a city of some size (having grown from an estimated population of 180,000 to over 400,000 people since 1988), it feels like a small
town. The city is still most vibrant in its central historical district, an
area of cobblestone streets, open-air markets, and colonial churches. In
1988 it would have been hard to guess from outward appearances that
the residents of this area were engaged in global processes only imagined
by the far more cosmopolitan Guayaquileños.

Although I came to Cuenca to study rural-to-urban migration, I was
soon convinced by local scholars to investigate transnational migration
to the United States. At the time, the rates of emigration from Cuenca
were increasing rapidly, which was interpreted as a serious social issue.
I was intrigued by transnational migration because so many of the rural-
to-urban families I was working with, like the Quitasacas, already had
relatives in New York. While the major focus of my research remained
issues of identity in relation to rural-to-urban migration, I decided that

this was an opportunity not to be missed and began to interview people about transnational migration as well. Eventually, I was introduced by a professor at the university to a rural community, Corpanche, just outside of Cuenca, where the rates of transnational migration were particularly high. Encouraged by local scholars, I concentrated my research efforts in this community. Little did I know at the time that this would lead to some of the most uncomfortable and stressful moments in my fieldwork.

Back in 1989 transnational migration from Ecuador was a topic that was not discussed easily or openly with strangers, especially North Americans. In Corpanche this meant that more than once I was asked if I was from the Central Intelligence Agency (CIA) or—by those better informed—the Immigration and Naturalization Service (INS). Sometimes during a conversation my informant would suddenly become frightened, and I imagined that she was afraid that she had said too much. If someone else stumbled upon our conversation, we would invariably change the subject. The clandestine nature of so much of the process of transnational migration—from securing loans and purchasing counterfeit visas to living illegally in the United States—produced a level of reticence and anxiety that I had not experienced when discussing any other topic.

Then the truly unforeseen happened. After I had spent several weeks in this town, an article on migration was published in a national magazine (*Vistazo,* July 20, 1989), highlighting Corpanche and a nearby community. The magazine used photographs of community members and portrayed Corpanche as a place where the women are immoral hussies and the men greedy fools. Even though I had nothing to do with that article, the community was (quite understandably) incensed by it and built roadblocks surrounding the town, effectively barring entrance to all outsiders, including me. Groups that were mobilized to patrol the community's borders threatened violence against anyone who dared to enter the town. Completely ruffled, I never returned to Corpanche. I did, however, continue to interview transnational migrant families in Cuenca. Although nothing as awful as banishment ever occurred again, I consistently found that my informants were hesitant to speak freely and openly. In 1989 the subject of transnational migration had to be approached extremely cautiously.

When I returned to Ecuador in 1993, everything had changed. The topic of transnational migration was on the tip of every tongue, and everyone wanted to discuss it with me. Given my problems with the subject four years earlier, I was surprised by the sudden openness. Of course, I was better known by people and perhaps was more trusted.

Still, that couldn't explain everything—even people I had never met before initiated conversations about migration. Something else was clearly going on. While I cannot say for sure what that was, I think that several factors combined to make the subject of transnational migration less emotionally charged and frightening. In the intervening years there had clearly been much more dialogue, both official and unofficial, about migration. Not only were people talking more to each other about it, but both local and international scholars had conducted numerous research projects, and the local media had covered the story many times over.

Indeed, the topic had reached such a level of familiarity in the popular consciousness that it could even be turned into parody. When I arrived in the summer of 1993, I found that a local musical group was getting a lot of radio air-time with its song "Cholo Boy." Using musical styles that ranged from rural Ecuadorian San Juanitos (folk songs) to New York rap, the song poked fun at the stereotypes of materialism associated with transnational migration to the United States. In a truly ironic twist, one of the band members was a North American sociologist who was studying transnational migration.

Probably most saliently, as more and more migrants made return visits home and reported on the conditions in the United States, it became clear to Ecuadorians that—despite rhetoric to the contrary and a few often-told tales of failed border crossings—the United States has made no real effort to detain or deport Ecuadorians. In fact, Ecuadorians, like many other undocumented immigrant groups in New York, move about freely and congregate openly in city parks to celebrate Ecuadorian holidays with music, dancing, and roasted guinea pigs. No one thought anymore that I was an INS operative. Indeed, often my informants were as interested in what I had to tell them about life in the United States as I was about what they could tell me about life in Ecuador. For many, talking to me about New York was the next best thing to being there and helped them to frame their loved ones' experiences.

At a time when transnational migration was becoming increasingly common, it was very clear that the state of the Ecuadorian economy was worsening. Not illogically, there seems to be a correlation between the condition of the Ecuadorian economy and the number of Ecuadorians emigrating from their country. As economic and political conditions deteriorate, the evidence (both official and unofficial) points to higher and higher rates of emigration. Because most of this migration is in fact illegal, it is almost impossible to obtain truly accurate statistics on the numbers of Ecuadorians living elsewhere. Estimates are that anywhere from 400,000 to 1 million Ecuadorians are living abroad, mainly in Europe, Canada, Venezuela, and the United States. This constitutes as much as 10 percent of the Ecuadorian population (Carpio 1992; Astudillo and Cordero 1990:23). It is not uncommon to hear educated Ecuadorians call New York City the "third Ecuadorian City" (Astudillo and Cordero 1990). In the early 1990s it was reported that Ecuadorians made up the largest group of undocumented immigrants in that city (Colloredo-Mansfield 1999). More recently, the U.S. Department of Justice (1996) estimated that there were 55,000 undocumented Ecuadorians in the United States, representing about 70 percent of all Ecuadorians in the United States (Jokisch 1997). Vicente, it seems, is in good company.

By 1999, when the Ecuadorian economy was by all measures in shambles, the issue of emigration was of acute national interest. The major newspapers in various regions of the country contained articles that speculated on the rates of emigration, what it meant for the future of Ecuador, and the conditions suffered by undocumented immigrants abroad. Of course, the assumption behind the connection between the economy and emigration that I have made here is that economic necessity, to some important degree, drives the processes of transnational migration (see Massey 1987).

While there is little doubt that migrants do seek to better their economic circumstances by leaving their own country, that fact is only a small piece of the transnational migration story. Migration, especially transnational migration, is not just about making a living or a better living; it involves complex negotiations on the individual, familial, and community levels about what really matters. Is a man being a good son or a bad one if he chooses to migrate? Can children be raised properly without the presence of an affectionate father? Does a migrant offer less or more to his family than a man who doesn't migrate? How does a woman who is thinking of migrating choose between her husband in the United States and her children in Ecuador? Does leaving mean that the migrant is giving up on Ecuador or simply earning investment capital for the future? What do migrants do with the money they make? To whom are they obligated? Whom can they trust? What constitutes a good life? How much money is enough money? What is real and what is only imagined about the migrant experience in the United States? Is the migrant a New Yorker or a Cuencano, an Ecuadorian or a Latino, a *cholo boy* or an *iony?*[1]

While the core chapters of this book discuss how these issues are articulated and negotiated by different members of one Ecuadorian family, this chapter explores these questions more broadly. First, I describe the political and social implications of Ecuador's historic inability to create a coherent and inclusive understanding of "Ecuadorian" identity; second, I describe the country's economic development. I look at these two areas in no small part because when I ask members of the Quitasaca family why people are migrating, their first response is invariably a commentary on the state of the Ecuadorian economy; and the second is an explanation of their perceived status within national and local society. "People like them" are leaving Ecuador because there are no jobs—there is no way to make a living. The Ecuadorian economy is troubled for complex and multiple reasons, but I argue here that many of the country's current problems are rooted in policies and practices linked to its historical and political articulations with the rest of the world. The roots of migration from Cuenca are deep, involving material and social conditions that span centuries, not just decades, as well as the intersection of global, national, and local processes.

As transnational migrants reshape the social and physical landscape of the city, multiple tensions and contradictions arise both for individuals and for communities. The second half of this chapter explores the concept of social identity in Cuenca. *Cholo boys* and *ionys* are stereotypes, no doubt, but they resonate in Cuencanos' understandings of individual and local identity and the longings that fuel so much migration. People often long for consumer goods, of course, but they also seek far less material and usually more elusive changes in social status, family position, or personal image (see Mills 1999). Given the entrenched class system of Cuenca, transnational migrants imagine that through their experiences in New York and their newly acquired consumption habits they can not only change the status of their families from poor to middle-class but also change themselves from *cholos* into cosmopolitans.

At one time the Quitasacas thought that education would provide the key to the success of their children, whereas now they think that going to the United States is the only way for Vicente to "do something" in life, as his mother said. The phrase "do something" is significant in that it implies both an economic and a social dimension to identity formation. No doubt these dimensions are interconnected, as an individual's abilities to purchase and consume are often interpreted as a key to perceived identity. Yet it is never that simple. As the core chapters of this book demonstrate, the making of identities through transnational migration is highly contested. While Vicente's mother struggles with the question of whether his basic character has been ruined, his sister worries that because he has no career he will always be a "nobody." In a transnational and global world where cultural borders overlap and where cultural and economic power is unequal, identity construction defies regularity and coherency (Marcus 1998:60).

Transnational processes ought to be considered from several vantage points that move between the local and the global, the personal and political, and the structural and the individual without resorting to making only causative claims (see Boyd 1989; Kearney 1986). For example, economic processes certainly influence individual decisions about migration; but they do not determine them or explain how they happen, how they are understood, and what they mean. Transnational migration from Cuenca has no single origin or uniform effect on individuals and communities, and it cannot be understood by models that analyze sending and receiving communities as distinct and unconnected entities (for more, see Hondagneu-Sotelo 1994). Rather, transnational migration concerns the intersections of time, place, people, and ideas and results in transformations that are not easily bounded. Indeed, the conversations I had with the Quitasacas taught me that discussions about transnational migration even within one family are multistranded and usually very ambiguous.

In the last two decades anthropologists have become increasingly interested in globalization and transnationalism, and this focus has changed how we think about the anthropological endeavor (see, among many others, Gupta and Ferguson 1997; Marcus 1998; Ong 1999). While it is more than obvious that "global" processes have always been occurring, the pace of the passages of people, goods, and ideas has intensified considerably in recent decades, changing the very nature of our world (Lomnitz 1994; Appadurai 1996). Anthropologists are attempting to de-territorialize their research and consider cultural and social processes as they transcend boundaries (Appadurai 1991:192). Cultures, like individuals, cannot be rooted to specific localities (Gupta and Ferguson 1997a:35), as Vicente's eating guinea pig on a sunny August day in Queens, New York, while his sister watches Madonna on television in Cuenca, surely tells us. Yet, in an effort to reveal the complexities of global interchanges, we cannot ignore the fact that differences in real power exist within and between the cultures engaged in these processes (Roseberry 1989). These power differentials are rooted in European colonialism, North American cultural imperialism (Roseberry 1989), and the spread of consumer culture that typifies late capitalism (Jameson 1984; Hebdige 1994). So it would be disingenuous of me to imply that Madonna and a roasted guinea pig enter the global scene with the same degree of cultural capital — they just don't. These power differences are not insignificant in the ways in which the cultural politics of migration unfold.

National Identity and Global Articulation: A View from Below

Vicente's wish to hold (but not too obviously) the Ecuadorian flag in the photograph that I described at the beginning of this book is rather symbolic of Ecuadorian feelings of national identity. Ecuador is a funny place. It is an Andean country, but it rarely identifies culturally with its neighbors and often sees itself as overshadowed by the more powerful nations that surround it. In fact, Peru (to the south) historically has been a very real threat to Ecuadorian national security, while Colombia (to the north) is popularly seen as being "culturally" better developed than Ecuador. Elites in Ecuador have told me many times about what is only semi-jokingly referred to as "Ecuador's national inferiority complex," which plays out in many ways. For example, foreign consumer products from lollipops to appliances are invariably considered superior to Ecuadorian ones, and Ecuadorian professionals seeking legitimation often brag about receiving their training "abroad." Throughout most of its history Ecuador has been plagued with an ill-defined sense of national identity, contributing to political instability and pronounced social inequality.

The roots of Ecuador's national ambivalence go very deep (see Becker 1992). Michael Handelsman notes that during the colonial period the region that is today Ecuador (then called Quito) was periodically reassigned to two different administrative districts, the Viceroyalty of Peru to the south and the Viceroyalty of Santa Fe de Bogotá to the north. Because of this, he argues, "the integrity of Quito as a fixed and unified place was fragmented," leading to frequent territorial disputes between the two administrative centers during the colonial and early Republican periods (Handelsman 2000:5). Indeed, Ecuador had serious threats to its territorial integrity throughout the twentieth century, with an on-again, off-again border war with Peru that ended only with the signing of a bilateral peace treaty in 1998. Because of the ambiguity and elusiveness of Ecuador's borders, Handelsman finds a certain irony in the name given to the country in 1830. He notes that the equator (for which Ecuador is, of course, named) is not a real line bifurcating the globe but only an imagined one — much like the country of Ecuador itself. Handelsman calls Ecuador a symbolic "imagined community," because it is a nation struggling to imbue itself with a distinct national identity in the face of countless obstacles.

One of the most difficult challenges for Ecuadorian nation-state development has been the intense geographic and political regionalism that has long characterized the country. Ecuador is composed of three distinct regions: the coast, the highlands or sierra, and the Amazonian lowlands or *oriente*. These areas not only are climatically distinct but more importantly have different relations of production, diverse ethnic groups, and ultimately different political orientations. Much of the political instability in the twentieth century was a result of regional antagonisms, particularly between the coast and sierra. The sierra, where Cuenca is located, is historically known for its conservative political and economic views; while the coast, which historically has had very different labor conditions (Striffler 2002), has been seen as more liberal politically. In a country with limited revenues, these tensions can often play out in the way money is allocated. For example, for much of the time that I was in Guayaquil there were insufficient funds to pay the salaries of municipal employees regularly. Understandably, city workers frequently resorted to work stoppages, and many services like garbage collection were halted. In the poorer sections of the city and around the municipal markets, bags of refuse and mountains of discarded fruits and vegetables rotted for days in the tropical sun.

A further difficulty for Ecuadorian nation-state development, and one that contributes to the country's identity politics, is the question of how to integrate the large indigenous populations into a unified national identity (see Whitten 1981; Salomon 1981). Indeed, this is a debate that began in the early Republican period and still has important political and social ramifications (Meisch 1992; Brysk 2000). The elites of Ecuador, as elsewhere in the new republics of South America, were essentially white people who claimed Spanish descent and who, Mary Crain (1990) argues, rejected any cultural alliances with indigenous populations. According to Crain, "Ecuadorian national identity was frequently modeled according to European patterns and its social orientation was towards the outside," especially Europe (Crain 1990:46). It was only in the 1960s and 1970s, after capitalist expansion into the countryside had already significantly altered indigenous practices, that the government attempted to integrate Ecuador's indigenous populations into a concept of national identity. However, these attempts, writes Crain, amounted to little more than "official nostalgia both for 'authenticity' and for an imaginary Indian of the past who no longer exists" (Crain 1990:56; see also Apolo 1995). It was not just a case of too little too late but of the elites' romantic ideal of an "indigenous" Ecuadorian that had long since passed.

In the 1970s Ecuador embarked on a national program to promote a unified concept of national identity and began a public campaign that defined national identity through the concept of the mestizo (mixed white and Indian). The idea of promoting a *mestizaje* identity was to subsume the social and cultural differences between races and ethnicities under a homogenized category that could include everyone (Stutzman 1981; Middleton 1981).[2] One of the hopes behind this public campaign was that by embracing a mestizo identity Ecuadorians could cast aside old barriers and work toward a more equitable society. Unfortunately, the cultural politics of the day resulted in little real change, and *mestizaje* really meant that the Indians would, or should, become more like "whites" rather than whites becoming more like "Indians" (Stutzman 1981).

In the 1990s, in a different global political landscape, Ecuador shifted its concept of national identity yet again, abandoning the "mestizo" label and its implied homogenization and adopting a pluri-ethnic position in which cultural and racial diversity were to be celebrated (Brysk 2000). The government began a series of public initiatives, including changes in school curriculums, to educate the nation about Ecuador's rich ethnic diversity (Meisch 1992). Despite the rhetoric, however, by all indications real ethnic integration has not occurred in Ecuador; the images of power and influence are invariably more white than brown or black and are often more closely oriented to European rather than indigenous cultural values (Rogers 1998). Indeed, wealthy Ecuadorians today are still much more likely to see themselves as more closely linked to the people of Miami than to those of the Amazon (Michel Poratais, quoted in Kyle 1995:71).

The Ecuadorian social scientist Marcelo Naranjo writes that there is a strong connection between Ecuador's "cultural dependency" on the west, its economic dependency on external markets, and internal social stratification (Naranjo 1981). Indeed, he concludes that Ecuador's participation in global economic and cultural processes has created and strengthened local patterns of social inequality. Since the colonial period the Ecuadorian economy has been and still is disproportionately oriented toward supplying commodities to external markets, while neglecting national needs, thus exacerbating extremes in income distribution. The top 20 percent of Ecuador's population in 1987 controlled over 50 percent of the wealth and the bottom 40 percent only 14.7 percent (Anderson 1997:235). Such unequal distribution of wealth is deeply problematic both socially and economically, as it limits the educational and occupational opportunities of large segments of the population. Indeed, the economic history of Ecuador is one of unpredictable booms and busts (starting with cacao at the turn of the twentieth century, bananas in the 1950s, and petroleum in the 1970s), and it highlights the vulnerability of a national economy based on commodity sales (Anderson 1997). This dependence on the external markets means that economic opportunities in Ecuador are always closely tied to consumer tastes generated elsewhere and that diversification of the economy is minimal. When market demand for a commodity evaporates, or when circumstances prevent Ecuador from supplying that commodity, the economy is crippled.

The current economic crisis that has caused so many to flee Ecuador has its origins in the short-lived oil boom of the 1970s. In an ironic twist, at the same time that Ecuador was profiting from this oil boom, it was also becoming increasingly indebted to foreign nations and banks. Anxious to modernize Ecuador's economy in the early 1970s, the government of General Guillermo Rodríguez Lara used oil revenues to increase state control over the economy by offering subsidies for goods and services and lowering taxes for businesses (Bocco 1990). This meant that more money was going out of public coffers while less money was coming in. When oil revenues fell, the government found itself forced to borrow money to complete its development obligations (Bocco 1990). By the mid-1980s Ecuador had a stagnant economy and a staggering debt burden. The government attempted to control inflation by devaluating the currency and invoking other austerity measures, such as removing subsidies for basic goods. These measures only slowed productivity and growth even further (Kyle 1995), and unemployment and underemployment rose considerably throughout the 1980s.

These conditions were exacerbated in the 1990s when a combination of national and global events continued the downward trend in the Ecuadorian economy (Larrea 1998). Among these events were a military confrontation with Peru in 1995, the El Niño floods of 1997, the decline in the worldwide price of crude oil to less than $10 U.S. a barrel, and the destabilization of international markets with the Asian economic crisis of 1997 (Hurtado 2002). Throughout this period Ecuador continued to borrow money from international lenders, so that by the end of the decade debt repayment became one of the most fundamental obstacles to economic growth (Hurtado 2002).

The economic and social costs of the debt burden had come home to roost by the 1990s, as Ecuador was pushed by international financial concerns like the International Monetary Fund to restructure its economy. In particular this means decreasing government subsidies for goods and services, including health and education, and a move toward privatization of many government-owned enterprises. Prices for basic products such as rice, cooking fuel, and gasoline—which were once heavily subsidized by the government—are now vulnerable to market fluctuations. The effects of structural readjustment have been severe, and Wendy Weiss (1997) argues that that they have disproportionately affected the poor. Prices of food and gas rose at the same time that wages remained stagnant and the currency was devalued, increasing overall levels of poverty.

By 1999 Ecuador's economy was in shambles, the insecurities felt by the poor were palpable, and little relief was in sight. Confidence in the government was critically low, and the national coffers were just about empty—a sign of the inability of the state to regulate banks, collect taxes from its citizenry, and convince foreign lenders of the country's solvency and political security and, most ominously, of the inevitable depletion of Ecuador's oil reserves. Government corruption was rampant, even at the highest levels. The poor resent the corruption of their government officials and the assistance that the government has given to failing banks. They see this as yet another signal that the government takes care of the wealthy first. Because of the financial crisis, public services have become increasingly ineffectual, sparking riots and demonstrations that have paralyzed the country several times. In 1999 it was not unusual to see several demonstrations a week in Cuenca, as one day the health workers and the next day the university students took to the streets demanding an end to privatization.

The bankrupt condition of the state meant not only that services were reduced but also that public employees—once the envy of others—were only sporadically paid. One informant that I have known for years, Carmela, is a public health nurse. When I met with her in June 1999, she told me that she had not received her salary for over three months. She was still going to work every day, but many others were not. According to Carmela, some government workers were so desperate that they were finding ways to make money illegally. Some of her colleagues working as health inspectors had taken to extorting money from the businesses they were charged with supervising. Moreover, since both Carmela and her retired husband had worked for the government (he had been a laborer

for the utilities company), they expected that through their social connections they would be able to find their twenty-year-old son a steady,
if not well-paid, government job. That was proving more difficult than
they had imagined; and for the first time since I had met this family,
the son was talking about migrating to the United States. By 1999 many
families in Cuenca made ends meet only because of the remittances sent
by loved ones in the United States and elsewhere.

Cuenca: The Athens of Ecuador

In 1998 an elegant coffee-table book was published by the city of Cuenca
(Aguilar 1998). The book is an effort to place "in one artistic volume"
a number of impressions about the city. It is filled with beautiful color
photographs accompanied by essays by some of Cuenca's most illustri-
ous scholars and artists. The photographs include pastoral rural scenes,
colorful pictorials of the numerous festivals that take place throughout
the year, and even some of the loveliest pictures of industrial production
that I have ever seen. I enjoy looking at the book tremendously, because
it portrays a way of life that seems effortlessly to combine the best of the
past and the present. Tradition is celebrated; the future is well in hand.
There is one photograph, however, that speaks volumes about what
lies under the surface. The picture appears among a number of others
illustrating the varied architecture within the city. The scene is the river-
bank that separates the *centro histórico* from the newer sections of the
city, and the caption reads: "The cliff-side: two architectural styles in
contrast" (Aguilar 1998:154). The picture shows an impressively well-
maintained colonial-era structure on one side and a "high-rise" of twelve
or fifteen floors constructed of glass and concrete on the other. The text
completely ignores the old woman wrapped in a blanket sitting on the
stairs leading down to the river. She is wearing a dirty "Panama hat,"
and her deeply wrinkled face is directly facing the camera—she does not
avert her gaze. Her toothless mouth hangs open plaintively, and her hand
is outstretched. She is begging. Her presence in the picture is not hard to
discern; on an eight- by ten-inch page she is fully two inches high. What
puzzles me about this photo is why the photographer did not return at
another time of day when she was not there—or perhaps give her a few
coins and ask her to move. I can only presume that in all the ways that
really matter this woman is invisible. She is not alone.
Cuencanos like to boast that their city is the "Athens of Ecuador," in

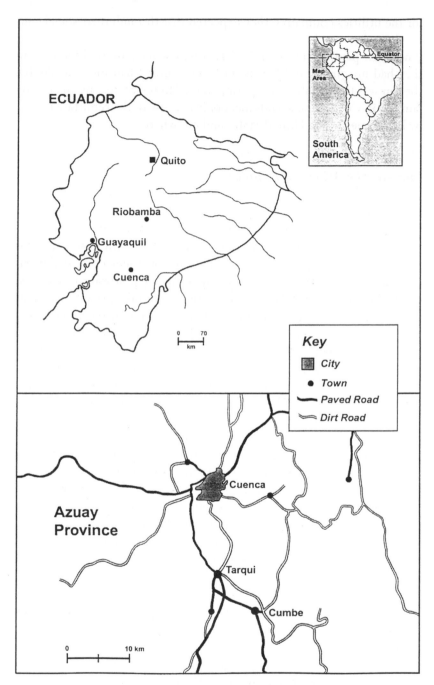

Map 2.1. Ecuador and Azuay Province, where Cuenca and Cumbe are located.
(Map designed by Art Desjardins with help from Richard McMullen)

part because of its temperate climate but also because of its rich intellectual, architectural, and artistic history. While Guayaquil is a bawdy port town and Quito a busy capital city, Cuenca cherishes its reputation for civility and "old world" (read: European) charm. Cuenca's downtown cobblestone streets wreak havoc on today's trucks and cars, but they are lovingly and painstakingly repaired rather than paved over. Cuenca has always been closely linked to the global marketplace, however, and its rural peasantry has a long history of adapting to changing local, national, and global interests (Palomeque 1990; Malo 1991). Because landholdings in this region were generally small and of relatively poor quality, the rural peasants of Azuay have always found it necessary to supplement their agricultural income—often through seasonal labor in other areas or industries or through artisan production. The products of this labor were generally oriented toward external markets.

The city has changed considerably in the twelve years that I have been working there. Mainly because of rural-to-urban migration, the city and its surrounding areas have grown considerably, and its suburbs now extend deep into the countryside. Drawing rural and urban boundaries is almost impossible. Transnational migrants are building new homes on the rural/urban borderlands—creating a unique kind of Ecuadorian urban sprawl where elegant two-story homes bump up against one-room adobe dwellings. Since the late 1990s, crime—or at least the perception of it—has increased, and many people tell me today that they no longer feel safe in Cuenca. Everyone has a story or two, true or not, of someone being robbed at gunpoint when coming out of a bank or a courier agency.

The Quitasacas moved to Cuenca from the small town of Cumbe in the 1980s so that Lucho would have a steady job, the children would get a good education, and the family would eventually reach a comfortable standard of living. While the faltering economy certainly figures in their perceived failure to accomplish this, the pervasive class structure embedded in Cuencan society contributes to making the family members feel truly impotent in their attempts to get ahead. Almost every conversation about transnational migration that I had with members of the Quitasaca family returned at some point to the ways in which social inequality circumscribes their lives.

Discussions of social inequality in Ecuador invariably turn on concepts of ethnicity and race, which are usually intermingled with notions of class. Norman Whitten notes that "ethnicity and class both interrelate and clash in modern Ecuador and boundaries between ethnic and class systems sometimes merge, sometimes rigidify, and sometimes dissolve" (Whitten 1981:17). Discussions of ethnicity and race in Cuenca usually center on cultural characteristics or social qualities rather than on membership in a particular group (in the case of ethnicity) or truly distinctive physiological traits (as might be the case for race). Indeed, social categories vary according to who is assigning them and when and the social purposes achieved by using one appellation or another. As Mary Weismantel (2001) indicates, the same term—such as *cholo(a)*—can serve to unite people or incite them to a violent clash. Therefore, I think it is not particularly useful to define static social categories, but it is crucial to explore the way they are used in particular contexts.

I learned about the situational nature of race/ethnic/class categories fairly early in my fieldwork in 1989 through my acquaintance with the husband of one of my informants, a man named Luis. Most days Luis could be found standing outside the building where he lives, talking to family and friends and watching the activities of the vendors on his busy street. Luis is skilled in the art of social bantering and spends his days pleasantly—joking with the market vendors and devising schemes for making money. His wife is the one who keeps the family afloat by selling food. Luis is not a rural-to-urban migrant but hails from a bustling rural town. I met several members of his family over the years and got the impression that Luis is a bit of a ne'er-do-well among his relatives. Most of them have a somewhat more middle-class lifestyle than he does. Luis is relatively tall (about five feet eight inches), his dark brown hair is slightly wavy, and he sports a lush moustache. His last name is a Spanish one. If I were to categorize Luis according to stereotypic racial categories, I would most obviously place him in the category of a mestizo. Not only would Luis object to this, however, but it would miss the point entirely.

Luis is a complex man who detests elite superiority and has a well-developed sense of class/racial consciousness. He speaks frequently of the exploitation of the poor by the elites, and one of his favorite topics for his pointed humor is the relationship between the rich and their maids. Calling all maids "María," a common name among the rural poor, he sarcastically imitates how the elites depend upon their maids: "María, oh María, come here and tuck me into bed . . . María, come quick and see if my bath water is hot enough . . . María, María, come and feed me." Luis takes great pleasure in these jokes and in turning the tables by infantilizing the elites.

When he spoke about himself, Luis identified himself as an Indian. "I am proud to have anyone call me an Indian," he told me more than once.

At first I did not know what to make of this, coming as it did from the informant least likely to "be" an Indian by all obvious markers. Herein lies the paradox of race/ethnic classifications. While I do not know if Luis calls himself an Indian to his peers, his pointed reference to me was not without its own meaning, regardless of what he calls himself at other times. I think that Luis identified as "Indian" when speaking to me, a "rich" and socially superior foreigner who in his perception must embody a core of the upper-class values and beliefs about social hierarchy, to usurp the power dynamics in the implicit status differences between us. In other words, by calling himself an Indian he is declaring (among other things) that he is not even going to play the game of trying to impress me with mestizo/middle-class pretensions and that he is painfully aware of the history of exploitation that race implies. His embrace of Indian identity is a political statement and a means of taking control of an unpredictable social relationship. By defiantly claiming he is an Indian, he preempts any judgments I might make about his poverty.

Similarly, in later chapters I explain, for example, why Rosa proudly referred to herself as a *chola* in 1989 but soon afterward abandoned the dress that identified her as such. Ultimately, the reader may notice that I never answer the question "What is the Quitasacas' race or ethnicity?" — because there is no appropriate answer to that question. Instead I explore how different family members talk about race, class, and ethnicity at different times and what that means.

In Cuenca there is a rigid and firmly established social hierarchy that is embedded in the very fabric of the social system and regional consciousness (see Brownrigg 1972; Hirschkind 1980). The elites of the city (most of whom can trace their lineages back to the Spanish invaders of the valley) have always considered themselves urbane city dwellers who have a cultured respect for the folkloric traditions of their area. Perhaps because of the historical relations of land tenancy in this region that led to *mestizaje* at an early stage, the relationship between rural and urban has generally been a harmonious one, although it is over-idealized by the upper classes (see Hirschkind 1980). The *cholos* — who are ideally associated with a rural lifestyle and a distinctive manner of dress — have long been admired for their perceived industriousness in contrast to the "Indians" elsewhere in Ecuador, who are traditionally scorned by the Hispanic urban society.[3] In particular, the elites of Cuenca have romanticized the *chola* Cuencana, with her swaying *pollera* (wide, pleated skirt), who stands as a symbol of that which makes the city unique and distinctly "Ecuadorian." Behind the professed respect, however, lie distrust and suspicion. As long as the *cholas* know their place, which is ideally in the rural areas producing crops and artisanry, they are viewed as important symbols of Cuenca's rich cultural heritage (Weismantel 2001). Once they begin to alter the social and physical landscape of the city in undesirable ways, their "*chola*-ness" becomes a burden and a barrier to employment, housing, education, and access to public services. The "folkloric" *chola*'s son turns into the grasping *cholo boy*.

Like many other places in Ecuador, Cuenca is deeply entrenched in a paternalistic tradition that emphasizes the importance of who you are and whom you know (McKee 1980; Stark 1981). Everything from registering children at a particular school to getting telephone service is more easily accomplished through *palanca* (literally, leverage). Those in the upper classes carry surnames that instantly bring respect, and they have dense networks of individuals that they can call upon for assistance. In contrast, those at the bottom of Cuencan society, like rural-to-urban migrants, are relatively bereft of *palanca*. For poor people in Cuenca, establishing influential networks is elusive. One of the most common ways to extend network connections is through godparent relationships, asking someone of significance to sponsor a child in baptism or some other ritual. Often, but not always, these relationships prove unsatisfactory.

Transnational migration is one obvious way of side-stepping the effects of a poor economy as well as the limitations imposed by a rigid social structure that impedes social mobility and relegates those without *palanca* to the social margins. Although the relative wealth and consumerism of transnational migrants and their families offer a jarring contrast to the elite image of Cuenca, they also provide a mechanism through which the marginalized can reconstruct their identity. While they indeed may never have the "right" name, skin tone, or social connections, they do have access to some economic leverage. Because this disrupts the elites' centuries-old hold on wealth—but no doubt also because it wrests control of cultural production away from them—the elites are often extremely disdainful of the money accrued by migrants. They consider the new homes built by migrants to be grotesque displays of conspicuous consumption and portray migrants in the popular media as victims of capitalist exploitation in the United States: they are ignorant peasants who have been blinded by the lure of earning dollars and do not really know what they are doing to themselves, their families, and, most distressingly, the cultural patrimony of Cuenca. In 1989 the wife of a transnational migrant who was living a very middle-class lifestyle in Cuenca complained to me that her daughter was shunned at school because she did not come from a "known" family.

Because social position is determined through social connections that may span centuries, transnational migrants may find that in the final analysis they cannot really alter the social hierarchy — at least as things now stand. The question is whether this will continue to be the case — and if so, for how long? As migrants continue to leave or return home, send money, and establish businesses, their effects on the economic landscape are not inconsiderable, especially in these dire economic times. When the national government and the municipality of Cuenca are literally bankrupt, the buying power of migrants cannot be dismissed. For example, in 1999, while the local newspaper in Cuenca reported a virtual depression in the local and national economy, Vicente's uncle (who had been in New York for fifteen years) spent tens of thousands of dollars in Cuenca, building a house and buying a new car.[4]

Whether the ability to buy consumer goods ever translates to real shifts in social standing, however, is far from clear and may be less important than understanding what buying power means to those who have newly acquired it (Featherstone 1995). For example, in discussing transnational migration and consumerism in Otavalo, an indigenous community in northern Ecuador, Rudi Colloredo-Mansfield (1999) notes that unequal participation in the consumer economy has led to increased divisions of wealth within these rural communities. It should be noted, however, that the Otavalan communities were originally far less stratified than Cuenca. Additionally, Colloredo-Mansfield writes that consumerism should also be examined to see how it leads to "cultural improvisation" (Colleredo-Mansfield 1999:29). In other words, consumption is also a means through which people interpret, express, and rework their culture. Cultural values and concepts of the "good life" are expressed and negotiated through particular choices made about consumer goods, while at the same time moral interpretations of these goods, those who have them, and those who don't are created and manipulated.

This, of course, is not an exclusively Ecuadorian tendency: North Americans also associate moral or social values with such things as clothing, houses, and cars. In the end, the cultural meanings of both old and new goods are — for better or worse — reevaluated and revalued (Colloredo-Mansfield 1999:47). This process can be dynamic, as new cultural forms are often created and expressed through the production and consumption of ever-changing consumer goods (see García Canclini

1993; Kearney 1996). This dynamism, as Colloredo-Mansfield notes, can also include a measure of loss or "destruction" when "in with the new" becomes "out with the old." While consumption per se is not the focus of this book, it is useful to look at the discourse surrounding consumption in Cuenca as a means to understand the processes of image and identity construction and transformation.

It is the notion of "loss" that resonates most clearly in the elite response to transnational migration in Cuenca. To the elites, transnational migration is synonymous with crass consumerism and is portrayed as leading to the destruction of traditional cultural values and to rampant immorality. They believe that migrants have traded family values and cultural continuity purely for material gain. Yet the inherent simplicity of the migrants and their families, so the cultural mythmaking goes, means that the values of the material goods are not really understood by those who purchase them; they are only empty symbols of conspicuous consumption.

While I heard this sentiment frequently in my conversations with middle- and upper-class Cuencanos, it was truly brought home to me in the national magazine article discussed at the beginning of this chapter (*Vistazo,* July 20, 1989). This reporter interviewed women in the same rural community where I was working; and no doubt he and I had been in some of the very same homes. His article describes palatial homes with unused indoor plumbing, stereo systems that no one knew how to use, and typewriters covered with rabbit and guinea pig droppings. Thus, he implies that the consumer goods have little use-value and are only important for their symbolic value. It is consumption gone amok. Furthermore, according to the author, a "mix of almost grotesque customs" (39) has emerged in the community as U.S. and Ecuadorian cultures blend. He is dismayed to report that children are now saying "okay" instead of "sí."

The article also panders to the worst stereotypes of migrant families by focusing on the sexual exploits and infidelity of local women whose lax morals he attributes to the absence of husbands. If that isn't shocking enough, he reports the dubious story of a woman who killed her illegitimate child before her husband returned home. Without the presence of a male "head of the household," women under the influence of rampant consumerism turn to illicit sex and murder. Finally, the author decries what he calls the developing "cult of illiteracy" (39) among migrant families. Mothers, he reports, are resistant to supporting education because they do not see the value of it. After all, teachers—who have so much education—earn little compared to a transnational migrant. What is the point of education when the road to material success is so clearly transnational migration?[5] These types of stories, which are far from true in most cases, are circulated by the elites and serve to perpetuate the popular cultural myth of the misguided peasant who, under the influence of North American–style consumerism, loses all perspective on what matters. Of course, this is not just an indictment of the local peasant but also of North American–style capitalism.

The other side of elite story-telling about the destructive nature of transnational migration is the frequently told tale of the failed migrant. This story, like the other, does have elements of truth; but I call it a "myth" or "story" because—as it is told and retold—details shift and alter so that in the end it becomes a parable. The general theme of these stories is how the migrants, or their families, suffer unmentionable emotional and financial distress when things don't work out.[6] In one scenario the migrant fails to reach the goal of entering the United States and falls victim to unscrupulous *coyotes* or bandits somewhere along the way. The migrant is usually left penniless somewhere in Central America and forced to ask already indebted relatives to borrow still more money. One particularly sinister version of this story describes how the migrant is told before leaving Cuenca to hide money in various places like toothpaste tubes or hems. The migrant is then robbed at every step of the way, with the thieves clearly informed ahead of time where the secret stashes of money are hidden. The toothpaste tubes are all taken in Nicaragua, the hems searched in Honduras, and so on until the migrant is left stranded and penniless in Mexico. The *Vistazo* reporter also tapped into the failed migrant myth by describing a particularly moralistic tale. According to the author, one miserable migrant took to drinking in the United States, was never able to save or send money home, and died in the midst of "the blue elephants of delirium tremors" (*Vistazo,* 39). His impoverished family had to sell all of their worldly goods to bring his body home for burial.

While the elites use transnational migration to expose North American capitalism, something that rightly figures prominently in Ecuadorian intellectual critiques of global inequality, the migrants and their families are much more ambivalent. In contrast to the elite image epitomized in the magazine article, the members of Vicente's family clearly value what money can buy but do not advocate consumerism at any cost. In fact, Vicente's most consistent admonition to his siblings is that they should finish school so that they will have more options and can stay in Ecuador.

It is even more telling to hear his siblings remark that, while Vicente only has a job in the United States, they have bigger goals and yearn to have a "career" with meaning and purpose. Vicente himself is not yet anxious to return to Ecuador and seems to be enjoying his American life. Yet he remembers too clearly the difficult periods when he first arrived and does not wish the loneliness he experienced on anyone. "Making something of oneself" in the United States has an emotional cost that must be weighed very seriously. The financial, emotional, and social costs of transnational migration are carefully and meticulously assessed by the Quitasacas and are discussed in terms that reflect various understandings of both gain and loss.

Cholo Boys *in an MTV World*

The nature and pace of globalization at the end of the twentieth century were clearly influenced by two fundamentally linked processes: the flow and development of capitalism and the intensification of communications networks and mass media (Appadurai 1996; Jameson 1998; Ong 1999). Transnational migrants generally move in relation to capital accumulation, so that in the 1990s poor Ecuadorians went to New York in search of employment with the intent (sometimes unrealized) of becoming participants in the transnational flow of capital back to Ecuador. Ironically, the postcolonial Ecuadorian model of development that benefited the elites created the very same conditions encouraging transnational migration that they find so deplorable. *Cholo boys* fundamentally disrupt the established economic and cultural order by buying into media-constructed images of an imagined consumer world and then acting on those images. They, in turn, become part of the process of image building as their newly acquired consumer goods become a means to renegotiate status and identity.

Over the years, I have seen many of these larger social processes play out in the daily lives of the Quitasacas. When I met the Quitasacas in 1989, their family was still relatively young, and they were hopeful about their future. The two eldest children were attending decent schools, Lucho was steadily employed as a poorly paid bus attendant, and Rosa supplemented their income by knitting sweaters at home. They frequently discussed options for earning more money by changing jobs or starting a new enterprise in the informal economy. While they wanted to take advantage of what the city could offer, they also worried about the social contexts in which they were raising their children. Neighbors in their dilapidated *conventillo* (tenement house) were considered strangers and were therefore suspect; and the children, especially the girls, were kept out of the "street" as much as possible because there were so many ways they could go astray. Rosa proudly wore the traditional *pollera* that identified her as a *chola,* although the children all wore modern clothing. The family owned a small black-and-white TV, and the children were keenly interested in the cartoons, soap operas, and reruns of *Starsky and Hutch* that dominated the airwaves.

As the years passed, Rosa especially made more and more concessions to the values of urban living; but she did not do this without a struggle. She was forced by economic troubles to allow the boys to tend a store to earn more money and by social pressures to adopt more Hispanic styles of dress and grooming. As the children grew and became more cognizant of social differences and how they are expressed in clothing and leisure-time activities, it became more difficult to provide them with what they wanted and to control their behavior and longings. Vicente and Alexandra's teenage years proved particularly troublesome, as they openly expressed anger at their parents for their poverty and the lack of opportunity it provided and what they interpreted as their parents' lack of urban sophistication. Anxious to appear modern and stylish, both Vicente and Alexandra have been frustrated about their inabilities to attend social events and buy new clothes. Desire always seemed to outpace their financial prospects. At some point everyone in the family realized that the parents' plan of achieving a middle-class lifestyle through hard work and respect for the dominant values will never be achieved. Furthermore, experience tells them that they live in a world of limited opportunity and are excluded in no small part because of their ethnicity. It is at this juncture that the illusion of the United States seems most compelling.

Doubly burdened by their ethnicity and their national economy, young, poor Cuencanos like Vicente yearn for the imagined life that they see on television and in the movies and hear that their friends and neighbors must be living in New York (see Appadurai 1996). Living in a nation that has historically defined progress in very "European" terms and that uniformly values foreign products and ways of life, Vicente from the time he was young was entranced by the images of U.S. lifestyles and technologies that he saw on television. And, like most of us when faced with mass-media images, he was sometimes unable to make the elusive distinction between reality and fantasy. So in 1989 he asked me questions such as: "Do most Americans walk around with miniature TVs on their wrists?" and "Do people have robots to clean their houses?"

Today the number of television channels in Cuenca has grown considerably; and while many of the programs are now originally produced in Spanish by mega-networks such as Univisión, the messages that are broadcast are primarily depictions of extravagant North American–style consumerism. Ricky Martin, the Puerto Rican pop star, may in fact be Latino; but his videos portray an over-the-top fantasy of North American consumerism (material and sexual) that is nonetheless interpreted as though it were real. The imagined world of television filled with fast cars and beautiful women is often understood, for better or worse, as the real world in which North Americans live, which is perhaps attainable through transnational migration. Because the "real" is virtually unknowable until one lives in New York, it is the image that seems to bear the most weight (see Baudrillard 1988). As Susan Bordo explains, for image-making in general, "it is the created image that has the hold on our most vibrant, immediate sense of what is, of what matters, of what we must pursue for ourselves" (1993 : 105).

For boys like Vicente, the identity images presented to him are hardly in competition with one another. On the one hand, there is the establishment image of the poor urban man (the one that the elites are comfortable with and would like to perpetuate), which is one of humility and hard work but with ultimately little reward. Limited in educational opportunities and bereft of *palanca,* the poor are confined to the bottom of the social system and are consigned to providing the needed labor and services to the elites. This image tells the poor *cholos* that they should not even hope for more than they have, a sentiment brought home to me when I read the phrase *La envidia te mata, cholito* (Envy kills you, little *cholo*) emblazoned above a driver's head on a crowded city bus. This construction is hardly an image that a young man whose head is filled with pictures of fantastic U.S. consumerism would find in any way appealing. Contrast that to the images of the cosmopolitan transnational migrant, who often sports the most modern clothing and styles and, most importantly, has a pocketful of money to use to set up a business that could make him financially independent. The fact that it takes migrants many years of sometimes brutal labor to achieve this is understood by most; but it usually becomes an afterthought, a small price to pay for the rewards that can be gleaned.

The family members left behind in Cuenca are perhaps the ones who are most aware of, and worried about, the price that may be paid for the financial success of the migrant. One of the most consistently articulated concerns is the veiled worry that their loved one will in fact turn into what is seen on television — someone consumed with style and money who has lost track of more important values. As desirable as North American consumerism may be, family members also offer very accurate and poignant critiques of the impact of U.S. capitalism on the "character" of their relatives. In the beginning they worry that the migrant will fall victim to loneliness and seek solace in alcohol, drugs, or risky sex. Later they wonder if the migrant will become taken with success and start to look down upon the family in Cuenca. The fear is always present that the migrant will adjust too well to North American life and no longer find the simple life in Cuenca, and the family responsibilities it invariably entails, in any way appealing.

The fears of family members are heightened by rumors such as those in *Vistazo* magazine but also by the stories of friends and neighbors whose sons or husbands seem to drift away when they go to the United States. In 1997 one family I know quite well begged me to look up their son who had left for the United States two years earlier. They were concerned because he contacted them only very sporadically, and they wondered if he was in some kind of trouble. I telephoned him numerous times when I returned to the United States, but he never returned my calls. Although he spoke to his family now and again, by 1999 he had severed all contacts with other Cuencanos in New York; his family was so worried about him that his 55-year-old mother was seriously contemplating going to the United States simply to find out what had happened to her son. The family worried that he was involved with drugs. My own suspicion, which I left unspoken, was that he was leading an openly gay lifestyle in New York — something he could never do in Cuenca.

Despite the fears of loved ones, for most migrants life in New York does not involve making radical changes in "character" or behavior but is a subtle and gradual process of adjustment and accommodation — one that usually takes several years. In the beginning phone calls to Ecuador are numerous and long, gifts and remittances are regular if not large, and plans for returning home are discussed with regularity. Over time this frequently changes. In fact, in Chapter 7 Vicente admits that — as time goes by and life in New York City becomes the daily norm — he is losing his strong emotional attachment to Ecuador. Now he can't be sure if he'll ever return there to live. Whether his father's presence in New York will reawaken his Ecuadorian sensibilities is yet to be seen.

3.1. Lucho and Rosa in the garden of her brother's house in 1999.

3 | *Family Matters*

There's a story about the devil that Rosa likes to tell her children. In the story there are two poor sisters. One marries a local man who drinks too much and isn't able to provide for his family. The other sister is unsympathetic to her sibling's unfortunate situation and brags that she will do better by marrying a rich man — one with gold teeth. One day while washing clothes in the river, the ambitious girl is surprised by the sudden arrival of a handsome man dressed in a white suit, with cowboy boots on his feet and gold caps on his teeth. She is dazzled by him. Right then and there he asks her to marry him, and she of course consents. On the day of the wedding, however, as the reception guests lie on the floor asleep from too much food and drink, the girl spies her groom transforming into a rat. She realizes then that she has just married the devil himself. With the help of an old witch and the timely use of some humble tools of women's work, such as a needle and thread that she uses to tie up her groom, she barely escapes the dire fate of being taken away by the devil. The now-chastened girl joins a convent, where she repents her selfishness and greed until the end of her days.

Rosa tells this story because it works on multiple levels to reinforce ideas about the moral order of life that are very important to her (Miles 1994). In particular, it highlights the value of good family relations at the same time that it warns of the threats to family unity that the blind pursuit of wealth can create. In this story, the greedy sister has clearly valued wealth, material comfort, and status over her relationship with her sister. She cruelly points out the difficulties of her sister's marriage and brags about her own better prospects. Such disregard for the feelings of one's siblings is a sign of obvious moral decay, since close sibling relationships are very highly valued in the Andes (Butler 1981; Allen 1988). By expressing a lack of sympathy for her sister and the desire to do her one better, the greedy woman exposes her moral laxity. It is not bad enough that the bride covets money and social status—she does so at the expense of her sister's feelings.

Embedded in this story is a symbolic critique of capitalism that I think is not insignificant. Consider for a moment the form that the devil takes here—something of a conglomerate of hegemonic images, including both local and international symbols of power and wealth. The gold teeth of the devil are a now largely outdated Ecuadorian affectation of wealth among the poorer classes, whereas the white suit is reminiscent of the Spanish/Hispanic plantation or hacienda owner—the traditional oppressor of the poor. The cowboy boots could reinforce the *hacendado* image or, perhaps, conjure up an entirely different one linked to U.S. economic and cultural imperialism. The Marlboro Man—that international symbol of U.S. cultural imposition—is now ubiquitous in Ecuador. Even the luggage carousel at the airport in Cuenca, often a visitor's first image of the city, is illuminated by the red glow of a Marlboro Man sign. Hence, the devil in this story is lurking in the very symbols of wealth that are, in and of themselves, so alluring and desirable.[1] The trick, it seems, is to figure out how to acquire the desirable without attracting the undesirable. One message from this story is that one way to accomplish this is to make sure that family obligations and relationships are not abandoned during the quest for wealth.

When I first heard this devil story in 1989, Vicente's transnational migration was on no one's mind. At the time I surmised that this tale helped Rosa teach her growing children moral lessons about how to live a good life in a modernizing city. This story, and others I heard like it, stressed the values of hard work and family responsibility and instilled a healthy skepticism toward the empty and usually unattainable symbols of wealth and influence. Through these stories Rosa was telling her children that the manifestations of wealth that are so valued in the urban setting (and so difficult for them to achieve) may in fact come at a cost that is far too high. Today, however, this story strikes me as just as appropriate as an allegory for transnational migration.

While transnational migration from Ecuador most obviously involves the movements of single individuals, migration is really about connections and connectedness. While these multiple connections start on the level of the family, they can and do extend across international boundaries and encompass a wide range of friends, acquaintances, and even unseen strangers. In this chapter I explore the linkages and bonds between transnational migrants and others in their families and communities and examine how gender roles and family position have an impact on transnational migration. The decision to migrate is rarely, if ever, contemplated by isolated individuals; it is usually part of complex family negotiations that take into account such factors as age, birth order, gender, and understanding of responsibility and duty to others (see Pessar 1982; Georges 1992; Chavez 1998). While the opportunity to engage in transnational migration is facilitated by the network of connections established through the years by Cuencanos moving between Ecuador and New York, it is usually an individual's family that ultimately makes the decisions and provides the wherewithal for a family member to leave.

Friends, Family, and Loan-Sharks

The celebration of the baptism of a child is a major event for a family. Billy's baptism at the age of two in 1995 was no exception. The ceremony took place in Cuenca, at the Church of San Blas, which is not far from the center of town. This is one of the older and simpler churches in town and is showing signs of neglect. Both its interior and exterior are badly in need of a paint job; its outer walls are chipped and deeply cracked. The baptismal ceremony was stiff and formal, and the priest gruffly rushed the proceedings along. When it was over, my husband and I were officially Billy's "co-parents." Calling on some of his taxi driver friends to provide transportation, Lucho then herded the guests into cars for the half-hour trip to their nearly abandoned house in Cumbe, where the real fun was to begin.

Cumbe is a small town about thirty-two kilometers south of Cuenca and is fairly typical of the towns in close proximity to the city. Over the years, as the rural population has grown, small towns like Cumbe have become increasingly integrated into the urban economy. Cumbe is a *parroquia* of Cuenca, which means that it comes under the administrative budget of the city. Cumbe has a population of about 5,000, one primary school, a technical high school, water service most mornings, and electricity twenty-four hours a day. Cumbe is today called a "bedroom community" of Cuenca—albeit one of the more distant ones. This does not mean, however, that Cumbe is like a North American suburb where the middle class goes to escape the pressures of city life. No one moves to Cumbe, and those who have lived there for generations are finding it more and more difficult to stay. Rosa's family is probably fairly typical in that her parents have always lived in Cumbe, making a living in agriculture. They have several fields scattered in the surrounding countryside where they grow corn, potatoes, and grasses for the guinea pigs and pasture cows. Because of the small size of their landholdings, however, none of their six children rely solely on agriculture. Indeed, by 1999 four had left Cumbe entirely: Rosa for Cuenca, and three brothers for New York. One brother remains in Cumbe, where he runs a small store, as does her sister, who commutes with her husband to Cuenca every day to work in a glass shop.

Despite the close ties between Cumbe and Cuenca, Cumbe still looks and feels like a rural town. Sundays are market days in Cumbe: the town plaza is filled with vendors of fruits and vegetables, a variety of plastic bowls and buckets, and inexpensive clothing. The town is best known, however, for its pigs. Located just off the Pan American Highway, Cumbe lures travelers to its central plaza with freshly roasted pig. On Sundays half a dozen women wearing *polleras* sit behind small tables where whole roasted pigs are displayed—the skin toasted to a golden hue and glistening with fat. The pig is slowly denuded of its crackling—served up in small portions with plenty of salt—and then the meat is fried into tasty morsels that can be eaten with the fingers. Busloads of travelers stop in Cumbe for a small bag of roasted pork to ease the boredom of the journey. On weekdays the town is a good deal quieter. Its one central street is virtually empty, because everyone is either out in the fields or off to Cuenca for work or school.

Rosa's unassuming house in Cumbe is fundamentally indistinguishable from those of her neighbors. The house is built of concrete and adobe and has only two rooms, with light bulbs dangling from the rafters in the ceiling. The rooms of the house are generally poorly lit, as there is only one small window at the front of each room. On the day of Billy's baptism, however, Rosa had festooned the uneven whitewashed walls with fluffy white, store-bought decorations. Chairs were placed around the room; and as guests arrived they worked their way around the circle, shaking hands and formally greeting those already seated. The room's occupants were a study in contrasts. In one corner sat friends and family members from Cumbe. The men wore straw hats and drab and nondescript pants and jackets; their faces had a rugged appearance that comes from toiling for years in the equatorial sun. Their wives, though, provided a splash of brilliant color. They wore their very best *polleras* in deep shades of blue, red, orange, and purple wool, embroidered on the bottom with small flowers encrusted with sequins. Shawls in shades of fuchsia and red were wrapped around their shoulders. Their hair was neatly tied in two braids. Many women, however, were dressed more like Rosa. She wore a simple, conservative skirt and a white shirt, and her hair was tied back in a ponytail.

Directly across from me sat a very distinctive group of young people. The girls wore tight skirts and high heels, and their dyed hair fell loose around their shoulders. They made eyes at me off and on, whispered among themselves, and smoked cigarettes with much delight. The boy accompanying them was dressed in baggy black pants, and his shirt was open to reveal numerous gold chains around his neck. He periodically flipped his long hair out of his eyes. Baptismal parties are filled with food, drink, and dancing; they serve to reaffirm relations of reciprocity with old friends and to establish connections with new ones. At the time I was ignorant of the identity of the young man with the gold chains, but I later learned that he was to play a vital role in helping Vicente get to New York.

One of the things I noticed when I first started researching transnational migration back in 1989 was that it could be mapped geographically and chronologically. By this I mean that there were apparently clusters of areas, particularly in the countryside surrounding Cuenca, where the rates of migration were very high. Nearby communities usually shared similar rates, with a pattern that one community began its transnational experiences a few years before the other. This, of course, is not a coincidence, as one of the most important means of facilitating transnational migration is through mutual-aid networks—people helping people. Mutual-aid networks emerge after someone, often a family member, has lived in the United States for a few years and offers to provide the financial and/or logistical means for someone else to migrate. There are geographic clusters of migration because people's circles of friends and family tend to live nearby. Crucial survival information about how to obtain safe passage, where to get a job, how to find a place to live, how to obtain an illegal social security card, and how to send money home is passed freely among migrants through their mutual-aid networks. Less positively, but perhaps inevitably, some enterprising individuals have managed to parlay this "aid" into a lucrative—and exploitative—business of providing loans to transnational migrants. These loans are frequently negotiated at extremely high interest rates, sometimes 10 percent or more, compounded monthly (Kyle 1995). It usually takes a migrant several years to pay off the loan in small installments.

The illegal journey from Ecuador to New York can cost anywhere from $3,000 to $10,000 U.S., depending on how one goes. At the cheaper end, $4,000 might buy a boat ride to Panama and the services of *coyotes* to guide the migrant through Central America to the U.S. border. Going this way, referred to as *andando por la pampa* (walking over the plains), can literally take months and include severe hardships. In 1999 newspaper articles in Cuenca documented how this route can occasionally involve incarceration in a Central American jail if the undocumented migrant is caught by the authorities. After serving up to three months in jail, however, the migrant is simply free to continue the journey north. For $8,000–$12,000 the migrant can buy considerably more comfort, safety, and time. In Vicente's case, it was a one-day plane trip traveling on a legal U.S. visa, albeit on a passport in someone else's name. Vicente used the services of a *pasadora* (smuggler), who arranged all of the paperwork for him, booked his flights, and prepared him for the likely possibility of being questioned by immigration authorities. *Pasadoras* usually work fairly secretly, and families are given little information about their loved one's departure schedule. Indeed, once Vicente gave the *pasadora* the down payment, he was told to be ready to leave at a moment's notice. He was able to get access to the closely guarded *pasadora* from that young man with the gold chains at his brother's baptism. *Pasadoras* often work with their own brokers, who provide the loans to secure the *pasadoras'* services; but Vicente was very fortunate to receive a loan from his high school graduation *compadre* (godfather), a transnational migrant himself, who became good friends with Vicente and the family.

What is theoretically important about these mutual-aid networks is that by understanding how they facilitate, support, or constrain transnational migration we can continue to shift the focus away from viewing migrants solely as victims of economic oppression and structural violence toward thinking of them as active participants in cultural construction (Hondagneu-Sotelo 1994).[2] In other words, migrants do not simply just react to poor economic conditions; they are themselves capable of producing flexible, meaningful, and dynamic social groups that are responsive to individual needs. Not only do transnational migrants count on established networks (like family or godparentage) for the financial and logistic support necessary to migrate, but the processes of migration often facilitate the creation of new networks and even communities (see Grasmuck and Pessar 1991; Miles 1997). Some of these new networks are supportive, and some are exploitative. For example, on the positive side I found that the wives of migrants left behind appear to form their own networks and connections with other women like themselves who are managing households without their husbands. These women informally share information about how to manage and spend the money flowing home, which courier services are most reliable, and who can be trusted when news is scarce or completely absent (see Miles 1997).

While the networks are very important in the lives of transnational migrants and their loved ones, even more central to this book is the argument put forth by Pierrette Hondagneu-Sotelo (1994) that migration networks are activated and managed not by individuals but by families and households. Transnational migration is rarely an individual act; it is "shaped by particular configurations of gender politics" that are culturally constructed and mediated, molded in part by the migration process itself, and that play out within individual households or families as they move through time (Hondagneu-Sotelo 1994:56). Decisions about who should go, when they should go, and how they should go are fundamentally negotiated on the level of the family or household. Considerations of an individual's position in the family and responsibilities to the family are always taken into account.

For example, even though Lucho has talked of going to the United States for the last twelve years, it was in fact Vicente who migrated first. Lucho's decision to postpone his migration was not accidental or circumstantial but was influenced by his and Rosa's shared belief that a father of young children should be present in the household. Now that his children are getting older, new concerns such as supporting himself and Rosa in old age have come to the fore, reigniting his thoughts about his own migration. In 1999 Vicente did not want to help his father to come to the United States, fearing that his own lifestyle would be affected by Lucho's presence. Quite frankly, I think he worried that his father would put a damper on his social life. By 2000, though, Vicente had changed his mind. Confident of his adult manhood, he was convinced that his father would not attempt to control his life. He was, in fact, looking forward to spending time with his father. In the following section I explore the concept of the family more fully, laying the groundwork for understanding how family and gender roles frame the Quitasacas' discourse about transnational migration.

Women, Men, and Family Life

Watching Alexandra grow over the years from a small, thin eight-year-old to a young woman of twenty has provided me with some of my richest understandings about gender and family in Cuenca. At eight Alexandra was most often seen and not heard. She quietly did her chores, watched over her baby sister Cecilia with surprising vigilance, and brought home good school grades. She spoke to me rarely and usually only if I spoke to her first. At twelve she was a little more expressive. She told me of her dreams to be a bank teller or a travel agent or to have any job where she could wear one of the snazzy uniforms of the meticulously groomed office workers in Cuenca. At fourteen Alexandra was my best baby sitter, and I was her confidante. She spoke to me of some family troubles and what she wanted from life. She also had lots of child-care advice for me. At sixteen she was driving her parents crazy. Alexandra was angry all the time and wanted the freedom that she thought other girls were getting but was always denied to her. She told me how frustrated she was to be poor and a girl in a place where neither one of those was much respected. Her future, she said, was completely bleak (see Miles 2000). Alexandra was not alone in these sentiments. I heard them expressed in various ways by several young girls. By eighteen, her discontent had subsided, and she was fighting to stay in college. She was articulate, intelligent, and opinionated and loved her medical classes. But, given the family's financial situation, Alexandra felt continual pressure from her parents to quit her studies and go to work. Against her parents' wishes (because they had other requests in mind), she asked me, as her godmother, for help to finance her education.

While this thumbnail sketch of Alexandra's life leaves out many important details and all of the raw emotions that characterize a real life, I present it in this way to draw attention to several major themes that are essential for understanding family life in Ecuador. First is the issue of gender. As a girl, Alexandra has behavioral expectations placed upon her that are sometimes heavier than (but always different from) the expectations placed on her brothers. She was given more household responsibilities at an early age, and she was much more heavily supervised when she reached adolescence. Girls turn into women, and the behav-

ioral expectations for proper female behavior are taught early. Second, gender and gender role expectations are mediated by birth order. As the second child in her family, Alexandra has often taken a backseat to Vicente, the eldest. Six years younger, she was never able to assume the level of authority he had over all his siblings or to achieve the intimacy of emotions that Vicente shared with his mother. She often felt left out and misunderstood—something that came to the fore in her adolescence. Third, the tensions Alexandra has had with her family over behavior, money, emotions, and responsibility point to the ways in which families and households really function. Despite often repeated romantic stereotypes about "family unity," within households there are in fact very real differences in access to power and therefore control over decision-making (Folbre 1986; Deere 1995). Some voices are simply heard more often than others. Finally, Alexandra has changed—and then changed again. All people do; all families do. As families grow or shrink over time, as individual members move through the life cycle, and as the objective conditions of life change, family dynamics, priorities, and decision-making processes shift. In other words, how a family functions in any given circumstances will surely change.[3] That does not mean that we cannot say anything about family dynamics, because I think we can; but we must be careful not to portray families as homogeneous institutions that move through time in a static way. Let us now look at these themes of gender, birth order, intrafamilial tension, and flexibility a bit more thoroughly and explore how they play out in the lives of the Quitasaca family.

Strong Men and Perhaps Stronger Women

One of the problems of describing gender roles in Ecuador, or anywhere in urban Latin America for that matter, is that it is often too easy to fall back upon simplistic stereotypes about macho men and demure women (see Stevens 1973). In this model, long-suffering women are often juxtaposed to their patriarchal, philandering, or authoritative male counterparts; and women's influence in the family comes only indirectly, usually through manipulating others by emphasizing their own sacrifices and moral superiority. While there is some truth to this stereotype, as there usually is, in the end it is problematic to make such broad generalizations (see J. Scott 1986; Ehlers 1991; Levine 1993; Gutmann 2000). On the ground men and women behave in a multitude of ways that sometimes reinforce, and other times deny, the stereotypes of Latin American patriarchy and machismo.

From my own experience, having worked fairly closely with many families, I know that they defy easy categorization. Women were sometimes the breadwinners and sometimes not; and the relations between men and women sometimes appeared easy-going and egalitarian and at other times quite the opposite. Some of the poor women I met in Cuenca were opinionated and assertive, while others were painfully deferential. In the beginning, most women were more expansive in their opinions when their husbands were not around; but even this could change as we became better acquainted.

By describing gender roles solely in an abstract way with sweeping statements about "women," we not only dangerously homogenize complex gender relations and in the process disempower social actors; we also lose sight of the fact that embedded in the institutional and cultural patterns of gender lie real human relationships. Gender analysis calls for complex social analysis that involves looking at men and women together and not in isolation (Lugo 2000). So even though Alexandra claims that she has little hope of finding a good husband, she is all the same very loyal to her father. Moreover, while Rosa has fought with Lucho, suffered under the yoke of his machismo, and acquiesced to and resisted his attempts at domination, she has also loved him and valued his role as husband and father in the home. One of my greatest concerns here as an anthropologist and a feminist is to write about gender in a way that bears witness to the patriarchy that is present but that does not forget that models for gender behavior are often most real as they play out in the joys, sorrows, struggles, triumphs, and even mundane details of everyday lives (Weiss 1988; Gutmann 1996). Indeed, Elizabeth Brusco (1995) argues that formulations of machismo in Latin America ought to be carefully considered, since they are often more salient as models for public rather than private or domestic behavior. This of course presents some real challenges for anthropologists, as our mere presence can create a "public" situation, even around a kitchen table.

With these cautions in mind, however, I turn to examining discussions of gender in Ecuador. Several authors have written that in mestizo Ecuador public cultural expectations for male and female behavior are really quite different (Anderson 1978; McKee 1980, 1999; Pitkin and Bedoya 1997). In particular, these authors point out that ideally men are responsible in the public sphere and act as providers and heads of household while women are most often associated with the domestic sphere and the maternal role. Indeed, McKee's work in the highlands has shown that, with some caveats, when men and women are asked about the ideal traits of each sex they both emphasize male strength and female submissiveness (McKee 1999). While I did not ask the same questions that Lauris McKee did, her description rings true to some extent, especially for Lucho's and Rosa's generation. Even in families where the woman was a primary contributor to the household income, I often found (especially early in my work) that the man acted as the "spokesperson" for the family with me. Men frequently played the role of gatekeepers, rushing to answer my questions before their wives could speak and quizzing me pointedly on what exactly I was doing in their home.

Elsa, a rather assertive woman I knew in 1989, loved to talk and was always ready for company. Although I saw her with her husband only twice, I did not notice a real change in her demeanor when he was around. Her advice to me about what constitutes a good marriage, however, revealed the strength of the cultural ideals described by McKee. Elsa, who was nearing forty, told me that she had a fairly unhappy marriage. She and her husband fought frequently and fought hard, but she told me that she was working on making her marriage better. According to Elsa, the success or failure of a marriage "is completely dependent on the woman"; when a woman protests and tries to asserts herself, the marriage is threatened. Marital harmony is achieved, she told me, when the woman gives in completely to the husband's wishes and demands. Elsa and her husband had "talked over" their marital problems and things had improved considerably, because she no longer contested what he said and did.

Lucho was the primary wage earner in the Quitasaca family, and for many years he closely guarded Rosa's access to the productive domain. He did not support her small attempts at income generation when they took her outside of the home and on more than one occasion prevented her from pursuing economic opportunities. Consequently, Lucho controlled the family's finances, sometimes putting Rosa in an awkward position when his expected wages weren't forthcoming. In fact, there were times when their marriage was seriously compromised. At the beginning of my fieldwork, Lucho portrayed himself as something of a rake—telling all sorts of vaguely off-color tales about his exploits as a long-distance bus driver. More than once there might have been some truth to his talk of other women. Over the years they have fought quite a bit; many times they would barely talk with one another; and at least one time he beat her.[4]

To understand how gender and family intersect, I think it is important to know that while Rosa sometimes found Lucho crude and brutish, she also often spoke appreciatively of his role in the family. In fact, even before I met him she told me about his sense of humor and his ability to bring laughter into their lives. While I don't wish to minimize Lucho's sometimes questionable behavior, I did come to agree with Brusco's argument that machismo is often expressed most obviously in "public" not private behavior (Brusco 1995). It seemed that Lucho saved his most offensive and sexist jokes for company, no doubt mistakenly believing that this is what outsiders wanted or expected from him. His violence against Rosa in 1993 took place in a semipublic setting: relatives and neighbors witnessed the fight. Even during some of the worst periods in their marriage, Rosa said that Lucho was always a good father and that he was concerned about, and fair with, all of the children. Indeed, Rosa has looked to Lucho to provide for the family, and he has worked very hard. When she has counted on his input concerning family affairs, he has not let her down. He was just as agitated, for example, about Alexandra's difficult period as Rosa was, and he took an afternoon off from work to sit with me and discuss his concerns alongside her. Rosa did not, however, look to Lucho for emotional fulfillment until Vicente's departure. Rather, the most satisfying personal relationship in Rosa's life for years was with Vicente. She found in him all that was missing in her relationship with Lucho: consistency, trust, companionship, and unquestioned affection.

As the eldest son, Vicente has long assumed a very prominent role in the family. By the time he entered *colegio* (similar to high school but lasting six years), he was better educated than both his parents; and by the time he was fourteen (if not sooner), Rosa shared family concerns with him in order to get his "educated" opinion. Rosa claims that Vicente suffered more than the other children, since the early days of her marriage were characterized by greater poverty and marital instability than the later years. Today he, of all the children, has the harshest opinion of his father. As Vicente matured, it was assumed that he had a degree of authority over his siblings; and he would often comment about their friends, social lives, and homework. Perhaps because of Vicente's easygoing nature, or perhaps because this authoritative role is fairly expected, his siblings have expressed very few objections to his authority in the household. Indeed, Alexandra claims her adolescence would have been much easier if Vicente had not been gone. Only Beto, at sixteen, expressed some jealousy over Vicente's good standing with his mother. Over time Vicente also began to assert some authority over his father. In the one incidence of violence that I know about, which occurred in 1993, Vicente took a strong stand against his father. He vowed to head the family himself if violence were to occur again. As far as I know, it never has.

Critical to any discussion of gender and family is a consideration of how class and ethnicity intersect with the ways in which gender is understood, conceptualized, and negotiated (Rothstein 1983; Moser 1987; Benería and Roldán 1987; Babb 1989; Stephen 1991; Buechler and Buechler 1996). Indeed, it should be understood that when I speak of gender roles in the Quitasaca family I am also explaining aspects of class and ethnic identity, because they are inseparable in so many ways. Such household patterns as the configuration of the division of labor, access to resources, individual responsibility, sexuality, and roles in decision-making are linked to understandings of how this family is situated, and how its members perceive their position, within the larger social contexts (see Deere 1995). Therefore, the gendered behavior and ideologies expressed by the Quitasacas make sense only by understanding how they see themselves (and how others see them) positioned within the hierarchical Cuencan society described in the last chapter.

To be sure, I do not wish to resort to class analysis as a means of excusing behavior that is otherwise inexcusable. So I hesitate to support the argument that poor men sometimes engage in domestic violence because they are themselves victims of larger structural (or even personal) violence (Gutmann 1996; Sánchez-Parga 1997). This argument claims that poor men who are beaten down by society or are victims of violence as youngsters (sometimes by their mothers) take out their mounting frustrations on women.[5] Such claims, while perhaps reflective of a certain truth, ultimately only diminish and homogenize poor men and justify something that by their own cultural standards is not admirable.

My interest in discussing class and gender reflects a concern for locating difference. Rosa sees herself as a *chola* (a female of country origins), and others easily categorize her that way too. Therefore, she behaves in ways that she thinks are appropriate for a *chola*. Thus, her humility and Lucho's bravado when dealing with bureaucrats and functionaries are gender-coded appropriate presentations of self for people of their social position. Sometimes the Quitasacas have found themselves awkwardly placed between competing models of gender linked to different class or ethnic orientations. For example, in the rural areas where both Lucho and Rosa grew up, women are fairly active in the production of cash products such as milk and cheese and in the marketing of produce from country to town. Economically active women are the norm. Hence, Rosa's idealized picture of marital life sees the two genders as economic partners. Her musings about Vicente's future include a vision of Vicente and his wife working side by side in some venture. This model of gender complementarity or egalitarianism may mirror more "traditional" Andean (in contrast to more hispanicized, urban mestizo) conceptions of male and female roles (Isbell 1978; Silverblatt 1987; Hamilton 1998; for an less idealized view, see Stolen 1987). Lucho's objection to Rosa's participation in income generation outside the home, a bone of contention for many years, is probably an urban affectation. He perceives, rightly or wrongly, that successful urban families have a single male breadwinner.

Indeed, the Quitasacas have long struggled with the disjunctures between their rural past, their urban present, and their children's cosmopolitan futures. Both Rosa and Lucho grew up in rural areas (she in Cumbe, he in the countryside of nearby Tarqui); and while they want their children to be successful in the city, they are very wary of the children adopting too many cosmopolitan ways. Therefore, although they stress that the children should do well in their studies, they also keep a very tight rein on their social lives. According to Vicente, Alexandra, and Beto, their parents are really "too" strict and rarely allow them the freedom to attend youth parties and gatherings. Rosa and Lucho's main concern is that they do not know their children's friends, or their parents, and cannot be sure that the events will be properly chaperoned. When they were having problems with Alexandra several years back, Rosa and Lucho complained to me that in the city no one would keep an eye on her and report back if she was doing something questionable, as they would do in a rural town. Interestingly, based on Rosa's stories of her own past, it seems as though she had much more freedom as a young girl to work and socialize than she allows her own daughters. The difference is that she lived in a rural town, where people all knew one another and the dangers were apparent. In contrast, the city holds unseen and maybe even unforeseeable dangers.

As the devil story that opens this chapter highlights, the Quitasacas must walk a fine line in providing their children with the necessary tools to be successful in the city (such as modern clothing and education) while trying to maintain a value system that emphasizes family responsibility over self-achievement and cooperation over accomplishment. Indeed, the Quitasacas know that family cooperation will last only for a while at best. Soon their children will be grown and will marry; and Lucho and Rosa know that—given the economic situation in Ecuador—their children will not be able (or perhaps will not want) to take care of them in their old age. It is this knowledge that has provoked Lucho's migration to New York. Even though he has worked all of his life, the family has never been able to save money; and, like the vast majority of poor Ecuadorians, Lucho has never participated in any type of social security system. They have nothing set aside for "retirement," and they have no prospects of ever being able to retire. Indeed, they never use that word, since it implies a pension, which they will never have. While the older children suggested to me that Billy, the youngest in the family, would "take care of Mami and Papi," Lucho and Rosa have no such hope. They assume that they will have to be independent of their children in their old age, just as their own parents are. Rosa and Lucho have no means to assist their parents, and they do not imagine that their children will either.

The effects of the poor economy have had an impact on everyone in the family in a variety of ways, from limiting school choices to curtailing social activities. The children all understand their position in the social hierarchy, which to a greater or lesser extent affects their attitudes toward and plans for the future. Yet, in many ways, the poor economy has had the greatest effect on Lucho and his role within the family. In his ideal urbanized vision of how the family should operate, he would be the head of the household and the sole—and successful—breadwinner. This has never been the case. Rosa has always engaged in income generation, much of it in the home. Moreover, Lucho and Rosa occasionally have had to borrow money from friends or relatives. For Lucho, the tension arises in the conflict between his desire to be a good provider and his desire to be a good father. To Lucho and Rosa, a good father is physically present in his children's lives, offering *cariño* (affection), guidance, and discipline (see McKee 1980). Children who grow up without a father present are generally pitied. As Lucho watched his ability to provide for his family diminish, however, both in real terms and relative to migrants to the United States, it became increasingly difficult for him to defend his position as a good father. He felt he was failing his children as well as himself, since he was unable to provide a secure living or, as he most desired, a safe and comfortable place to live. By 1999 it was clear that, as his children aged, the balance seemed to shift for Lucho; he was beginning to think that his presence in the home was less important than his ability to provide financially for his family. A little more than fifty years old, he heard the clock ticking.

Household decisions in most families (including the Quitasacas) are not democratic; and often self-interest (economic or otherwise) takes precedence over issues of family harmony (Wolf 1990). As Carmen Diana Deere notes, "There does seem to be general agreement that rather than by cohesion and coherence, as implied by altruism, intra-household relations are governed by relations of domination and subordination, hierarchy and inequality and struggle and conflict" (Deere 1995:59). While I might quibble with the inflexibility of the word "governed" in Deere's analysis, in general there is a great deal of truth to this statement. Rosa and Lucho have struggled over issues of domination, as have the children. As the children aged, they began to assert more authority in the household; but, as Alexandra found out, that influence is much more easily granted to boys than to girls. Indeed, the power of Deere's statement is revealed by the Quitasacas as they discuss Vicente's transnational migration, which—they have come to learn over time—has much more to do with him than it ever did with the family. My point here is not to paint a picture of family as a collection of manipulative, selfish, and wholly self-interested social actors but to emphasize that families, just like communities, are involved in struggles over power, influence, and authority.

Yet, despite the many instances I could describe where the patriarchal stereotypes were sharply drawn within this family, just as often it was unclear to me how pervasive and impermeable they really were. Even though Rosa is a softspoken woman, for example, it is apparent to me that she never took Lucho's peccadillos quietly; and she fought back in a variety of ways, both overtly and covertly. Some of these are discussed in Chapter 4. I noted as well that the distribution of household tasks was fairly egalitarian. While it is true that the boys were more likely to be called upon to run errands for Rosa, they also shared to some extent in the "typically" female tasks of caring for younger siblings and helping in the preparation and clean-up of meals. Indeed, the public (male)/private (female) split (see Rosaldo 1974; Maurer 2000; Díaz Barriga 2000) was never complete or total; Rosa and her girls (to an even greater extent) have developed real competencies in negotiating the public spheres of school and work. Both Lucho and Rosa consider it very important that the girls have a career so that they may always "defend" (or fend for) themselves.

Moreover, while male "strength" may be desirable, Rosa has told me more than once that she thinks that women are really "stronger" in the end. Women's bodies endure more over a lifetime, they usually suffer emotional troubles without resorting to drinking and violence, and they often work harder and more consistently. Her girls, she notes, have always been much more directed and dedicated students in school than her boys. Certainly, Alexandra's influence in the household continues to expand as she matures (see Levine 1993). She is now the best-educated person in the home and indeed in the extended family; and with Vicente gone her worldly experience is highly valued.

Finally, as Lucho and Rosa age, they have become much better companions to each other. They seem more united in their concerns than they ever were previously, and in 1999 Rosa spoke of Lucho in truly affectionate terms. When I returned to Michigan in 1999 after a summer in Ecuador, I was surprised by a photograph of Rosa and Lucho that I had taken. In the picture they were both laughing, and they leaned subtly toward each other in a manner that hinted at an ease and affection that I had never seen from them before. Perhaps the improvement in their relationship is an effect of Vicente's leaving, perhaps it is due to aging and life cycle, or perhaps it is due to their common struggles against an impossible economy. I suspect that all of these matter to one degree or another.

One thing that seems clear to me is that Rosa's daughters, and Alexandra in particular, do not seem to share her tolerance for living a lifetime with a patriarchal partner. Alexandra continues to frustrate her parents by periodically challenging Lucho's authority, and her refusals to submit quietly to parental will never cease to confound them. Alexandra views her suitors with a very critical eye; she rejects middle-class men from her school because she perceives that they do not respect her, while simultaneously requiring that poor men from her neighborhood who do not go to school must keep up with her intellectually. Alexandra believes that good men are too hard to find and is fully prepared to stay single rather than marry unhappily. Indeed, all the girls hope to marry a man who helps out at home; and while the younger girls uncritically accept that their father does not, they resent Beto when he doesn't help and want to avoid a marrying a man who won't. One way to do that may in fact be to marry a transnational migrant: because of their experiences in taking care of themselves, migrant men are commonly perceived as more willing to help out at home.

The following four chapters introduce the reader to each of the family members in turn. While relations with extended family are very important to the story that unfolds here, I include interviews only with nuclear family members for two reasons. First, while dense extended family relations are the norm in the Andes, rural-to-urban migration often serves to "nuclearize" the family. Extended family members are frequently left behind in rural areas, and their influence in day-to-day life is diminished. This is true for the Quitasacas, and Rosa in particular was often saddened by it. Second, transnational migration frequently erodes family relationships even further. My interviews with the wives of migrants in 1989 indicated that many of them had troubles with their extended families over sharing remittances (Miles 1997). One woman I interviewed, Eugenia, went so far as to sever all contact with her extended family. When I met her in 1989, her husband had already been gone for two years; she was often overwhelmed by raising two boys by herself, managing the household, and supervising the construction of a modest new home financed by her husband's remittances. Eugenia was very lonely and always exceedingly grateful for my visits, yet she continued to isolate herself from her relatives because they were relentless in asking her for money. If she gave to one, then she would have to give to all of them. It was easier in the end to refuse them all.

I begin the chapters about the family with Rosa because I know her best, but also because it was through her that I came to know the others. Rosa's chapter functions in part as a general history of the family as well as a narrative of my interactions with them. Her chapter is followed by Lucho's, then by the chapters of the four eldest children still at home: Alexandra (eighteen), Beto (sixteen), Marisol (fourteen), and Cecilia (eleven). I have watched these children grow up over the years; and the sections dealing with field notes focus both on my interactions with them at various times and on observations I made about Rosa and Lucho's child-rearing preferences. While their narratives all touched on similar themes of sadness at Vicente's absence and concerns for the family's financial problems, I was also struck by how different they were as well. Gender, birth order, character, and life experiences all influence the lives they have led and how they talk about them. Finally, Chapter 7 focuses on Vicente and his experiences in New York. Vicente and I had an easygoing relationship with one another in 1989 when he was fourteen, but we were not able to spend much time with each other after that. When I interviewed him in 1999 and again in 2000, I found him to be thoroughly delightful. He is thoughtful, honest about himself, and surprisingly good-natured. He reminds me of his mother, because he is quite concerned with living life as a good person; but he combines that with his father's ability to poke fun at himself and his circumstances.

4.1. *Rosa at her mother's house in 1989 with Alexandra, Marisol, and Cecilia. She is still wearing the two braids and* pollera *skirt that identify her as a chola.*

4 | *Rosa*

Introduction

One of the first things I noticed about Rosa was how she laughed. She didn't laugh loudly or with wild abandon but gently and shyly, with her eyes dancing and her whole face lighting up. In the course of many interviews with rural-to-urban migrant women in Guayaquil and Cuenca, I would regularly joke with the children to lighten the mood, which was often far more somber than it needed to be. It usually worked: women would relax a bit, and sometimes smile, although few laughed. Rosa did. She was not laughing at me, however, but at her own children's obvious pleasure. It struck me right then that I liked her because she took real joy in the laughter of her children. She was dressed that day in the "typical" outfit of the *chola* Cuencana, with her hair in two long braids, wearing a blue *pollera,* a white blouse, and a blue paisley sweater.[1] She listened carefully when I spoke, obviously taking pains to understand me despite my accent, looked me squarely in the eye, and gave thoughtful responses to my questions. When I asked her at the end of the interview if I could come back someday to talk more, she smiled and replied, "Of course."

And, indeed, I did go back. I got to know Rosa and her family as their lives and routines were revealed to me in bits and pieces over lunch or afternoon snacks and on trips to their home village of Cumbe. Over time Rosa became my most trusted informant as well as a reliable friend. During the first field trip from late 1988 to December 1989, I experienced all of the angst and loneliness of the first-time ethnographer; and on those occasions I found comfort in her warm kitchen. Many an impromptu afternoon was spent there making and eating empanadas, drawing pictures with the children, learning to knit, and, always, gathering anthropological "data." I found Rosa easy to be with because she was gentle with her children and patient with me. She found me easy to be with because I ate all her food with gusto. We always had something to talk about, and I was continually surprised upon leaving her house to find that night had fallen and the cobblestone streets of Cuenca were jammed with people returning home at the end of the workday. Whole afternoons would pass this way, sometimes several times a week.

From the start, my relationship with Rosa was for the most part an easy one, as our personal styles suited one another. For example, she and I share a tendency not to push each other to talk about things that make us uncomfortable. This meant that sometimes her family stories or personal problems took months or even years to be fully revealed to me. It was also not unusual for Rosa to gloss over an answer to a question the first time I asked it and then spontaneously discuss the same issue later. I once asked about "envy illness," which at the time she dismissed as something "only old people believe in nowadays."[2] I was rewarded a few weeks later on a trip to her rural home with a long and detailed story about her personal experience with envy illness. Rosa never pushed me for answers to questions that made me uncomfortable. It was not uncommon for people in Cuenca bluntly to ask how much money I had, how much I paid in rent, what my father's occupation was and how much he earned, how much money my grant gave me to live on, or what consumer goods I could call my own. Some of these questions, of course, seem shockingly rude to a North American, and I never really got past bristling at them. I know that sometimes I was barely able to control my annoyance—especially if the interlocutor was especially tenacious. Over the years I have come to depend on Rosa's sense of propriety, which remarkably often coincides with my own.

Rosa and her husband had moved to the city of Cuenca around 1983, mainly, she said, so that they could provide their children with better educational opportunities. Schools in the rural areas are generally thought to be of poor quality; urban schools offer more choices, but they cost a good deal more. In 1989 Rosa's main goal for the future was to educate her children, with her stated objective of seeing them graduate from high school. She wanted them to have a "career" so that they would not face the economic insecurities that she and Lucho have had to deal with because they work mainly in the informal economy. Rosa herself has only a third-grade education, and she struggles to read and write. Both Alexandra and Vicente, the two school-aged children at the time, attended private Catholic schools. This is common in Cuenca, where the public school system is of greatly variable quality and insufficient to serve the burgeoning population. Their particular schools catered to the urban poor; they were of average price for private schools and perhaps of slightly lower than average academic caliber. Nonetheless, Rosa was proud of her children's school accomplishments and often liked to hear Vicente tell about what he had learned in school.

Toward the end of my first trip in September 1989, I became Alexandra's godmother and therefore Rosa's "co-mother." She called me *co-madre* from that day on, emphasizing the fictive kin bond that now existed between us. Godparentage in Ecuador changes relationships with the whole family, not just with the godchild. Curiously, Rosa became simultaneously more respectful toward me and freer with her thoughts and feelings. By participating in the baptismal ceremony, accepting the gifts of roasted guinea pigs, and dancing the night away at the party they sponsored, I had publicly demonstrated a willingness to solidify my relationship with the family. At the same time, once the baptism party was over — and given our extreme status differences — the obligations were now almost entirely on my side. I know Rosa harbored the hope that I would fulfill the vague obligations as a godmother to be "of help" to Alexandra and the family. But even under ideal circumstances there were no guarantees that the godparent relationship would, or could, endure through time.[3] In fact, I was scheduled to return to the United States in three months.

Our relationship did in fact endure, however, and even flourish. With each return visit to Cuenca, I am treated more and more like a member of the family — one who is privy to the joys, problems, and conflicts that every family suffers. While my later field visits (in 1993, 1995, 1997, and 1999) were centered around research topics other than migration, I continued to visit and keep notes on Rosa's family. They are always the center of my social life when I am in Cuenca. Many a Sunday has been spent driving through the countryside in their aged Datsun taxi. The children frequently accompany me to cultural events in town, Alexandra has been a reliable and willing baby-sitter for my daughter, and Rosa's warm kitchen is still the best place to spend a rainy afternoon. Over time I have come to know most of their extended family members; and they have met and fed my sister, husband, mother-in-law, and daughter. In 1995 my husband and I became the baptismal godparents of Rosa's youngest child, Billy, born in 1993.

Yet I do not wish to romanticize our friendship too much; like all human relationships, it has had its moments of frustration, annoyance, and misunderstanding. Even more importantly, there is no way that I could honestly deny the fact that we come from different worlds, not just culturally but—more crucially from my perspective—economically. The ways these differences played out on occasion did not make either one of us very comfortable or pleased with ourselves or each other. More than once Rosa has wanted more from me financially than I was really willing to give. Finding a way to ask me for money so that it didn't offend me clearly put her on edge. I sometimes felt manipulated but played along, mostly because I didn't want either one of us to lose face. I have had moments of acute discomfort as I mentally wrestled with fulfilling her requests (which in the big picture were never that large) and my own feelings about what both the ideal anthropological relationship and friendship entailed. Do you give friends or informants money? What does that do to the friendship, and how does it affect the data? How do you preserve a measure of equality (the signpost of friendship in North America) when one person regularly gives money to the other?

Of course, what I finally had to realize was that any friendship Rosa and I have has to be negotiated on terms that are very distinct from those of friendships with people in my own social system. There are few rules in transnational relationships, but many possibilities. As other anthropologists have noted, in the Andes reciprocity and the mutual giving of goods, labor, or hospitality are an essential element of most good social relationships (see Allen 1988). Indeed, medical anthropologists have documented how a lack of reciprocity in important relationships can even lead to illness, especially in women (Finerman 1989; Tousignant 1989; Larme 1998; Oths 1999). Yet that mutual reciprocity does not have to turn on the exchange of similar items. So, while I may have more economic capital, which Rosa and her family desperately need, she has "cultural" capital, which I very much want and which, in the long run, contributes to my professional success and therefore my economic capital. We are, in fact, in a relationship of mutual dependence predicated on the reciprocal exchange of both knowledge and wealth. I realize that this can be viewed in a cynical way as "paying" for anthropological data, but I like to think that Rosa and I really do like each other too much to reduce it to that.

Over the course of the last twelve years both of our lives have changed considerably, going through the ebbs and flows that all of us as human beings experience. In general, things have worked out for me the way I planned in 1989. I have made several important status shifts, moving from being an unmarried graduate student to being a wife, a mother, and a university professor. These status shifts have not altered my relationship with Rosa a great deal, although (as I discuss later) they have had an impact on my relationship with Lucho. I'm not sure what Rosa really can know or imagine about my life in the United States; but the few glimpses I do occasionally get don't surprise me too much. I know she believes that my lifestyle is far grander than it really is, but who can blame her? She thinks this for multiple reasons. First, even though the pay is pathetically poor, university professors in Cuenca frequently come from elite families; and some teach because they want to, not because they need to. Some have other, more lucrative jobs in addition to their university positions. Also, the mass media (for Rosa, primarily televised soap operas and music videos) present a fantasy life of the glamorous and monied "other" that is interpreted not as an illusion but as a desirable reality experienced by someone else — possibly even me (Appadurai 1996). Finally, I own a car, a computer, and a house; both my husband and I have steady jobs; and we have only one child. What else could she think? And, in fact, relatively speaking, she is right. We take so much for granted.

Rosa, who was thirty-six when I met her in 1989, has changed considerably over the years as she has moved from being the mother of very young children to seeing herself as middle-aged. With this has come something of a shift away from concerns about how she will be able to care for her children to worries about how she will live when they all grow up and leave her. She seems physically smaller and more delicate, and she is clearly more disappointed with life than she was twelve years ago. This is understandable. She has gone through a lot of personal upheavals in that time, including a terrible and lingering family feud over remittances sent by her brother in the United States; the difficult pregnancy and birth of Billy in 1993; serious marital problems with Lucho; Vicente's departure to the United States; worries about Alexandra when she was a teenager; and the daily grind of living in a series of unpleasant or insecure housing situations. Moreover, although Rosa and Lucho have made all sorts of plans to improve their economic prospects, like the vast majority of Ecuadorians they can never seem to get ahead. She accomplished a major goal in 1989 when two of her children graduated from high school. The rest are making good progress. But, given the downturn in the economy, Rosa does not imagine that they will really get ahead in Cuenca. No one does. Many of her plans for a better life have dissolved in the face of impossible economic conditions, leaving her disillusioned and physically weakened but not altogether bitter. Despite their hard work, she and Lucho are no closer to their long-standing goal of having a house of their own than they were twelve years ago. In fact, they may be still further from it. In 1999 Rosa's father began to threaten to take away the house he gave her in Cumbe after her marriage. Since she has no paperwork showing ownership of the house, he may very well do that.

Vicente's departure to the United States was devastating to Rosa. Even in 1989, when Vicente was only fourteen years old, I noted in my field notes that he and Rosa had a very close relationship. Specifically, I wrote that she spoke to him about daily events much as a wife might speak to a husband. In 1999 my god-daughter Alexandra said something similar to me, noting that in Ecuador the eldest son is "almost like a husband to his mother." The "almost" here is important, as it implies an emotional not a physical attachment. Relationships between husbands and wives among the poorer classes I worked with in Cuenca are often ambivalent and can be emotionally unsatisfying for women (see Chapter 3). Sometimes they are downright painful. In Rosa's case, there have certainly been some ups and downs. Until recently Lucho was often absent while traveling for work; when he was home, he was demanding of her time and energies. In the early years of our acquaintance I knew that Rosa appreciated Lucho's sense of humor but also that the household was more peaceful when he was gone. Over the years Lucho has hurt Rosa deeply and limited her economic chances by insisting that she stay home when the children were young. As Rosa and Lucho age, however, they seem to grow more comfortable with one another. He has become less demanding in recent years and more circumspect in his manner, and she appreciates the fact that he has been a good father to their children.

Vicente has always been his mother's confidant. In 1989 he was the apple of his mother's eye, and she spoke to him in ways she could not speak to Lucho. As Vicente matured and became a young man, Rosa looked to him for advice and emotional support. Once Vicente entered *colegio,* he was better educated than both of his parents. His departure affected Rosa deeply, and by her own admission she has never really been the same physically and emotionally. She cannot speak about him for long without dissolving into tears.

In writing about Rosa, my biggest concern is to do justice to her complexity as a person. She has a warm heart and a generous nature; yet she has done something that by her own Ecuadorian standards is unequivocally and seriously unethical. In 1992 she took money that was not hers to take, causing grave family ruptures that have only partially healed over the years. My goal here is not to have the reader sit in judgment of her but rather to consider the circumstances of her life that made this move understandable, if not admirable. In what follows readers will see that even when women like Rosa "play by the rules," the culture of subordination in Cuenca limits their opportunities and how the need for money in an ever-shrinking economy lies at the roots of Vicente's migration to the United States.

Field Notes: 1989–1998

1989

During my initial fieldwork in Ecuador in 1988–1989, I met a number of rural-to-urban migrant families and documented how their lives were affected by migration and by the influences of modernization. These families represented the urban working poor, who lived in substandard housing and worked in various menial jobs in the informal economy. I visited most families several times a week, but I was always most at ease with Rosa. In the following field notes my personal relationship with Rosa develops, as I learn about Cuencan culture and the lives of rural-to-urban migrants. These elaborated notes also document how my own analytic and anthropological sensibilities evolved. Descriptions of social facts give way to more analysis of social problems as my understandings of the culture and my abilities to analyze it improve.

MARCH 3

I went to see Rosa today. At first she kept me in the doorway, ashamed of her "poor house." After about ten minutes she let me in.

They live in very small, dark rooms in a building in the center of the Centro Histórico district. As in all of the *conventillos* in Cuenca, it's impossible to tell that behind the old wooden door with peeling blue paint are the homes of countless families. She lives off the hallway as you first come in, and there is a courtyard beyond where the toilet and sink are. There are about six or eight "apartments" in the two-story building. There is no running water in her rooms, so they store it in pots in the kitchen. I imagine when they wash dishes or clothes they have to work around the schedules of the other tenants, as there was only one large sink. There is a pervasive odor of musty wood, kitchen grease, and inefficient plumbing in the dank passageway.

The apartment is small—the door opens onto the kitchen, which is dominated by the table, a gas stove, and a refrigerator. When she opened the fridge to put something away, I saw that it was nearly empty. The second room has two beds against each wall and a small TV. The rooms are really quite dark, since the only window is in the bedroom and it overlooks the musty hallway. They have covered the window with paper. Once inside you have no way of knowing if it's night or day, sunny or rainy.

Rosa grew up in Cumbe and only attended school until the third grade. Although there were schools in the country in her day, her parents didn't send kids to school since there was so much to do at home.

MARCH 7

Rosa told me today that she has one brother in New York. He is undocumented. His plan is to stay there for five years, make money, and come home. He lives with someone else from around Cuenca. She said her husband thought about going to the United States too, but he doesn't want to leave his wife and children. "What good is money if we are alone?" she said. The husband works for a long-distance bus company, and he is gone quite often.

MARCH 17

Ecuadorian expectations for children's contributions to the household are so much greater than our own. Rosa is always interrupting the children's play or TV watching to have them fetch water, wash something, or go to the store. They never complain. While it seems to me that the kids are always ready to help out, Rosa told me that she thinks the children don't help her enough.

When she told her husband about me, he made a joke that he might fall in love with me and then what would Rosa do? She said that when I meet him he will surely keep me laughing because he is very funny.

Rosa, like everyone else I've noticed, asks my pardon whenever she feeds me. She told me she is asking to be excused for the poor food she is giving. It makes me uncomfortable because her food is always so good and it's so kind of her to feed me.

MARCH 24 — GOOD FRIDAY

Lucho was out today, but all the kids were home. We talked about a lot of different things, including a discussion of the *chola* Cuencana. I was looking at a schoolbook with the kids when we came upon a picture of the *chola* Cuencana. I asked Rosa if she considered herself a *chola*, and she replied yes. She said that she prefers to wear the *pollera* but that her husband doesn't like it and so she doesn't dress her daughters in them. Besides, she added, the *pollera* is expensive. Jeans and T-shirts, which I always see the kids in, are simply cheaper. Lucho, she said, doesn't like *polleras* because they are costly, but Vicente piped in that it was really a matter of *vergüenza* [shame]. Rosa said, "We do it to ourselves," meaning that people who used to wear the *pollera* have adopted the dominant values that associate it with backward country folks, so they make fun of women who still wear the *pollera*. She pulled a tweed skirt out from under her bed and said that she puts it on when she goes to the bank or to her children's school functions. If she wears the *pollera,* she will be made to wait longer in lines and people will be more likely to treat her poorly or cheat her. Even though Vicente was clad in modern clothes, he seems not to be ashamed of his mother's preference for the *pollera,* and he said at school they were taught that they should respect their parents' use of "traditional" clothing and it represents part of Cuenca's rich "folklore." Were it only true that being "folkloric" is really appreciated!

APRIL 5

Rosa is the oldest of six children, and she said that the oldest and youngest child in the family are always the *más queridos*—the most loved. I didn't sense that she sees anything really wrong with parents having favorites. In fact, it seems to me that she is repeating this in her own family, where Vicente and the baby, Cecilia, clearly get the most attention.

After she and Lucho married, they lived in Cumbe, first in a rented house and then later in a house right next door to her parents. Her parents gave her the land for the house. They lived there until Vicente was in the fourth grade. Over the years Rosa and Lucho have been engaged in a variety of economic ventures and have moved back and forth from Cuenca to Cumbe. They had a small truck and sold milk from Cumbe in Cuenca and peddled goods in Cumbe that they bought wholesale in Cuenca or Guayaquil. Rosa has cooked food, sewn *polleras,* and knitted sweaters. The most lucrative business they were in was the milk business. Rosa claims she had clients from wealthy neighborhoods and that they were doing really well. But she also called the milk business a "dirty" one. There is a great deal of competition between truck owners over both milk providers in Cumbe and clients in Cuenca. One day Lucho had an accident, totaling their truck. They had to sell many of their personal belongings, including some gold earrings, to pay off the truck. Soon after, they moved to Cuenca so that Vicente could go to better schools.

We spent most of the time I was there out back in the courtyard taking in the sun. A neighbor woman was clearly curious about our conversation, but Rosa wouldn't include her. Similar to what other women have said to me, Rosa doesn't trust any of her neighbors and she has few friends, if any, in the city.

APRIL 16

Rosa asked me today if there are bad husbands in the United States, as in Ecuador, or only good ones. She wondered if everyone married as late as me and whether people use birth control or whether they have so few children because they marry so late. Rosa is the only one in her family with so many kids; the others have only two or three each. She said she has so many because she got married young, at seventeen.[4] After Vicente was born, she tried birth control, first the IUD, which she had taken out when someone told her it causes cancer, and then the pill, which gave her headaches. That's why there are six years between Vicente and Alexandra. She doesn't want any more children, saying if she has one more it will be "half a dozen—what a fright!" After Cecilia was born the doctors wanted to sterilize Rosa, but she claims that she is still a young, strong woman who has lots of work left in her. She thinks the sterilization would weaken her.

When I arrived at the house it was almost 4:30 and Vicente was at a friend's house doing homework. As it got later Rosa became more and more agitated at his absence and said she didn't like it when he stayed out late [it was not yet 6 P.M.] "in the street."

APRIL 23

I met Rosa's parents today when they came to her house to wait for a phone call from her brother Carlos in the United States. A neighbor has a phone, and they make arrangements well in advance so everyone is there to receive the call.

MAY 9

I asked Rosa about "evil eye" and whether her children were ever victims of it. She told me that Cecilia had it once, not too long ago. As she turned to Vicente for confirmation on the date, he said, "It wasn't evil eye, it was just a sickness from God." His priest at school taught him this. When I tried to get Rosa back on the subject, she just repeated Vicente's line that it was "just a sickness from God," saying that only old people still believe in it. So much for the direct approach. I wonder, though, what would have happened if Vicente wasn't there? I think that even though I didn't get the "answers" I wanted about evil eye it is interesting to see the ways that "tradition" is admired (Vicente's teachers liked the *pollera* as folkloric) at the same time that other folkloric ideas are unacceptable. The *chola* is symbolic of Cuenca's past—and of each one knowing her place and being able to tell that place in a flash of a swinging *pollera* hem—but the ideas of the *chola* are to be erased from her children's minds.

MAY 16

Rosa came by on Wednesday night to borrow $80. They need it to pay school fees. I had always thought I would never give informants money—it could only be bad for the anthropological relationship. But when the moment came, my heart took a lurch and I agreed to do it. I console myself that $80 isn't really all that much. Rosa took the matter extremely seriously. She seemed very unhappy about asking for the money, and I was unhappy for her. I have decided not to think about getting the money back. If I think of it as a gift, I won't get mad if I don't get it back.

MAY 20

We spent the day in Cumbe. Rosa's parents live just up the hill from the central plaza and have land scattered all over. A river runs about 100 yards behind the house. The river is also the bathroom, but canals for sewage have supposedly been recently laid. There is a water spigot right outside the house, but water is unreliable and is usually off by 2 P.M.

The two old people live alone. One of Rosa's brothers lives on one end of town, and her sister lives out of town in the opposite direction. The grandparents' house has two stories and is made of crumbling concrete, wood, and adobe. The kitchen is separate.

Rosa keeps her heirlooms and memorabilia in her house. I noticed in a picture that Rosa used to be much heavier. She explained that she has been sick for twelve years—only getting better in the last two years or so. She said she had *envidia* [envy illness] caused by a neighbor here in Cumbe who wished to do her harm—for no apparent reason except that Rosa was a good person with a beautiful baby boy [Vicente]. She was finally cured by a *curandero* [traditional healer].

The day centered on food and eating. We had a huge lunch of potato soup and *mote* [hominy] with some *carne asada* [roast beef], then we spent most of the afternoon shucking dried corn and grinding it to make *humitas* [tamales], and finally after nightfall we had roasted guinea pig. I was given far more food than I could comfortably eat, but eat it I did.[5]

MAY 24

Rosa told me her stereotypes of *gringas* [female foreigners] today. She said that most everyone thinks that *gringas* are loose. She hears a lot of stories from Lucho about how flirtatious they are on the bus and how they are willing to talk to most men they meet. Rosa saw a *gringa* kissing an *indio* from Otavalo [north of Quito] publicly in a restaurant. She seemed a bit shocked by it, but she thinks that *gringas* are really attracted to Indian men from Otavalo. Public displays of affection, especially sexually laden ones such as kissing, are downright shocking to Cuencanas like Rosa. Between the American movies that come here like *Fatal Attraction* and the young tourists [both European and American] they have a pretty odd view of American women and sexuality. I find that their stereotypes of us can be extremely revealing.

JUNE 6

Lucho has been home all this week because of the transportation workers' strike. Rosa said that he is driving her crazy because he insists that she prepare complete meals [a soup and rice dish] every day.

JUNE 13

Rosa launched into a litany of woes today—all about expenses. Over and over she said, *me da pena* [it pains me] about their mounting debts and school fees. Because of the transportation strike when Lucho did not work, they have fallen behind. Rosa is also upset because her mother isn't feeling well and Lucho will not let her go to Cumbe to see her. He doesn't like it when she leaves the kids even for a few hours.

JUNE 21

Rosa was in much better spirits today. The school fees have been paid. We talked some about *compadrazgo* [godparentage] today because Rosa's brother Miguel will be baptizing his children soon—he wants them baptized because he is planning to go to the United States. As it turns out, of Rosa's five children only Vicente has been baptized. When I asked if she preferred *compadres* from Cumbe or Cuenca, she said Cuenca. While those from Cumbe are more generous with what they have, people in the city simply have more to give. Vicente's *compadres* are from Cuenca. She has yet to baptize the other children because of the expense.

The illegal trip to the United States costs about $4,000, which has to be borrowed, often from those who have already gone. Lucho is thinking about going, but he wants to see how Miguel fares first. Rosa doesn't want Lucho to go since she is afraid that he will "forget" about them— that he will get used to life in the United States and will not want to come back. As many other women have reported to me, she is afraid he will start a new family in New York.[6] "I've grown accustomed to him," she said. She also worried how the children would fare without the "warmth" of a father. If he did leave, she would have to move to a more secure home because she gets frightened by the drunk men living there.

JULY 20

Rosa was very upset today about the money that her brother Carlos in the United States is sending home. Her father is taking the money and loaning it to others in Cumbe who want to go to the United States. But they need the money to pay off Carlos's loan. According to Rosa, Carlos has been sending the money to his mother, who is "too timid" and turns it over to Rosa's father. Her father is only paying the interest on the loan and using the rest for various purposes. Some he gives to the one son still living in Cumbe, and the rest he is loaning to others. They want Carlos to send the money directly to Rosa so she can pay off the loan. However, they hesitate to tell Carlos too much of what is going on because Rosa fears that her father will accuse her of turning Carlos against him. Rosa said that her father was never a nice man but that the money has "made him crazy" and that now the siblings are fighting among themselves because of money.

AUGUST 10

I have promised to help make a cake for Miguel's children's baptism. I took Rosa to Mi Comisariato, the American-style grocery store. She had never been there before and she kept saying "how pretty" about all the fancy packaged goods. I could tell that she was uncomfortable there, and it was odd and sad that I, so new to Cuenca, walk so freely into places that she would never go.

AUGUST 13

I write this while sadly suffering from the *gran chuchaki* [a big hangover]. The baptism of Miguel's girls in Cumbe was a real bash. The *compadres* were two couples from Cuenca who seemed out of place among the other guests, who were mainly from Cumbe. There was a lot of drinking, and when the *compadres* left around 10 P.M. everyone was worried that they left annoyed. People were saying that 10 P.M. is too early to leave. The price to pay, I guess, for selecting *compadres* from a higher social status. As the evening progressed many people got very drunk, but Rosa watched over me. She would stop people from forcing more drinks on me and finally took me out back when the drunks became too forward. I guess that is one advantage of being a female anthropologist—as a woman I could hide out in the kitchen—something I don't think a man could so easily do.

The next morning Rosa's mother summed up the party by saying rather matter-of-factly, "Well, at least Miguel has completed his *cargo* [burden or responsibility]." No one really seemed to have had a good time.

AUGUST 29

Rosa and Lucho came to the house today to ask if I would be Alexandra's godmother. They asked Alexandra who she would like, and she chose me. We discussed planning it for when my sister and two friends come for a visit in mid-September. [As it turned out, a friend of mine from graduate school who was traveling throughout South America was able to act as godfather.]

SEPTEMBER 3, CUMBE

More details continue to unfold about the brother in the United States. It seems he got his loan to go from a bank, using the father's agricultural lands as collateral. Carlos then loaned half of that money to a friend so that he could also go to the United States. The friend has now abandoned Carlos, denies he ever received money from him, and refuses to pay back the loan. Rosa's father was fuming mad about all this and kept saying how they received the guy as a friend in their house, fed him guinea pig and all. So, it seems, at least on some levels, that the father has certain rights over Carlos's money since one loan is actually in his name. The other loan uses the land where Rosa's house is in Cumbe as collateral. That is partly why she is so concerned that the loan get paid off and not just the interest. I am amazed at how complicated it all is and how many different people are involved in the process. I have a hard time imagining them all in some bank office somewhere negotiating terms. It is clear that people are a lot more sophisticated than I am giving them credit for.

I spent the morning with Rosa's mother taking care of the cows. That sixty-something-year-old woman put me to shame. I could not keep up with her as she practically raced down the steep slopes to where the cows were tethered, milked them, took the surly beasts to water, ran the milk back to the road, and then returned to cut herbs and grass for the guinea pigs — which she hauled in a huge pack on her back. Milking a cow is a lot harder than I thought, but leading them to water is even more difficult. Vicente had a hard time keeping up too, so the two of us ended up lolling about by the stream at one point while the old lady did all the work. How utterly shameful!

The baptism will be held in about two weeks. Rosa is getting frantic with all the details of cooking, cleaning, and paperwork. I'm asking everyone I know what is expected of me; and in addition to party favors, which I have to order, I am supposed to buy Alexandra's dress and shoes.

Everyone tells me we are going to have a great time—they all mention the guinea pigs I'll be eating!

SEPTEMBER 18

The baptism was great fun! The *compadres* of the other children were really *alegres* [happy], and they showed their goodwill by dancing and eating. We received these enormous plates of food, which, I was relieved to learn, we did not have to eat on the spot but could take home. In contrast to Miguel's party, Rosa kept a pretty close watch on the alcohol. While there certainly was plenty to go round, no one was drop-down drunk. The strangest moment for me at the baptism is when I danced the first dance with my *compadre* [Lucho]. The music was a waltz, "Oh, how we danced on the night we were wed . . ." I felt like "giant woman," towering over my partner dancing to a Muzak version of a wedding waltz in a cement room with bare light bulbs and a plastic-tarp ceiling. I wanted to laugh out loud at my awkwardness except that both Rosa and Lucho took it very, very seriously. One of the nicest parts of the party was how young and old and city and country mixed the entire evening.

OCTOBER 5

In an interesting twist on the dynamics of race here Rosa told me today how she is "afraid" of the Indians from Riobamba [Riobamba is a province to the north]. She thinks they are "dirty" and don't brush their teeth. She admits she shouldn't feel like that, but she can't prevent herself from feeling frightened of them. I took this as a real indication of how small differences in skin tone and culture create great divides between people. Rosa is herself a victim of prejudice by others in Cuenca who put her down because of her rural background, but, as a *chola,* she sees herself as very different from the "Indians" of Riobamba. In the pecking order they are lower than her, and while she knows she shouldn't judge them, she does so anyway.

OCTOBER 18, CUMBE

Rosa talked about love today. She likes the idea of couples knowing each other for years before they get married. Love in Ecuador is "crazy," according to Rosa; sometimes couples know each other only for a few weeks before they run off and get married.

NOVEMBER 20, LUCHO'S FAMILY IN TARQUI

Rosa and her sister-in-law spent quite a while talking about the *pollera* and why young girls, even those in the country, are not wearing it anymore. Their discussion centered on the fact that *polleras* are more expensive than skirts. Frankly, I thought they were skirting around the real issue of shifting social status and the *pollera*. The stigma of rurality associated with the *pollera* and the women who wear it is implicit, but too dangerous to talk about openly or casually—at least with me around. To wear the *pollera* is to self-identify as having rural roots and therefore to open oneself to prejudice when in the city. Rosa says she prefers the *pollera* because she was raised in one and that she would feel ridiculous— like she was wearing a carnival costume—if she changed. Despite what Rosa told me when we first talked about this, wearing the *pollera* seems for the most part to be an all-or-nothing proposition. In other words, women don't move back and forth between the *pollera* and skirt. Rosa owns a skirt, but I have never seen her wear it even when Lucho is displeased—as I guess he was at the baptism. He wanted her to wear a skirt, but she refused. She doesn't defy him on much, so this must really be something that is important to her.

Here's a real testament to how some women see marriage and relations between the sexes. When Rosa's sister-in-law found out that I was twenty-nine and unmarried, she said, "So much the better!" Marriage, she said, "ruins" a woman. The reason I look so young, she said, is that I am not saddled with a husband and children. She noted that in Ecuador there is too much pressure put on girls to marry. A woman could not live on her own as I do—she lives with her parents until she lives with her husband.

DECEMBER 2

Last Sunday I was at Rosa's house in Cumbe when Alexandra came out and asked me to go into the bedroom where Lucho and Rosa were seated. It looked very serious. As it turns out, they were worried and didn't know how to tell me that they didn't have the $80 from the loan. Lucho said he felt very bad that I was leaving with them still owing me money. I told them I had long ago forgotten about that money ever being returned and I saw it as a gift. They seemed much relieved.

DECEMBER 12

The last few days in Cuenca were busy but also filled with lots of ambivalent feelings. I love Cuenca but I also remember many of the difficult times . . . struggling to fill my days sometimes, wondering if I was doing the "right" thing, constantly pushing myself to try to do more and always, always fighting loneliness. Somehow, except at Rosa's, never feeling exactly like myself.

June–July 1993

This was the first trip back to Ecuador since my initial fieldwork, and I was accompanied this time by my husband, Rich. He stayed only a few weeks and then returned to the United States, while I spent almost two months there. Although Rosa had sent me her phone number and new address, I had forgotten to take them with me to Ecuador; so at first we had difficulties finding her. My main research agenda during this period was to study ethnomedical conceptions, and I was working with a traditional healer who lived outside of Cuenca; I was often out of town. I saw Rosa only about once or twice a week. I found the family in some disarray during this trip for multiple reasons that are revealed below.

JUNE 2

We just could not find Rosa. I knew she lives somewhere on Pío Bravo, so we walked up and down the street trying to find her. I thought it would be like the old days on Luis Cordero, where everyone knows where everyone else lives—even if they don't know them! We finally had Luis [a friend] drive us to Cumbe to find out from her parents where they live. When we got there, I met her brother Patricio—the old folks were out in the fields. We stayed only briefly. Patricio got me really worried because he said that Rosa had been very sick. We turned back to Cuenca immediately and Luis brought us to their house on Pío Bravo, where we knocked on the door. The upstairs window opened and out popped Alexandra's head. She was flabbergasted to see us. When we got upstairs Rosa was in bed, something I had never seen before. I was really worried and as I approached the bed I saw a little, teeny, tiny baby wrapped up in swaddling rags. He looked like a football, he was so tightly bound. So that is what Patricio meant by "really sick." A baby! She explained that it had been a really difficult pregnancy, and I know that she really didn't want any more children. The baby seems rather listless, and she says that he doesn't eat very well. She breast-fed all of her children; but for some reason, she says too many worries, she has no milk for this one. They are feeding him with bottles, which makes me nervous—I kept saying that they must be sure to boil the water and not dilute the formula too much. So far the little guy has no name.

This apartment is much bigger than their last one. It has three good-sized rooms. The boys have their own room, while the girls sleep in the same room with Rosa and Lucho.

From her bed Rosa said she knew that I was coming, or that she would hear from me soon, because yesterday a dove was just outside her window. The arrival of a dove foreshadows good news.

JUNE 9

Rosa is still not out of bed. She is too weak, and while she can't maintain the traditional forty-day *dieta*,[7] she is trying to stay in bed as much as possible. She seems somewhat removed from the baby, not at all as I remember her with Cecilia.

A lot of Rosa's glum mood has to do with some kind of a family fight that is going on—I only got a few details, but it seems that everyone [siblings and father] is angry at Rosa. The fight has something to do with money that her brother has sent back. I gather that she was in charge of the money and some is missing. The details are sketchy.

JUNE II

Rosa talked today about how difficult life is and how women suffer. Lucho has been very annoyed with her lately because she is ill and is not doing things around the house. He says he's "dying of hunger" since she hasn't been able to cook meals. Her kids aren't used to doing things around the house, and yesterday she asked someone to make her some tea and they all ignored her. The baby apparently needs a bath, but she is afraid to put her hands in water for fear that she will become more ill.[8] I think this is pretty typical of rural-to-urban migrant women in the city. They do not have the support of a wider network of kin to help out in times like these. She complained that she has no milk for the baby, and she is worried about how he will grow without it. She feels terribly when he cries in the middle of the night and no one will get up to make his bottle.

JUNE 15

Rosa is still in bed. We talked about names for the baby. Rosa likes American names because they are different. She thinks she will name the baby Bill, after Bill Clinton.

JUNE 27

Boy, I am really sad. This was the first day Rosa was out of bed and I saw that she no longer wears the *pollera* and she has her hair in a single ponytail and not two braids. I was shocked and I must say disappointed. I love the *pollera* and the way it swings as a woman walks. I thought it gave her some distinction. She is wearing a tweed skirt, but it doesn't mean she looks more modern at all. She looks shy in the skirt and more self-effacing—just like, as she said years ago, she was wearing a costume. The reason for changing is even sadder. Vicente had been consistently late for school so the priest called a meeting of the mothers of the late kids. As he looked over the room he pointedly addressed some of the mothers, including Rosa, calling her a "woman of the plaza." This means a market woman, and he implied that market women are too wrapped up in their own business affairs to take proper care of their children and see to it that they get to school on time. She was so embarrassed that she put the *pollera* away.

We went to Cumbe over the weekend. Carlos, Rosa's brother from New York, was there when we first arrived. I didn't care for him. He tried to speak English to me but then got mad when I couldn't understand him. He clearly didn't understand English well at all but wouldn't speak Spanish to me. I think he wanted to show off for his family and then he got annoyed when it wasn't working too well. When I asked him questions he would give me short, terse replies as if he didn't want to be bothered with me. I found out later in the day what his problem was, and it turns out it is *the* problem. Boy, is it messy. A few years ago Carlos had paid off his loan to the banks but was still sending money back to Ecuador. Rosa was in charge of picking up the remittances at Delgado Travel [a courier service] since she lives in Cuenca and taking them to the bank where Carlos had a savings account. Well, it appears that Rosa "borrowed" from that account to pay for Lucho's taxi without really ask-

997 I returned alone to Cuenca for a very brief time. I saw Rosa's
ly pretty consistently over the two weeks—usually having meals
them several times as week—but I spent more time with another
ly, whose granddaughter died of diarrhea while I was there. My
s about Rosa from this brief visit are therefore more sketchy than
rs. By this time Vicente was gone, the family had moved again, and
s were not going all that well in the new house. This time around
biggest concerns were with Alexandra, now sixteen: they thought
as a bit wild. Economically, Ecuador was reeling from an economic
, Lucho was earning very little, Vicente had not sent much money,
hings were tight financially.

RY 1

s new apartment is in a half-constructed house way out past the
Libre [open market]. It takes a good half an hour to get there by
nd I make Alexandra or Beto come and get me in town to take me
house, as I am sure I will get lost. I don't really like the house very
; it is noisy and cold and damp. Rosa complained about the neigh-
od, saying there were a lot of thieves and bad sorts. She doesn't
e kids to be out.

sa said that while Vicente has sent them very nice presents for
mas and money on Mother's Day, because of the debt he owes to
padre in New York who helped him get to the United States, he is
able to send them much money. Things are as difficult financially
ays, and they moved to this house, even though they don't really
because it was simply a lot less expensive than the old one.

a begins to cry at the mere mention of Vicente's name.

2

nd Lucho for a while, spent a long time talking about Alexandra
They are clearly upset. They will not let her go out with boys, but
ys they keep coming around—she can see them outside waiting
They think she lies to them about where she is going and what
oing. A neighbor told them that she is hanging around with an
oy in the neighborhood who is married. They think she is "hard-
" and has a "dirty heart" because she is angry all the time and

ing her brother. When her brother returned to Cuenca for a visit, he
expected to find that money in the bank. He needs that money to get
back to the United States. Rosa is particularly upset with her sister and
other brothers, who are mad, because it doesn't really involve them. I
think they have taken this opportunity to air all sorts of other grievances
they may have with her. She argues that she and Lucho hoped to earn
the money with the taxi and return it before anyone even knew it was
gone. Rosa knows that what she did is wrong, but she is still terribly hurt
about things being said about her. No wonder Carlos was such a snot to
me—he is harboring a lot of resentment about anyone and anything associated with Rosa. She continues to visit her mother even though no
one else there will talk to her—I think that takes some nerve.

This was one of those days that I learned a lot more than I wanted
to know. Another piece of the puzzle was put in place today and that
is Lucho's very reserved manner—not just around me but with Rosa as
well. I was sitting outside with Marisol [now seven] and Cecilia when
Marisol told me the most awful story. I guess things have been worse
than I thought. Rosa and Lucho have had an awful fight. Rosa has been
working occasionally in the small store that they put in the house in
Cumbe—in an attempt to make extra money more quickly. There isn't
much there, just soap, some sugar and flour, alcohol, candy, and cigarettes. One night while Rosa was in her early pregnancy she was there
while Lucho was out drinking. He came back, they got into a fight, and
he beat her. The girls didn't know what it was about, but Rosa later told
me that it had to do with Lucho's frustrations with money and with her
since she has been sick. Vicente intervened and told his father that he can
never lay another hand on his mother. So far he hasn't, and Rosa claims
he has been humbled by this.

JULY 10

I wanted to take Alexandra out and buy her some clothes, but Rosa suggested that I get her glasses instead. She is having problems reading the
board in school.

JULY 22

The last year or so has been a really difficult time for Rosa and her family,
and it is clear that relations have been strained on all sides. We had a few
good afternoons together, but Rosa has more than enough on her plate

these days between a new baby and thc money issue. I don't know what to make of that. On the one hand my loyalty is to Rosa, who is clearly hurt by how her siblings and father have all turned against her—but it also seems like she really messed up here. From her perspective she is now the victim of unnecessary hostility, rather than Carlos the victim of unapproved "borrowing."

1995

In 1995 I returned to Cuenca for the summer, this time with my husband and three-month-old daughter, Isabel. My research agenda was to examine commercial natural medicine, but my social time was most often spent with Rosa and her family. Things were much better now, and the family was happier and more relaxed. My mother-in-law also came for a brief visit and was completely overwhelmed by the kindness the family showed her. During this visit we also formalized my husband's relationship to the family when he and I became Billy's godparents. The family was living in a new apartment again, which, as it turns out, set the stage for many of the events concerning Vicente's emigration the next year. The nephew of the landlord was a man named Bolívar who visited Cuenca every year from his home in New York City. He became good friends with Vicente and not only loaned him the money to go but also housed him on Staten Island for years. My notes this time were not kept on a daily basis, but I made periodic entries throughout the two-month period.

ENTRY 1

Rosa and the family are now living in a nice apartment near the bus terminal. They now have some orange Naugahyde living room furniture. They were very happy to see us and were quite taken with Isabel. She looks so big compared to little Billy, who is two years old now. He doesn't talk much yet, but he is fussed over by everyone. It's a far cry from how I perceived their treatment of him two years ago. It bordered on indifference.[9]

ENTRY 2

Rosa is still stinging from the family problems. but she has made up with her sister while her husband was in the hospital. They thought he was

going to die, so her brother Patricio camc to get [...] ever, she is still not talking to her other brother, [...] claims, is telling lies about her in Cumbe. Accor[...] wife is afraid that Rosa will get money from Mi[...] United States], so she does whatever she can to[...] keep brother and sister apart.

Rosa has moved everything out of the house[...] said she doesn't like to go to a place where pe[...] about her, including her father. When she move[...] the store, that was the last act of "giving up on [...] brother Carlos is now almost paid off, and he ha[...] them again.

ENTRY 3

Another baptism is being planned—this time [...] thing to wear! Rosa said I should be *muy elegant*[...] and sweaters. They will have to rush plans al[...] we leave.

ENTRY 4

Rosa came by the apartment this afternoon[...] afternoon talking. It was like the old days. We[...] including Vicente and marriage. They are real[...] finish high school. He has been held back at[...] they really need the money from a job he co[...] that he finish. Rosa said she blames herself[...] cess because she let him go "into the street'[...] making sure to keep Alexandra home more[...] of a problem. Vicente is talking about goir[...] wonders why he should finish high school i[...] the United States.

Rosa said that Lucho has caused her a[...] years—making jokes that aren't funny and[...] She doesn't know if he has been unfaithful[...] ing his stories. He has calmed down consi[...] She told him when things were bad three[...] if he wanted. Vicente would go to work a[...] out him.

doesn't even care that they are upset with her. Lucho hit her once when she lied, and he was shocked that she only looked at him and said she didn't care. They think she is sleeping with boys.

Interviews: 1999

By 1999 I knew that I wanted to write this book, and I spent the majority of my time that summer with Rosa and her family taping interviews. They were excited about the idea of doing the book because they thought it was important that North Americans understand the ways in which migrants are exploited in the United States. Economically, the country was in its worst shape since the Great Depression. Stores were empty because no one had money to buy anything, and no one was riding taxis. Gas prices hovered around $2.50 a gallon, making it almost impossible for Lucho to earn much money. Rosa had opened a small store on a busy thoroughfare in Cuenca selling packaged foods, treats, milk, cigarettes, and alcohol. The children took turns minding the store. Lucho continued to drive the taxi but earned, according to him, only a few dollars a day after gas, endless repairs, and dues to his taxi cooperative.[10]

The family was now living in a house built by Rosa's brother Carlos, who was still in the United States. Relations with him had improved considerably, but all had not been forgotten. Rosa's brother Miguel was still very angry and even tried to keep them from staying in the house. Rosa said she asked her brother if they could stay there, for the sake of the children, and watch over the house. Empty houses were an open invitation for thieves, who would steal even light sockets and plumbing. The construction of the house was not entirely finished; the walls and floors were still bare concrete. It was really the shell of a house with windows and plumbing. The house was located in a better neighborhood than the last, on the edge of the town, where the countryside begins. Beto and Billy shared a room and a bed, as did the three girls, Alexandra (eighteen), Marisol (fourteen), and Cecilia (eleven). For the first time since they had children, Rosa and Lucho had their own bedroom. Physically, Rosa, now in her late forties, really was showing her age. Her once robust frame seemed small and delicate, and her hair was thinning.

As our interviews unfolded, it became apparent to me that Rosa did not know what to think about Vicente. He had not been able to help them much financially, first because of his debt, then because he was out of work for a while, then because he needed to buy a car to get to work.

Rosa vacillated between concern for his well-being and concern that he had "changed" in some undesirable way, like so many others before him, because of his residence in the United States. Although Rosa for the most part denied that Vicente had changed in any really significant ways, a few days after this interview she asked me to talk with him when I returned to the United States. She wanted me to tell Vicente that having fun was fine, but that he should not have too much fun. She said that his friends were saying he was enjoying himself too much and that perhaps he might listen if a "mature" person like me gave him good advice. Even though he had been gone almost four years, Rosa was still extremely emotional about his absence and cried several times during the interviews. What follows is a mother's understanding of her son's emigration, peppered occasionally with romanticized notions of their relationship and of the hardships he has endured in New York.

Rosa's Story: To "Have Something in Life"

Vicente left because there is no work here—there is no place to find a job and no way to make money. He left too so that he could be somebody—have something in his life. You just can't get ahead here. Vicente was thinking about going to the university here, but he said to me, "Mami, who's going to pay for that? I'm a young man and I need money to go out with my friends, and who's going to give it to me?" And he wasn't just thinking about himself but about all of the children. He said, "The others are also going to need things too—it's better, Mami, if I go. I know you are going to suffer a lot, but I need to go to work. Maybe if I do we can reach the point where we have something." For me this was the saddest thing ever, Anita—it was like my husband left. Vicente was everything.

You know, young people need to be able to enjoy themselves, to go out with their friends and have fun—maybe drink sometimes. But because of the economic situation no one is able to do that. With the little we make and after all the things we have to pay for, there wasn't any [money] left. He felt bad that he was never able to go out with his friends. It got to the point that he even argued with us about it. He was really sad and upset because he had the misfortune of having parents who were really poor. He didn't have money the same way some of his friends did. "How is it," he asked, "that some people can have so much and others have nothing?" I think that all of this was really difficult for him . . . that's why I think he's always wanted to get good work. But it's so difficult to want to do something and not be able to.

Soon after he graduated from high school, he started talking about migrating with Bolívar. Vicente said to him, "I'm not a boy any longer. I need to work and I'll be responsible." Bolívar said that Vicente needed to talk thoroughly with his mother and father — and with the family — about what he wanted to do. Vicente told him, "I would like to study, but if I went to the university who would pay for it? I need more money. I'm not a boy, I'm not a kid — I'm a man. I've talked about it with my friends and my family and I have to go." He talked to Lucho and me and said that he wouldn't go if I really didn't want him to but that he wanted to go and work. What could I say? I couldn't really say, "No, don't go," could I? He has to make his own life. So little by little he started to get his papers ready.

After he got his passport, he was thinking of going, as they say, *andando por la pampa.* But one day he ran into a boy he knew. This boy said he was leaving soon for the United States and that he would introduce Vicente to his *pasadora* [smuggler]. The boy knew the *pasadora* well because, you see, she had arranged for him to leave for New York that very week. You know the boy, Anita: he was the one with all the gold jewelry at Billy's baptism. His uncle is a friend of Vicente's Uncle Carlos in New York. He told Vicente that it was really difficult to go *por la pampa* and that in Baños there is a really good *pasadora.* So Vicente told Bolívar about her and that it costs $7,000. Bolívar wanted to meet the *pasadora* with us. He acted like he was Vicente's father. He said to us, "I'll be happy to help Vicente by giving him more money because I don't want him to go suffering."

It was difficult to locate the *pasadora,* and we spent three or four days walking around looking for her. She was nowhere to be found. We would knock on her door and they wouldn't answer or someone would say that she wasn't at home. We wondered if she thought we were immigration. She is a Cuencana who lived for seven years in the United States. Finally, the boy from Checa left for the United States and we still hadn't met the *pasadora.* We waited to find out if the boy arrived safely. We learned that the boy had arrived after only a three-day trip. He said he spent two days in Quito but that he had no problems in getting out. He left Quito and in eight hours he was in New York. Bolívar said he wanted Vicente to go the same way that boy went, so he asked the boy to call the *pasadora* for us. It's more expensive to go directly like that. It costs about

$7,000 plus you have to have about $800 in your pocket for the trip. We finally talked with the *pasadora.* I was surprised—she was a young woman. Bolívar told Vicente that he would lend him all the money to go with the *pasadora* even if he had to borrow some of it. Finally he had the money for us. Here when someone lends you money you need to fill out papers, like a guarantee that you will pay it back. Sometimes I can't believe how good Bolívar was to us. He never asked for a single paper to fill out. He got the money, and one night we took the $1,000 deposit to the *pasadora.*

After we gave the money to the *pasadora,* we had to wait for the papers. I told Vicente to think hard about what he was doing—and to make sure he understood the great favor that Bolívar had done for us. It was September. We waited and waited, and Vicente was nervous—we all were. We bought a suitcase and some new clothes. One Friday evening at 8 P.M. Vicente and the young ones were getting ready to go to a youth party in Cumbe when the telephone rang. It was the Señora *pasadora.* She said that he had to be ready to leave the next morning at seven. The next morning! We didn't know what to do. At that moment we left to see the Señora to learn about the details. She said that it was for sure that tomorrow would be the trip. He had to go no matter what—whether he was ready or not. We had given her $1,000 already so then we had to give her the other $6,000. We all helped Vicente get his suitcase ready—making sure all his clothes were properly ironed. No one slept that night. I lay down, but I didn't sleep. I cannot even remember all the things that were running through my head.

In the airport the next morning we gave the *pasadora* the rest of the money. We were so worried that she might keep the money and cheat Vicente. Who knows what can happen? We were thinking all kinds of things . . . it was really sad. I mean, we didn't have a receipt [for the money already given]—nothing. Right there in the airport we handed over the money, trying to hide it so no one could see. We were so scared—that's a lot of money to just give to someone like that. She took the money and said, "Don't worry. It's certain that he will go." So that's how Vicente left Cuenca on October 7.

He left at eight in the morning, and at three or four in the afternoon he called us. He was in a hotel somewhere in Quito—it was a secret where he was—he couldn't tell us. He had the papers of someone else, someone who had been to New York before, so he had to know all these many details. He was given a paper with important things he had to learn about New York: where he was going to stay, with whom he would be staying, what they were going to do, other places he knew in New York, the names and numbers of streets, the telephone number where he would be. He had to learn all this. He said it was a really big piece of paper with all these details he had to memorize. There would be so many things he might have to answer when they asked him. He had to learn that if they [immigration officials] said his passport was falsified, he had to always say, "No, it's mine." He had to be sure about it. He had to say that all those things [details on the passport and visa] were about him.

Señor Bolívar has helped Vicente like a father. On the one hand I think that he has done us such a great favor, but on the other I think—well, when Vicente left, he left as a dreaming boy; he wanted to earn dollars and learn about so much. He wanted to work, to buy land and build a house, but it wasn't easy. It still isn't easy, because really, up to this point, he really doesn't have anything. I know that he has a car and that he has a license, but he told me that it cost him a lot of money. Lots of money. And for a while he was sick and for six months he had trouble walking. I'm not really sure what it was, but he couldn't work for quite a while. He told me he was always going to see a doctor. Because of all of this he really hasn't been able to make all that much money. Right now he is working, but I know that you really have to work a lot to get ahead there [Vicente was working in a restaurant as a busboy]. You have to stay there a good long time before you are able to return and visit your family. He would like to be here together with us one day, but I don't know when. He always says, "I don't have the money to come back."

He hasn't really sent us much money. When he was first there, he didn't work because he really didn't know anything yet. He wanted to get used to things for a while before he started working. But he got tired of that; and after a while he was sad because he wasn't working so he started to look for a job. Then once he had one he had to pay off his debt, pay his rent, and buy food. This is why he's not really been able to send us any money.

I think he is working now, but there have been other troubles. He told me that a nephew of Bolívar's was always bothering him, he was always giving him a hard time. I guess they just didn't get along. He couldn't stand Vicente or was jealous of him for some reason. They fought all the time, and Vicente told me that for a while they just ignored each other, with each one pretending the other wasn't there. But Vicente was un-happy, so he had to try to find someplace else to live for a while. It cost him a lot of money to move somewhere else, and then that didn't work out. Now, of course, he's back at Señor Bolívar's house.

Even more, Vicente is suffering because the work there is really hard. Just to be able to have a little thing he has to work from eleven in the morning until eleven at night — sometimes he doesn't leave work until almost midnight. He doesn't really have a fixed schedule. He has to work really hard in that restaurant. There are lots of people to attend to. Sometimes he has to stay at work even when there aren't many customers. He has bad nights when he doesn't earn very much, and that makes him really sad. He sacrifices a lot at work, yet they pay him very little. The ones who are legal, they get paid a lot more. But Vicente, no, he earns just a little bit.

When he had been there about three months he started to feel really bad. He was really sad and said that he wanted to come home and go to the university, maybe to study to be a doctor, cut hair . . . anything. He said that things were so difficult there. He said, "Mami, you wouldn't believe how you have to clean the table. If you don't do it right, the waiters yell at you." He didn't understand a word they said. So one little guy took to stomping on Vicente's foot. When I heard this, it was really painful. I told him he had to put on a strong face, that he had to get used to cleaning the tables but good! He told me he only understood a few words of what people were saying — and that he felt stupid. His boss really liked him, he treated him well, but the other workers were always treating him badly. They were always stepping on his feet or trying to make him fall. He said every time he went to where they fill up water they would stomp on his feet. They didn't do it for any reason, just to bother him.

On his free day he tells me that he cleans his room, washes his clothes, irons, and then he goes out. He has only one day off from work, and he really needs to take advantage of it. Sometimes he sends cards to us telling us what he is doing. He has friends from here that he goes out with and some he met there. They go to a lot of different places because New York is so big. So he doesn't stay at home sad and lonely. He says he goes out in the morning to do some shopping and get some things and then around eleven or so he says he goes out. Sometimes he asks for Sunday off of work and they [friends from Cumbe] all get together. I know he has to go far to get to them. When they are all together he tells me they celebrate their birthdays, their saints' days. I'm sure that they make all these arrangements through the telephone. They call and decide who will bring the cake, the colas, the beer, they make a barbecue — and that's all — after that they say good-bye until there is another reason for them to get together. They all go back to their own rooms so that the next day they can be ready for work.

Usually he calls once a month, but if things aren't going well he may call every two months. The call from there costs so much. When he calls, we talk for about an hour. He asks about the family, he asks about his brothers and sisters, asks if they are all well, if their studies are going well. Sometimes he'll talk with everyone and sometimes only with me. That's how the hour passes. Vicente tells us that "work here is really hard, so you need to make sure that you do everything to see that the others stay in school and study hard. Do anything so that they can stay there and find work."

He does not want his brothers and sisters to go, because it's too hard. Beto sometimes is thinking about going. He thinks that work there must be like it is here, but Vicente tells him that "without work there is no way to live there. You have to do everything yourself, pay rent, buy food and cook, and there is no one to take care of you. You have to learn to do everything. Both men and women have to do the same work—cook, wash, clean." "This is really hard," says Vicente, "because here [in Ecuador] the mother does all that." He says, "They [his siblings] come home and there is food ready, they eat well, and then they get sleepy and lie down. But here [in the United States] it isn't the same, you have to do everything yourself. It's especially hard in the beginning. Lots of tears fall when you first come because there is nothing here for you—only an empty room."

Things just aren't the same when you can't see each other. It's not the same as talking face to face together. Everyone changes. I think because of the loneliness. Like my brother Carlos. He left when he was just a young boy of eighteen years old, and he is not the same. He comes back now, walks around, and looks at everything, but he doesn't have the words [conversation] anymore. He doesn't sit talking and laughing with us. He never has a smile. Now he won't eat the food we make. There he only eats sandwiches that he takes to work—really big sandwiches made with ham, cheese, I think he told me, and something really, well—some special thing, no? This is what he is accustomed to. He's also told me the same thing Vicente has, that he works like, excuse me for what I'm going to say, he works worse than if he were an animal. Construction work there is really difficult, and he had to work really hard all the time, especially before he got all of his papers. When he was illegal, they tried to pay him only a small amount and work him even harder. Now that he is legal he tells me that they pay him better. He told me he now makes about $800 a week, but he only gets this much because he is legal.

Carlos comes back for visits, but he said that he will never come back to live. I don't know why he built this house. He doesn't think very well. He is used to life there and his work is there, but then sometimes he thinks about his family here — that's why he built the house, I guess. Sometimes he wants to help us because I have so many children. Then he turns around and he says he wants to sell the house. You see, his thinking is all wrong — first one thing, then he turns around and it's something else. He tries to help us mainly because he wants the children to go to school.

When they say that when you go to New York you live like you are in heaven, it's a lie. There you work double. You work hard without having anyone [family] around you. Here, in contrast, people want to work, but they get there late, they stand around talking. This is why Vicente says the other children have to go to school. The sad thing is, we couldn't help Vicente. We were backward too. No one knew what things would be like, and we listened to the older people who thought that if you worked you would see money. But it's a lie. There's a necessity, Anita, for a person to be well prepared in order to have work — maybe it's not big work — but you have it all the same. If you don't, well, that's why the people are leaving the city to migrate. They leave with pain, leaving their sad mother and father and family behind, sometimes even a wife. So many people go like this.

I say sometimes that Vicente has changed there, but then sometimes I say he is just the same. But I do think he has changed, Anita. Because of the loneliness. Of course, we talk, but only by telephone. I don't know if he's fatter, thinner, or sick. No doubt so that I feel all right, he tells me, "I'm fine, Mami." And we do the same. We have to say that we are all well so that he doesn't suffer more. We all say we are fine. Because if I say to him that I am sick he's going to feel even worse. Therefore, all of us have to try to be strong. There are so many people who have family there. Even if you are really sick, they say that you have to say, "No, we are all well." What I tell him is that we are always thinking about him as though he were still here.

Lucho does talk about going too for the same reasons Vicente left, because there is no work. We don't even have enough for food; we have to pay the tuition for the kids, telephone, lights, water, everything. We don't pay rent because it's my brother's house, but if we didn't have that we would have to pay rent. With all this, Anita, the money just doesn't stretch. With this crisis everyone would leave if they could.

When we are old, we're going to say, "We don't have anything!" Right now what little money there is we spend on school. Lucho says, "I'm still a bit young—I want to go." He said he wants to borrow a little from this person and from that one and with that money he'll go. He doesn't want Vicente to give it to him, because Vicente doesn't want him to come. So he says he'll stay with his friends—people he met at the cooperative. He says, "I don't want to go and be a bother to my *compadre* Bolívar— I'll go completely on my own. I want to go so that I'll have something. Everyone has something but me. Vicente is making money for himself, and the other kids are getting big and soon they will have homes of their own, but they won't have money to help us—they'll need it for their own necessities. I can't ask them to give me money for food. No, I couldn't do that." He [Lucho] has his papers all ready to go. The problem right now is that he doesn't have the money—$8,000 is needed. But he says sometimes that he'll just go *andando por la pampa*. I don't want him to go. It would be very sad for the kids because they are still young. But I can't say no to him because he can't make money here. He gets annoyed with me when I say, "Don't go." I know that without money you can't do anything.

My father has begun to cause us worry again. You know the land he gave us for the house—well, because we never got the papers to say it was our land and our house, he wants me to give up the house. I don't really know why he's doing this. He seems to have changed his character as he has gotten older—he has gotten very selfish. The one who is changing his mind is Miguel [her brother]. Miguel used to get along really well with me but not now. Miguel is always looking around trying to get more land—he's always trying to figure out how he can have more. Now he is saying that our land is for everyone and how can it be just for me? Especially since he says he has done more for the family than anyone. Miguel wants our parents to leave him more. We've been able to work on the house only little by little, and now that it is almost done they want to take it away. Just this Sunday it was rented out. I didn't tell Vicente about this because he would be sad. My father is saying that he no longer wants to give us the land and house and that he wants to split it up—everyone with an equal part. I'm really worried about this. Miguel is ruined now, and he is always walking around looking at things greedily. He just walks around eyeing everything.

Miguel was in Cuenca for a couple of months with Carlos, and he told Carlos that I should be paying rent. You know, Miguel still wouldn't even talk to me. He spoke plenty about me to other people—but to me he wouldn't say a thing. Carlos said he was coming to Cuenca to finish the house, but once he got here Miguel got Carlos drunk and convinced him to buy the car instead. The car is paid for now, but he didn't do anything to the house. He didn't even want the car, but he bought it anyway. So now the house still is like this, but there is a brand-new car down there that just sits there. What good is that? I had no idea of any of this—it never crossed my mind he would do that. I didn't know anything about this until it happened.

Vicente always talked a lot to me. He'd come home in the afternoons, usually just he and little Billy, and he would tell me everything. He never had a single secret from me. I knew everything that he did. He loved going out with his friends, but he was a really good boy. He always asked me, "Mami, give me permission to leave until six this afternoon." And if he was later he always called me. He had a lot of trust in me. We would sit, much as we are now, talking. Sometimes he would bring café and we would sit on the bed, just the two of us together. When children are little they are all affectionate, but Vicente always stayed that way with me, even when he was older. Vicente was my companion. It is just so difficult without him. Sometimes I just think about if he were just to walk in again. He was the one person whom I really confided in . . . the others, well they don't feel the same way—they stay alone. The little ones are still too young, but the rest don't talk to me as he did. If he saw something when he was at school or when he was out, he'd come home and tell me about it. He held nothing back from me.

Because he was the oldest, he knew how much I had suffered. The others really don't know. They were too young, but Vicente knew all that had happened. He really understood our situation because he was little when things were still so difficult. When Lucho was young, he was crude. He drank too much. Now he's much more tranquil—but when he was young, he could really be a brute. Vicente remembers all these bad times. When we were young and we were selling milk—hauling those buckets—Lucho was always cranky and gruff. He would yell at me, call me names, and be rude. Vicente remembers this and he says that "Papi doesn't know how to behave himself and present a good image. He doesn't know how to run a business." The other kids never saw any of this. Sometimes we even would make money by walking around and selling apples and fruits, and Vicente always had to go with us. One time we had a really old car—this thing was so old the windows were all out—we were out selling milk, and Vicente must have been five or six years old when he fell out of the car. The door flew open, and he just fell out. He was OK, just bumped his head because we were going so slowly, but all of these things he remembers and they make him feel bad.

He told me that he doesn't like to think about how things were when he was really little, that it just makes him feel bad that he had a family so poor and that his father could be so brutish. Of course, now that he's far away we don't talk about these things. I don't know, maybe he's just forgotten this. But he really suffered a lot when he was little.

Now Lucho wants to go so he won't be dependent on anyone. He wants to buy a small piece of land in the countryside where we can live contentedly. This is what he has been thinking. I think that you can work to seventy years old, more or less. Now we work only to put the kids through school. But we can't afford it anymore. Lucho is saying that we have to change the kids' schools because the two littlest ones, Billy and Cecilia, have only gone to public schools, and one day they are going to complain to us that they didn't have a chance [in private school]. So we are thinking of telling Beto and Marisol that we can't help anymore with their private schools [that would mean public school for them]. There just isn't enough to cover it all.

Well, now that we have arrived at a certain age, my hope is that all of the kids will marry, and someday it will be the two of us again, as it is for my mother and father. We'll have to work until we can't anymore in order to maintain ourselves because they [the kids] aren't going to be able to care for us. They are going to have their own families. It's hard, for as much as they would want to help us, there wouldn't be a way. Even if they wanted to, they wouldn't be able to. Maybe if they lived nearby they could help with a thing now and then, but they will have their own families to worry about and they will have to work for their own families. The two of us will just have to continue working until we are little old people [*viejitos*]. This is what we have been thinking. This is why Lucho is thinking of leaving. He wants something for his old age. He thinks that when we are old the kids won't know us or come to see us. He thinks that nobody loves old people.

Vicente tells me that he would like to get married someday so that he can have his own nice family. He should get married here, no? He had a girlfriend here, and I think you know the girl. She told him that she loves him, and he was upset when she told him not to go. But if he wanted to marry her he would have, despite what anyone else thinks or says. I don't like the girl. She comes from a family that is only bad. The mother of the family is married, but she is always looking for other men. She tells them she loves them for a while, and then she throws them out and sets out looking for another. All of them in the family do this—not the girl yet, but she's not married either, right? But I think that if all the others in the family do that, so will she. The mother separated from her husband, was off with another, then another. This is what that family is accustomed to doing. They get a man and they throw him out and look for another, and so on. The older sister of the girl, she's married, but when my brother Carlos was here she was after him. Because he's my brother I told him everything I knew about her. She cried to my brother that she wanted him to take her to the United States with him, that she loves him so much . . . and she has a little boy of only five or six! Was she just going to throw him out too? I don't think Vicente should be with someone whose family does things like this. It would be a better thing if he married a different girl; that way he could make his own house and work. Once he gets married, it wouldn't be good for the husband and wife to be separated, so he should stay here. I don't believe that you should marry one person for a while and then marry another. No, you should marry and have your child and make your house. Either here or there, but the two of them together. They should marry and from then on not live separated.

I think that Vicente should do the kind of work that he wants to do. He's been working in a restaurant now for a while; maybe he could come home and open a restaurant. He should work in whatever is best for him, but I think that if he were to do a different kind of business that he knew nothing about it would be more difficult and the business would probably not work out. Or if he is married they can have a business together where they both work together. But, of course, this is all his decision. He really hasn't said anything to me yet about this. Sometimes neighbors and friends [from Cumbe] ask me about him. "He's very handsome," they tell me. "What are his plans?" So far he doesn't really know, or he hasn't told me. But you see, that really is the big question: will he get married? Will he stay there? These things we just can't know. Who knows what would be better?

I think Vicente regrets going to the United States. He says that if he had been able to study in the university he could have stayed here and worked. "I didn't think about what I was doing," he said. He said, "I always wanted to go to the United States to visit. That to me was marvelous. But it didn't happen like that. Sure, when I first arrived it was so beautiful, but then later when I started working it was just hard." He says he wants to come back soon, but he wants to come with something, some money to build a house, or to have money to put in some type of business. He is staying there so long because he wants to do something for the family. He's thinking about how to help us.

When he left, it was so sad. I fell ill, and I am still not well. The doctor told me that my vision is completely bad. The doctor told me that I need to stop being so sad all the time and that I can't cry all the time as I have been doing. He said I need to stay busy, go out for walks, take little trips, and try to forget about crying. It's all this crying that has ruined my eyesight. I also have such bad headaches, and the doctor said I need glasses. But you need a lot of money to get glasses, and I don't have the money. I'll just have to wait and perhaps one day I'll have the money. Of course, it's not that I can't see, but I can't see letters very well, I can't read, and when the time comes to sign things I can't see it very well. I can't see where I'm supposed to sign. This is my problem, Anita. It was so very sad when Vicente left, leaving us alone here. He has also suffered so much. We will both suffer until he is home again.

5.1. Lucho serving champagne at the children's baptism in 1989.
(Photo by Irene Miles)

5 | *Lucho*

Introduction

As I reviewed my notebooks and journals to write this chapter, it became very clear to me that my opinions of Lucho have vacillated considerably over the course of our twelve-year acquaintance. Indeed, during that first year I even wrote that knowing him was a lot like eating *cuy* (guinea pig). The more I saw of him, the more I liked him. But in the long run it was not even that simple. So much would happen over the twelve years we knew one another, and my feelings about him would inevitably be affected by those events.

My first information about Lucho came from Rosa, who painted a rather good picture of him. Before I even met him, she spoke fondly of him, pointing out his sense of humor. He'd have me in stitches, she predicted; but that did not turn out to be the case. In fact, in the beginning I found that Lucho's sense of humor was not at all in keeping with my own. Most of his jokes centered on portraying an image of himself as a worldly womanizer, and his one-liners were often about his exploits with other women or my perceived wealth. Even though I understood that these statements were meant to be humorous and were not really spoken to offend, I still found them unpleasant. I thought his jokes were frequently insulting to Rosa or to me. At an early stage I found myself frustrated that our conversations were often very limited and trivial — or nonexistent if he was not in the mood to talk. Occasionally he took me to the edge of my patience as he pushed me to laugh or comment about something he said that I thought was just plain stupid. For example, once (long before I was married) he teased that I should marry Vicente so that he would have the advantages of living in the United States and I could know the pleasures of having a much younger husband. He provoked me in countless ways.

I often tried to mitigate my annoyance with Lucho by attempting to analyze why he behaved the way he did, with the hope that his behavior might carry a different meaning if I understood his world. Indeed, I knew it was intrinsically unfair to judge him by my western, feminist standards. I should note too that his behavior was not at all aberrant — it was repeated in various ways with many of the husbands of my primary female informants. Poor men would often find the easiest way to deal with me, at least in the beginning, was to joke with me — often about my untold riches.

I think this was the case for a variety of reasons, not the least of which is that they had very little experience in dealing with foreigners, especially female ones, who come from far more politically and economically powerful places. My informants' experiences with monied people in Cuenca had never been very positive, and men in particular showed a healthy skepticism about me. I cannot blame them for that. While it was never hard for me to strike up conversations with women about children, food, or family, it was much harder to sustain conversations with men. Men quizzed me more thoroughly than women did about my work, and they always tried to show that it all made sense to them. In general, I think that men were much more acutely aware of the vast economic differences between us, and they feared that as men and providers they would be judged poorly. Put bluntly, these men were accustomed to being insulted by the dominant society when they left their homes — and now it appeared that someone from that society was sitting in their kitchen. Jokes, often at my expense, were a good way to get the upper hand. While what I was doing as an anthropologist made sense to me, I cannot discount how odd my presence must have seemed to my informants. There is no precedent for strangers insinuating themselves into peoples' lives, and common sense and experience encourage caution. Much of Lucho's bravado over the years was, I've come to believe, an attempt to assert an image of strength and competence in the face of a demeaning world.

The fact that my own status was so ambivalent did not make things any easier. When I began my first fieldwork I was twenty-eight, an age that everyone saw as fully mature (if not a bit long in the tooth); yet I was unmarried, living alone, and not obviously employed. Most people, including Lucho, viewed this as odd but also accepted that I could not be held to Ecuadorian standards of behavior. As a foreigner, however, and one who represents a powerful other, I was also sometimes treated in social functions more like a man than a woman. I was included in political discussions in ways that women never were, and I was often called upon to agree with someone who wished to assert his position. "Isn't that right, Anita?" they would query. On occasion I was used as a pawn in a simple game of one-upmanship that had been going on long before I ever arrived. In this game one person who saw himself as socially superior to another would try to get me to agree with him in order to demean the other. In one family, for example, a cousin had married quite well and lived with his small family in a nice middle-class neighborhood. He would often come over to his poor cousin's house and — looking down his nose at my informant's home and family — would make comments about having too many children or not working hard enough. He would then turn to me seeking agreement. I developed my own method of avoiding involvement in these conversations: on those occasions my Spanish seemingly failed me completely, and I pretended that I couldn't understand a word that was said.

With Lucho I found that there was a real shift in his behavior to me when I became Alexandra's godmother and my position in their lives became less ambivalent. I now have a social status that makes sense to him, and one for which there is a ready and understandable code of conduct. I am his *comadre* and his daughter's *madrina,* which means that I should be treated with a degree of respect and consideration. Since Alexandra's baptism he has been much more careful about what he says to me and how he says it. He still likes to joke, but his comments are of a different nature. He now focuses on the difficulties of life in Ecuador, trying to put a humorous spin on how they are "jerked around" and "screwed" at every turn.

I did not see that much of Lucho during the 1993 trip, because my research took me away from Cuenca much of the time and Lucho was working very long hours. As noted previously, this was the time of greatest turmoil within the family, and relations among them were frequently strained. Lucho met my husband, Richard, during this visit and used his sense of humor to break the ice with him. Lucho is a small man, probably under five feet two inches, and Rich is relatively tall at six feet two inches. Lucho was relentless at first in teasing Rich about his large size, especially his "enormous" feet. He made Rich's physical dominance appear to be almost a deformity. Rich's halting Spanish became another subject for joking. I think that much of Lucho's joking with Rich was an attempt to equalize status with the big, tall, "rich" American who comes bearing gifts that can never be reciprocated by a poor Ecuadorian man. Lucho was able to draw attention away from the status differences between them by pointing out the linguistic incompetence of this far too big American. None of his joking was really mean-spirited, and the fact that Rich was never offended went a long way toward solidifying the relationship between the two. During most of that trip, however, Lucho was in fact fairly quiet, and it seemed to me that he was walking on eggshells—no doubt because of his strained relations with Rosa. For the most part Lucho and I were polite but distant with one another, which suited me just fine.

When I returned with my family in 1995, the despair of 1993 was still fresh in my mind, and I wondered about the lingering effects of those times. I looked for signs of stress and probed family members about it, but it was all seemingly forgotten. Lucho appeared more deeply involved with his family than he had in the past, and there was already some talk of Vicente migrating. Lucho was really taken with my infant daughter and enjoyed holding her and bouncing her on his knee. This was the first time that Lucho spent significant amounts of time with us; he took several Sundays off from work while we were there, and we all piled in his taxi for visits to the countryside. Lucho is an inherently impatient man, so he hustled us quickly from one place to the next, acting as an impromptu tour guide. We were surprised to learn that even though the children have lived their whole lives about two hours away from important Inca ruins, they had never had the opportunity to visit the site before. Sunday excursions cost gasoline money and take time off from work, so they just don't happen. Lucho seemed genuinely honored that Rich's mother came to meet them and have lunch, and he treated her with a great deal of respect and dignity. He did, however, comment afterward about the money that the *vieja* (old lady) must spend on cigarettes, noting, not incorrectly, that they could eat for a week on the money she spent on cigarettes.

Since this time my relationship with Lucho has gotten easier. He is much more circumspect now and in a general sense has mellowed. Lucho is a very good example of how gender identities shift throughout a lifetime and how they reflect changing life and social conditions (see Gutmann 1996; Hamilton 1998). I respect that he is very careful around me now not to make too many sexist comments and that he always goes out of his way when we come to Cuenca to drive us anywhere we want to go at any time. I also really appreciate that, while it is fairly accept-able for men of this social class in Cuenca to drink heavily at parties or celebrations and lose control of themselves, Lucho has never done this in front of me. In all the years I have known him and all the countless parties I have attended with him, Lucho has behaved with dignity. This is something that I cannot say about many of my other male informants, most of whom have drunk too much at one point or another. In the early years I think Lucho made a conscious effort not to act the drunken fool, while in later years he simply didn't care to drink.

At the time of the interviews in 1999 it is clear that Lucho was wres-tling with his own decision to migrate to the United States. While it would have been nice if Vicente could have sent money home, Lucho recognized that he had his own future to prepare for and was uncomfort-able asking him for help. As a father he was upset that he was presented with the impossible decision of making a choice between providing for his children or being with them (see Miles 1997).[1] He was worried that if he went away they would never have the same affection for him that they did then. He was proud of his children and their school success; but, because Rosa seemed to favor the oldest and youngest children, both of whom were boys, Lucho worried most about the girls. He knew that unless they went to school they would be very vulnerable. The girls returned his affection easily (see Chapter 6). During the course of the interviews he told me over and over again that if he had some way of making an independent living in Cuenca he would never consider, even for a moment, leaving his family. Obviously, things did not get better for him economically, and a year later he was on his way to New York.

Field Notes: 1989–1998

1989

During the last few months of 1989 I found that I enjoyed my time with Lucho and that, like Rosa, I had begun to appreciate his positive outlook on life. He was a tough survivor, just trying to make it in a world where the deck was stacked against him. Lucho worked hard and seemed as engaged with his kids as he could be, given his job as a long-distance bus driver. I couldn't help but notice how the children, especially the little ones, clustered around him when he was home. Even when I could find fault with how he treated Rosa, his devotion to his children was always readily apparent.

MARCH 19

I met Lucho today. They were all lying down (it was about noon) because Lucho needed to rest for his trip to Guayaquil later that evening. I showed them a lot of pictures of home—some postcards of Chicago and Syracuse and some family shots. They seemed really interested and asked some intriguing questions. Lucho wanted to know who owned the ducks in the public park and why they weren't stolen.

As with most husbands I meet, Lucho seemed to feel the need to impress me. He kept trying to make jokes—most of them at Rosa's expense—about all of his girlfriends. I pretended I didn't understand them because I couldn't bring myself to laugh. He also kept asking me if he could keep the postcards I had brought from the United States. He literally said that I don't need them so I should just leave them with him. He was joking . . . but he wasn't. I didn't want to give them to him since I show them to all the families I work with.

I don't know what I was expecting based on what Rosa said, but I was surprised to see how short Lucho is.

MARCH 29

Lucho returned around 7 P.M. He made the joke—it was only a joke I think—that he went to see his girlfriend. When he came in, Vicente was telling me stories in the tape recorder. He greeted me, went into the other room, and picked up the baby. A few minutes later Rosa started preparing supper. There was a little conference between Rosa and Lucho—over what I cannot say. I wondered if they were uncomfortable with me staying through dinner time—but I was anxious to finish up with Vicente. I left about 8 P.M. Lucho played with the baby in the other room most of the time I was there, but when she fussed too much he called Alexandra to come and take her away.

APRIL 5

I stayed with the kids while Rosa and Lucho went to see a tailor. When they got back, Rosa made hot chocolate and we drank it with bread and bananas that Lucho brought back from the coast. He stayed in the other room lounging on the bed most of the time I was there. When I left about 7 P.M. all of the kids were draped over him on the bed watching TV. I learned that at one point Lucho used to be a tailor, but that he makes more money driving a bus.

MAY 6

I invited Rosa and Lucho and the kids over to my house for apple pie. It was interesting to see Lucho out of his own house. He was clearly uncomfortable but prattled on all the same, making all kinds of jokes. Most of them, predictably, about other women. Rosa laughs a pained little laugh, but I thought even she had had enough. Whether I believe his jokes are true or not, I think it is rather telling that he feels he *must* make these jokes—even when we don't laugh. To be a man in his eyes is to make these kinds of macho presentations of self. Lucho said that in Ecuador if a woman doesn't marry by twenty-five she is presumed to stay single for the rest of her life. He was surprised to hear that twenty-eight is still not that old to be single at home.

MAY 16

When I asked Rosa the other day about her relationship with Lucho, she said that because he travels so much he is often not there and he lets her do as she chooses. When he is home, though, he seems demanding—he'll ask for café or something to eat without ever saying please or thank you and will often complain that whatever he wants isn't coming to him fast enough. I have noticed that when he is in the mood to talk to me Rosa has to take a back seat. When he's not in the mood to talk to me, he just hangs out in the other room. I'm trying not to take this personally. Lucho treats Vicente really differently than does Rosa. Rosa is almost deferential to Vicente, while Lucho teases him. He pulled on his ears and laughed when Vicente didn't really pronounce English words correctly.

JUNE 5

Lucho is starting to be a bit less of a show-off around me. I suspect that all the jokes are really a way of easing tensions. Much like Radcliffe-Brown's analysis of the mother-in-law relationship, this joking relationship makes interactions go smoothly and steers us away from discussing anything too personal.[2]

Because of the transportation workers' strike [over rising gasoline prices] Lucho has been home for a while. In contrast to Pedro [another informant], Lucho does not take on the purpose of the strike as his own cause. It is almost as though the strike is something that happened to him, not something he as a transportation worker has a real stake in.

When I arrived on Saturday, Lucho was out back washing his own clothes. He said he learned to do it in the military. He seemed proud of the fact that he served his time in the military and didn't buy his way out of it as so many men do.

JUNE 9

I went to Rosa's for lunch, and when I got there she had gone to buy a flower that Alexandra needed for school. Lucho was there but clearly in a testy mood. He had just gotten back from Machala at 10 A.M. and was scheduled to leave at 2 for Guayaquil. The house revolved around Lucho for the whole time he was there. There was palpable tension in the air. He was lying on the bed with Cecilia when I arrived; he got up, shook my hand, excused himself, and went back to lying down watching TV. He talked with Cecilia the whole time, encouraging her to talk to him. Every five minutes he would ask if Rosa had come back, and Vicente would run out in the street to see if she was coming. Just before she arrived, he got up, went out back, and washed up. He grilled Rosa on why she was gone so long. When she tried to explain that she had to find a particular type of flower for Alexandra, he interrupted her explanation and just barked, "Hurry up with the food." He ate in the other room, and Rosa kept jumping up and down every time he called her. When he left, Rosa seemed instantly relieved and the air of tension over the house lifted.

AUGUST 20

Lucho was talking to all of us about how important it is not to trust people. He said that most people you meet are bad and that the good ones are few and far between. The lesson for all of us was that you need to be careful about trusting people you meet casually.

We talked about why Lucho didn't make it to Miguel's daughter's baptism in Cumbe. He said that his boss has been ill lately and that because of that he has more responsibilities. Getting drunk and dancing for one night isn't worth it if it could jeopardize his job.

AUGUST 29

When Lucho came with Rosa to my house to ask if I would be Alexandra's godmother, he put on a clean white shirt. He was all politeness and took this social ritual very seriously. None of his joking today. He is actually quite nice when he wants to be.

SEPTEMBER 18

Lucho was really the perfect gentleman and host of the baptism. He spent most of his time passing drinks and encouraging people to eat and drink.

OCTOBER 2

Today Lucho told me that Ecuadorians could never stay in the United States because it is not their *tierra*. People always need to go home to where they come from. Besides, he added, life in the United States for Ecuadorians is all work, work, work, and they miss the parties and dances of home.

NOVEMBER 20

This is the first time we have visited Lucho's parents, but he wasn't able to come. He's on another trip somewhere. Rosa once told me that his parents were "cold" and "strange," and I now understand a little of what she means. They run a small store right off the Pan American Highway, with their small house much higher up the mountain slopes in Tarqui. There is practically nothing in the store—a few bars of soap, cigarettes, some candies, spice packets, and alcohol. When we entered the store, they seemed somewhat aloof, neither pleased nor displeased to see us [Rosa, all of the girls, and me]. Rosa seemed somewhat uncomfortable with her in-laws, and she is far more formal with them than she is with her own family. Rosa told me once that Lucho has a very large family and that he sometimes feels like he has been forgotten by them since there are so many. Rosa thought there are eleven siblings, but she wasn't sure.

DECEMBER 3

We just got back from Cumbe and my "good-bye" party there. Lucho's relatives were supposed to come, but they didn't show up. That was fine with me. It was a nice party though. Miguel brought his guitar and sang. I really got a chance to see Lucho relaxed and happy. It made me like him. He was the life of the party, making all sorts of jokes about himself (appropriate, I would say, when you are with your in-laws). He makes fun of his height (or lack of it) and some of the things that happen while on the road. He portrays himself as something of a bumpkin. Rosa seemed to enjoy him, and she laughed the hardest at his jokes. It was good to see them together like that—laughing and relaxed.

June–July 1993

I saw very little of Lucho during this visit. He was now driving a taxi and working double shifts, leaving the house at 6 A.M., returning for lunch and café at some point, and calling it a day and coming home as late as 9 P.M. Given the fact that they owed money for the taxi and had just had a new baby, Lucho was feeling pressure to make extra money. Perhaps because of the family troubles at the time too, Lucho often seemed uncomfortable around Rosa and was probably just as happy to be out of that gloomy house. Lucho is a very energetic man who never enters a room quietly and rarely sits still for very long. Even at mealtimes he is the first one finished eating and does not linger at the table. The contrast between his vitality and Rosa's calm was never more pronounced than it was in 1993.

JUNE 2

Lucho looked very much the same as he always did, and he was quite surprised to see us when he came home as usual for lunch. He was the only one so far who seemed even a bit happy about the baby. He pointed him out to us, saying "otro más" or another one. He helped Alexandra get lunch ready since Rosa is in bed. He also commented, though, about the poor quality of the food she made—and it wasn't the usual, formalized "begging your pardon" comment that people always make when they hand you food.[3] He was really unhappy with it.

Lucho always seems to enjoy playing host, and he turned the gathering into a small party with *trago* [cane alcohol] and toasts.

JUNE 11

Lucho is having some tensions at work since his cooperative has recently decided to upgrade the quality of service. Not only does he have to wear a necktie, which he dislikes, but he is worried about doing all the little things they asked drivers to do, like opening doors and carrying packages, etc. He said that the cooperative wants to provide *servicio de lujo* — luxury service. This means drivers have to be clean, polite, and helpful. They are inspected every morning before they head out. This makes him nervous since he worries he will do the wrong thing. I think it is a real testament to the class system that Lucho, the guy who often prattles on in social settings and is the life of the party as it were, was nervous about how his passengers — perhaps from the middle and upper classes — would judge his manners.

JUNE 27

Boy, Lucho is in the doghouse. While Rosa is polite if not a little reserved to Lucho, her mother more or less ignored him the whole time we were in Cumbe. They went through the ritualized greeting, but that was about it. Lucho seemed uncomfortable. Rosa's mother was more quiet than usual, and I noticed that she put me ahead of Lucho when serving food [order indicates position of respect]. Before, she always served her husband first then handed us our plates almost simultaneously. This time I was given my food very pointedly before Lucho [see Weismantel 1988]. He did not say much at all to his in-laws and spent most of the day tinkering with his taxi.

1995

ENTRY 1

Lucho looks physically different to me this time. He is about forty-five years old now, and he is developing a round little belly like a middle-aged man. Since he is so short, it really pops out. I used to think that he looked younger than Rosa, but that is no longer the case. He also talks more like a mature man. He said that Bolívar, Vicente, and he were up late last night drinking and that he is too old to be doing that.

ENTRY 2

We spent last Sunday touring all around Inga Pirca [Inca ruins] and the surrounding areas in Lucho's taxi. I felt like a really irresponsible mother. Back home children are put in car seats, and here we were careening around the Andes, Isabel on my lap, in this ancient car with the loosest steering imaginable. Lucho had to turn the wheel about three times just to go around a curve. The good news is that the taxi doesn't really go above 40 m.p.h. Lucho was in a jolly mood, and he kept trying to get Billy to talk. When he did, Lucho would burst out laughing.

ENTRY 3

Rosa and Lucho came to talk about Billy's baptism plans. They talked about how selfish people are here and how they do not want to attend to you in offices. They are having trouble fixing Billy's birth papers for the baptism, and the people in the Civil Registry are giving them the run-around. They think they made a contact in the registry here in Cuenca who will expedite the process — for a small bribe.

ENTRY 4

At Billy's baptism some of Lucho's work colleagues came late, accompanied by their wives, who wore these really flashy red party dresses. What a contrast they were to the peasants of Cumbe, who wore ponchos and *polleras*. Sometimes I forget that Lucho and Rosa really do interface with two very different worlds.

1997

Lucho is as concerned about Alexandra as Rosa is. He says that he knows the boys she is seeing are up to no good because if their intentions were good they would have done the right thing and come to see him first. Honest boys would come and pay their "respect" to Lucho before going out with his daughter. He regrets moving her from the high school run by the nuns (an all-girl school) to the one she is at now, which has more boys than girls. As a measure of his conservatism he even complained that Alexandra had cut her hair to shoulder-length. I had to tell him that he shouldn't let something as small as that bother him and if he wants his girls to succeed they have to adopt more "modern" hairstyles. I was thinking to myself that they should be happy she didn't get a tattoo or pierce some unusual body part.

Interviews: 1999

By this time Lucho seemed like a very different man than he had when I first met him twelve years earlier. He was truly middle-aged; but even though he was very frustrated about the economic crisis and his inability to make money, he was usually in good humor. In fact, for the first time in our long acquaintance I actually found that I looked forward to his arrival home at lunch. Whereas Rosa had gotten sadder over the years, Lucho had simply smoothed over the rough edges. When he came in for lunch, he'd liven up the room with a quick joke or story. His one-liners to Rich and me were now clearly laced with affection, and he was truly at ease with us. Lucho has always liked little children, and my Isabel was no exception. He laughed good-naturedly at her when she prattled on in what was for him unintelligible English. His children have always been much quieter, and he found her verbal antics unusual and terribly amusing. Like Rosa, Lucho had gotten thinner in these last years and had lost the round belly he had been developing. His hair had just a hint of gray in it on the top, and his face was beginning to show soft creases around the eyes and mouth. Lucho was not happy with his thinning waistline and said it was all due to a life of too much worry.

Lucho was nervous about the 1999 interviews because this was the first time I had taped interviews with him. Even though he was enthusiastic about the book and said from the outset that he thought it was a good idea for people to understand the lives of poor Ecuadorians, when it came right down to it he was worried about saying the right things. He tried to put me off for a while, but once we started he was a natural. He likes to talk, and I think he enjoyed the idea that someone thought that what he had to say was worth something. He is a pragmatist (in contrast to Rosa's romanticism), and while he too misses Vicente he does not paint the same picture of a suffering exile. Quite the contrary, he states that he "sent" Vicente the easy way—"he didn't suffer at all." I think it is significant that Lucho claims that he "sent" Vicente the easy way when it was Bolívar who gave the loan and Vicente who paid it off. I don't think Lucho is really trying to take credit for something he didn't do here but rather pointing out that he still had a role in the decision-making process. Even though his son felt it was necessary to go (maybe because Lucho couldn't provide well enough), Lucho behaved like a good father and saw to it that his son went as comfortably as possible. Whereas Rosa focuses on Vicente's emotional anguish in the United States and the loneliness he feels away from his family, Lucho equates suffering primarily with physical discomfort, such as an arduous trip, back-breaking labor, and hunger. His son experienced none of these. Indeed, according to Lucho, Vicente spent his first eight days in New York sightseeing with Bolívar, a luxury that Lucho (who has worked seven days a week for as long as I've known him) cannot fathom.

I conducted these interviews with Lucho during the lunch hour on the third floor of the house of Rosa's brother Carlos, where they were living. That floor was a constant source of agitation for the family, as it was a reminder of the pettiness of some of the extended family relations. When Carlos and his brother Miguel had returned to Cuenca for a visit from New York, Miguel (who has never forgiven Rosa) rented out the third floor of the house to a taxi cooperative to hold its weekly meetings. Lucho said Rosa's brother had done it not for the money but simply "for spite" and to annoy them, as once a week or so twenty or thirty men would go tramping up their stairs. Meetings always involved some drinking. That floor stood as a tangible symbol of Lucho's inability to control his living conditions.

Lucho's Story: "We're Screwed"

Vicente left because, well, because he wanted to. He was young. He was in high school, and between the kids they all agreed that they would go when they graduated. And that's how it all started. Others had gone before, but some left in the middle of the school year. But the rest wanted to wait until they had graduated. So the group of them decided to go. Really, they were driven by youth. On top of this he always dreamed, as young people always do, that he wanted to do something. Some kind of work where he could earn money. He figured that if he went to the university he would be in school for a really long time. It seemed to me that for him this would be really hard. He would rather dedicate himself to his friends. He didn't want to study something that would take a long time, so he went. Really, he didn't want to study anymore, that's what I imagine.

From my way of thinking I don't think it was a good idea. Going there [the United States] you suffer too much, you struggle too hard, and he had never really worked hard before. Really, when he left he was a boy as far as work went. He had never really worked hard. He went to school, came home and had lunch, studied, and went to bed. This was all he did. I think that, well, I really didn't like it that he went. I felt bad when he left, a little, no, a lot bitter and sad. And even now I still feel for him since he was our first. But because he was a young man of twenty, there was nothing I could do.

When he first went, he tried to help us out economically. He sent a big package with presents for each of us, with our names on it. Backpacks, pens—he sent us everything. Well, now he really doesn't send much anymore, and I think that with time passing he has changed. Of course, once in a while he sends something—so I can't say he doesn't at all. But there is nothing I can do. I don't feel right demanding it from him. He's a grown man, and I can't say to him, "Send us something!" You can't force him. But once in a while now he takes it upon himself to help us out with a little something—for example, he sent things on Mother's Day or Father's Day. But even when he couldn't help us with money he always talked with his brothers and sisters about their homework and he tells them to stay in school so that they can finish their studies. He doesn't want the others to do what he did. Sure, in the beginning he thought it was all wonderful, but then things got difficult. He just wasn't prepared to work the way he has. There everything is different. He didn't think it would be like that, and he started to feel bad. "Why did I do this?" he would say. And I would say to him, "Well, you are there now so you have to do something so that you can come back. If you don't, you won't ever make it back or it will all be a waste." In the first days he really wanted to come back . . . now I don't think he does anymore. Now things have changed. But his character, I mean the way he was, that hasn't changed. He is still easygoing, tranquil. He is just like he always was. Even though he's been there, what, almost three years. He still is very respectful. Sometimes I think he has changed, and then we talk on the phone and I know that he is still the same as always.

I don't know if Vicente will come back. He says so, but I can't really know his thoughts. When he first left, he felt bad and said to me, "Papi, how could everyone lie that the United States was a paradise?" And I said to him, "You know, you didn't suffer the way others did to get there. You went in a plane. I sent you in a plane from Cuenca to Quito, from there to New York. So you didn't suffer." But we all suffered when he left—he was my first son. We were all crying in the airport in Cuenca. We stood there watching him with his suitcase in his hand as he left. When he called when he first got there, around eleven at night, he was so happy. Everything was beautiful, he said. But time passes, and then he said that it was a city that, well, how can I say this, well, he just couldn't get used to it. And things got more difficult after that. I don't think he's happy there. He's always saying how much he misses us and wants to come home. That would be such a happy day for me because having everyone together is very important. Someday that will be! But who knows when?

We all felt bad when he left, and so for a while we walked around in circles crying. But little by little time passes and we get used to it. Now we just know that he is there and we are here. Over time you begin to forget your suffering. It's all about getting accustomed to things. Now the custom is a phone call or a card every month or so. He's had his hard times there. He was robbed outside the subway once of $1,000. They were waiting for him at the stop and they had a knife, but they didn't use it. He's a bit scared now, and that's why he doesn't want me to come. He said it's a bad place and too many bad things can happen. He says that it appears like it's a good life there but that's a lie. Life is really ugly and hard there. But I know things can't be that bad, because he's in the house of the *compadre* [Bolívar], who is very nice and educated. I know Bolívar's wife leaves him food that he only needs to heat up. At least as far as food goes, I know he doesn't suffer. And the same thing for his work. I don't know if it's a hotel or restaurant, I don't know what it is, but he's fed there too. And the *compadre* has children, maybe Billy's age or so, and Vicente has them to laugh and play with. So he hasn't had things too difficult.

His plane that left Quito made a stop in, well, I can't remember where, but there are no direct flight to the United States. Maybe it was Panama, I don't know. The *pasadora* gave him a false passport; he went as a tourist. She also made him buy all new clothes. He wore a tie, even, and all this gold jewelry she loaned him. A gold watch and gold chains with a crucifix. In New York she had someone take back all the gold jewelry. Vicente had a special sports bag—I think it was a special tourist suitcase. After he left Quito, the plane made the stop, and it was there that he was almost sent home. They pulled him aside there and kept saying that he was illegal and that he should give them his money and all his gold. They kept him there for a really long time, but Vicente stood his ground. He was tough, and he told them he wouldn't give them money and that if they really thought he was illegal they could just send him back to Ecuador. Finally, right before the plane left, boom, they let him go.

Once he arrived in New York, everything was fine. El Señor [Bolívar] had his own car, and he picked up Vicente and took him home.[4] For eight days after he got there they did nothing but get to know the city. Sometimes in a car or sometimes by train. They went here and there sightseeing, coming home at night to have dinner and watch TV. Eight days he spent like that! I thank the Señor [Bolívar] for all that he did for my son. Eight days showing him one thing or another. For eight days no one asked him for anything. After that he started to look for work. Really, he didn't suffer at all — it was a nice trip.

I think about going too, but the problem is the money. Making money here is too difficult, so I think about going for the rest of my children. Vicente is taking care of himself now, but I want to be able to help the others to get ahead. I really want my kids to finish their schooling. But the bad thing is that we always like to put our kids in private schools, so it always costs money. Now, because there is no way to make money, it's made me, um, how do I say it, now that there is no money I feel, I feel, I don't know how to explain myself, but I feel bad. I am in a bad state because there is no money to make as there was before. Before, I was able to pay for school for everybody, but now I can't. This is the reason I want to go. If I go, I won't be thinking about building some grand house to show off with — no. The first thing I want to do is help my kids finish school. Right now I really worry about and feel for the two little ones, Cecilia and William. The others are in high school and they'll make it no matter what, but those two are still young and in grade school. So I think about them when I can't earn any money here. The way it is now I go out every day and drive around in circles until I run out of gas, and I have nothing to bring home. So you start to think "Should I go or not?" It seemed to me that it is too difficult here right now. It's not that we are lazy and don't want to work — really, right now there is no money even to buy a soda. This is how it is. We go about with life screwing us. That's why sometimes I feel like going but then again sometimes I don't. That's the place I'm at right now.

You also have to think about the money. It costs so much to borrow the money to go. The interest is really high — more than 10 percent on $7,000. Vicente said he could give me a part — he couldn't pay the whole amount, just a part. When I think about the money, I get worried, because what happens if I don't pass [across the border]? Imagine that, and being $7,000 in debt? I'm really afraid of this — of borrowing the money, not making it across the border, and then having no money to pay back that loan. All of this you have to think about if you are going to leave your home. Will I pass or won't I? Nothing is for sure, but then I see some of my co-workers from the cooperative and they've gone now. One even took his wife, and they are building a big house. The money from there goes a long way here. If I could send $200 here monthly, everything would be different. So this is what I think about.

I really worry about the kids, you know. I've thought a lot about this. I think differently than Rosa about this. We all have our different ways of thinking, but I'm going to tell you what I really think.[5] I worry most about the girls. The boys are different. As men they will always find a way to take care of themselves. But I feel for and suffer for the girls. Sometimes I say things like, "Any day now I'm going and I'll leave you here." I do it so that they will laugh. For them I try to joke around. But, you know, if nothing changes, we'll stay like this — going nowhere. I also think a lot about what would happen if I went. With Rosa on one side, and me on the other, as the time passes my life would start to be really different. I would get used to things there, different people and different friends. And Rosa too would have the right to have her friends here. And then when I came back I wouldn't have anyone to share all this with. I know when I came back I wouldn't find my family the way it is now. Everyone here would become distant to me. I would be older and more worn out, as you know I'm not that young anymore. They wouldn't care about me as much, and they'd grow used to me being gone. I don't want to see my family only on videos.

The way I'm thinking about it now, I would go for [pause] three years or so. The first two to pay off the debt, and the next one or two to have a little something. I've got my passport all ready. I know some people who have gone to Quito or Guayaquil to try to get a visa, but usually you have to have your own house, things like that. But I heard there are other visas that cost $40, and you don't need to have a house. I'm thinking of trying to get that visa. That way I won't go illegally. With the visa you stay three or five years and you just pay for the plane and you are set.[6] I would like to go and work for about a year then come home for a few months and then go back again. So that's it. I'm thinking of going to the consulate to see if I can get this visa. Sometimes you have to try your luck . . . maybe it will work.

My friend from the cooperative works as a taxi driver in New York.

He rode around with his brother for fifteen days or so and then started driving himself. But once I get there I don't care what I do—the thing really is to earn money. I can paint buildings, I'll wash bathrooms, whatever. The thing that interests me is to work. I work here so I can work there. The thing I have in mind is to make money quickly; and as I told you, because of the exchange rates if I just eat, work, and sleep, I can save money quickly. I heard that driving a taxi there is different. There are streets with really big numbers and anyone can drive a taxi in the Hispanic neighborhoods. It's not like here, where there is really strict control. Here the police are always looking to cause you trouble. There, if you do something wrong, well, that could be a problem, but otherwise nobody checks for your license. They tell me it doesn't matter if you have a license or not. Here at every moment they stop you to see your papers.

Things are really bad here, and there is no work because of the bad government. I'm not talking about this government [Jamil Mahuad] but about the others before this bunch. A few years ago they tried practically to, well, I'll say this directly, to rob us all. They took all the money. They were really carrying away the country. They left it with one bank broken, then another, until the last. So many of the presidents have been like this. For example, Alcón, who was the last one, he's now in prison. In prison! The other, the vice-president, he has big houses in Los Angeles and I heard in Mexico too. All of this they have because they took all the money from Ecuador. Now they have their good life. And here we sit with a broken bank. There's no money. What are we going to do? All of this was kept quiet, quiet, quiet. I don't know how many millions of sucres they took—they just wrote checks. So many presidents have come, taking, taking, taking the money, and the country falls further, further, further behind. Now there is no work, there's nothing. Now this President Jamil froze all the money. He froze it all. Before, with two or three million sucres you could open a business of some kind. But now no one can because the money is all frozen.[7] There's no way to take out money. I don't know if it will be returned to people. Now the factories have closed because there's no money and everything is paralyzed. So what happens? The people are here without work. So what do they do? They migrate. Why? Because there is no work! If I had 40 million sucres or so I wouldn't even think of migrating. I would just turn around! I'd have just what I need to put in some small business, I don't care what kind. But you have to have your own money—without that you can't do anything.

The thing that I am thinking about is to have a little bit of my own money to start a business or buy a small piece of land and to be comfortable. Pretty soon it will only be the little ones left with us. The rest will soon marry. I can't know how things will be.

I don't want to migrate, because I really like being with my family. I feel happy with them. If I had good work or a good business I wouldn't even think about migrating. For the little bit I have left to live—I feel middle-aged—I wouldn't go far away. There [in the United States] I will get tired and worn out faster, especially because I will miss my kids. I want to be close to my kids, make sure they finish school so that maybe they could be professionals. But right now I can't give them anything. Right now it's really hard for me to pay for Alexandra's school. Sometimes she and Rosa fight about her school, but I told her, "Don't get married, stay in school." But it's hard to pay for this. No, if I had some way to make a living here I would be proud and happy to be here with my family. Sometimes I feel so bad because there is just no money. There is no way, and no how, to make money.

Since I was married I haven't really been separated from my wife and kids. When I was working for Express Sucre, the big bus company, I always felt bad when I had to stay in Quito or Santo Domingo. I felt really sad. I would worry about what was happening with the kids: "What's going on with my son or daughter?" I would think while I was away. These were always my thoughts. So if I go, I am going to have to toughen up. I can't go even for one year. No, it will be for a long time. All of my children so far have been good students. No one is doing badly. They're all doing well. So I don't want them to stop school. But it doesn't matter how much I want to help; without money, I just can't.

6.1. Alexandra, Cecilia, Beto, and Marisol celebrate their baptisms with cake and candy in 1989. (Photo by Irene Miles)

6 | *The Children*

Introduction

For two summers before I went to Ecuador in 1988 I worked in a day-care center on the Syracuse University campus. It was a great summer job. I spent much of the day outdoors, I had time to read anthropology during the children's nap time, and I never took my work home. As it turned out, however, that job was more than an easy way to make money; it became central to refining some of my anthropological interests. Like most young North Americans, before that job I had not spent much time around small children once I was no longer one myself. Working with toddlers who were just on the cusp of becoming culturally appropriate beings, I was fascinated with analyzing their cognitive development and the ways in which cultural values are transmitted to children. I closely watched how parents interacted with their children, how the staff consistently moved children toward certain behaviors, and how the staff discussed and thought about their work. Child-rearing is one of the few times when we take what is generally implicit cultural knowledge and make it explicit. But, even then, much of teaching culture remains unspoken. Later I was able to refine my understandings of how such seemingly small things (like when or how often a caregiver interrupts play) can reflect culturally important ideas about proper socialization (see Honig and Lally 1973; Conroy et al. 1980; Sinha 1985). Anthropologists and others have argued that observable patterns in child-rearing reflect important cultural values about gender, personhood, and morality (Levine 1974; Whiting and Whiting 1975; Harkness and Super 1983; Reid and Valsiner 1986). Indeed, as Robert Levine explains, the patterns reflect how "[m]ost parents in most societies produce children with the virtues the parents most desire and the vices they are most willing to tolerate" (Levine 1980:80).

Primed by these fresh experiences in the day-care center and independent study classes in child development, I went to Ecuador with a keen eye for watching children and their families. In addition to observing children within families, I also spent some time in two day-care centers, one in Guayaquil and another in Cuenca. The day-care center in Cuenca was located in a busy market and was established for the children of the women who sell produce in the market. What I saw in Ecuador was often vastly different from the mainly middle- and upper-middle-class values promoted by the day-care center I worked at in the United States. Issues of self-esteem, confidence building, and independence were promoted in that day-care center, and the explicit philosophy was to redirect children who were behaving inappropriately, not to castigate or punish them. The staff members were encouraged to avoid words like "no" and "don't" when correcting a child, to discuss the behavior, and to redirect the child toward positive activities and behaviors. We were not supposed to say to children who hit another child, "No, don't do that," but to explain why it was wrong and try to have the children reach their own conclusions about how their anger could be better handled by talking, not hitting.

Through this method, the children were supposed to learn to control themselves not because an authority figure told them to but because they came to understand the ramifications of their actions. It was deemed important for children to reach their own conclusions about how they would like to be treated and therefore how they should treat others. While we completely sidestepped the fact that in reality there was only one truly acceptable conclusion to these child-teacher discussions, the process of discussion and the rejection of blind allegiance to authority were considered central in promoting independent, confident children.

The child-care settings that I observed in Ecuador were far from middle-class, so a direct comparison to the Syracuse setting is very problematic. Both the homes and the centers in Ecuador were poor, with few toys and supplies for the children. The day-care centers had very high child-to-teacher ratios. I offer this comparison between the Syracuse center and what I saw in Ecuador not because I think it is accurate or fair (there are equally large differences between middle-class and poor populations in the United States), but simply to orient the reader to my perspective. I had the educated, middle-class, predominantly white, North

American example most directly in my experiences. Much of what I observed and recorded about children in Ecuador was refracted through that experience. For example, one pattern that stood out for me in both the institutional and the home settings in Ecuador was that children were not encouraged to be "independent" as in the United States but rather to be mindful of others and their connections to them.[1] Even children as young as two or three were expected to comply with the needs and demands of their families, especially if they had younger siblings. The one exception to this is that the youngest child in a family is sometimes given special considerations; but that child may also, in the end, have to bear the greatest expectations.

At home, children are taught to put family first, often before school and always before friends. In the day-care settings they were expected to help younger children and to follow the teacher's instructions carefully. In the Guayaquil center teachers were so few that they simply had no other option but to demand total compliance from the children, or bedlam would soon prevail. In that center, "coloring within the lines" was both metaphorically and actually encouraged. I found Ecuadorian children to be remarkably well behaved. While I suspect that "temper tantrums" must occur sometimes, I never observed a child having one either at home or at a day-care center; nor did I often see a small child openly challenge a parent's or teacher's directive.

In 1989 I had the closest relationship with Vicente. At fourteen, he was curious about his world and filled with questions for me about the United States. He would often sit in the kitchen with Rosa and me, participating in conversation and helping take care of Cecilia. I found him an articulate and energetic conversationalist. I saw much less of Alexandra in 1989 since she went to school in the afternoons when I was most likely to visit, but even when our paths did cross we communicated only a little. She was generally quiet and reserved and always had a serious look on her face. Whereas Vicente's innocence made him seem younger than fourteen, Alexandra's seriousness made her appear much older than eight.

As the children have grown, my relationship with each of them has changed. When I returned to Ecuador after 1989, I never spent much time with Vicente again. He had matured into a young man with a life of his own. I did, however, spend more time as the years progressed with Alexandra. When she was having difficulties with her parents, she spoke to me with pained honesty about her feelings; and I have come to count on her for insightful critical analysis of her life and of Cuencan society.

Because I am her godmother, I have helped Alexandra in ways I have not helped the others, including in recent years financing her medical studies in college. I am very proud of the progress she has made in school. Alexandra is smart; she has a probing mind and a wonderful sense of humor. While she was considered something of a problem teenager in 1997, by 1999 she was mature and responsible. Although she has never said so to me, I have always felt that Alexandra was underappreciated in her family, given that so much was expected of her as the eldest daughter. Her adolescent anger did not surprise me at all, but I come from a culture that expects teenagers to rebel, even when they don't have an obvious cause.

When I met Beto, he was about six and was quite a character. I found him endlessly amusing. He never understood what I said to him because of my accent, and I never understood what he said to me because he spoke incredibly fast. He would roll up into balls of laughter as we each in turn said "¿Mande?" (a polite way to say "What?" among other things) every time the other spoke. When we finally did figure out how to communicate, I had loads of fun teasing Beto. He would often believe my tall tales until they got too ridiculous, and then he would pretend that he had known all along that I was kidding. In later years, when I returned with my husband, Beto enjoyed talking more to Rich than to me. They mainly discussed sports. Within his family, however, Beto is a bit of the odd man out, and he knows it. Whereas Alexandra and Vicente have shared a close relationship over the years, as have Marisol and Cecilia, Beto was too much younger than Vicente (eight years) to be a real confidant to him. He is not particularly close to any of his siblings and seems to feel that loss. Beto spoke to me in 1999 of having no one he is close to, except his mother — and his relationship with her is rather ambivalent. He was deeply hurt by some things that she had said to him. At sixteen, he was very aware of and very angry about the slights that he had experienced both at home and in school. His interpretation of Vicente's reasons for migrating and his behavior since was tinged with a skepticism all his own.

In 1989 Marisol was four years old and was glued to her mother's *pollera*. She was a very pretty little girl with delicate features, and she both laughed and cried fairly easily. That has not changed. Marisol has remained the most emotionally sensitive and expressive of Rosa's children. She has given her parents few worries over the years. Marisol is a skilled needleworker and spends her spare time crocheting, knitting, and embroidering. Her school grades are invariably good. At fourteen,

Marisol's sensitive nature was still readily apparent. During our interviews in 1999, she started crying when talking about Vicente's absence and continued right through to the end, when she discussed how the family's financial worries created problems for her at school. Marisol seemed most concerned about doing right by her family — which meant helping out at home and listening to her parents' advice. She was angry that her siblings were not always completely honest with Rosa.

I include here only a brief sample of Cecilia's interview because at twelve years old she was still very much a little girl. She answered my questions honestly but did not elaborate much. Cecilia has always been an easy child for Rosa, as she is good-natured, undemanding, and likes to be helpful. She can always be counted on to run errands cheerfully. Vicente left Cuenca when she was only eight years old, so to her he is less real than he is to the others. She knows him more as the symbolic older brother than as a flesh and blood presence in her life. Cecilia has always been extremely affectionate with me; when she was younger, she would sit as close to me as possible and often hold my hand.

I chose not to interview Billy, who was only six in 1999. He was very different than Beto was at that age: he was extremely quiet, and making him laugh was next to impossible. He rarely spoke two syllables in a row to me except for the time when he counted to one hundred as fast as I have ever heard anyone do it. Even then he barely cracked a smile when we all laughed and cheered at his performance. Billy is by far the most inscrutable Quitasaca.

Field Notes: 1989–1998

1989

As I read over my notes from 1989, it is clear that two things stood out in my mind about Rosa's children. First, I was constantly impressed with how courteous and responsible they were. They would all greet me at the door, saying, "Buenos días, Anita," while giving me a hand to shake. I rarely saw the children fight among themselves or defy their parents. Over and over in my notes I mention the responsibilities the children have in the household and to one another. Despite some difficult periods, this overall impression has not changed very much over the years. Second, I frequently noted how much Rosa relied on negative reinforcement to assure compliance from her children. Rosa is among the most loving mothers I met in Ecuador, or anywhere else for that matter, and she took real pride in understanding her children's different personalities and needs. Yet her primary means of directing her children's behavior was through negative reinforcement. This means that the children were rarely praised for what they did right, while their transgressions were often remarked upon. In the beginning I found myself surprised at Rosa's negative comments to and about her children, since they seemed by my standards to be an incredibly well-behaved group. I later interpreted this as part of her overall strategy to raise children who are acutely responsive to family needs.

MARCH 7

Vicente goes to school in the mornings, so he is usually home in the afternoons. The other girl who goes to school, Alexandra, is eight, but I have yet to meet her. Except for Vicente, who is brimming with questions, the children are all quiet. Marisol clings to her mother but gets pushed away now and then to accommodate the baby.

MARCH 12

Alexandra came in after washing clothes outside and gave me her very cold hand to shake. When I asked her what she does in the morning before school, she said, "Wash dishes, make the beds." It seems to me that between doing that and caring for the little baby there isn't much time for homework or play. She is shyer than the other children.

MARCH 17

The baby seems to be held almost continually, often by Alexandra. Rosa complained to me today that the children don't help her around the house as much as she would like. She has to ask them several times to do things and they just don't have the *voluntad* to do things on their own. Vicente is the only one she praised.

APRIL 5

Alexandra arrived just after I did [5:45] and immediately changed out of her school uniform and started helping with the baby. When I mentioned

I was impressed with this, Rosa said, "She works hard," but continued by saying that because Lucho is gone so much the kids have to help her. But, she said, they are better behaved and obey better when Lucho is home.

Beto was in a crabby mood today. When I asked Rosa about it, she said he often gets that way and he was mad because she didn't let him go out and play with his friends. Rosa worries that he'll get hit by a car. She called him *muy wawa,*[2] which I took as a way of saying he was still too young to go off on his own. I teased him about his cranky face, and he looked like he wasn't sure whether he should laugh or get even madder. Poor kid, no one took him too seriously.

APRIL 10

I talked a lot with Rosa about toilet training here. She said [and my experience at the market center is similar] that kids here begin to "advise" their parents around a year and a half when they are going to go to the bathroom. They pull on their bottoms or start to squat. She said that it's the odd child who isn't toilet trained [using a chamber pot] by two. Back home many a three-year-old isn't toilet trained! It's hard to know why kids here train so much earlier, but I have noticed several things. First, people here are really relaxed about a baby's urine. After a year and a half or so they often leave off diapers [which are often—as in Cecilia's case—old rags tied together with a plastic bag on the outside] and let the kid pee wherever. I've been peed on more than once. Because no one really seems to mind, toilet training never becomes a control issue for a toddler as it can in the United States. Also, I imagine the diapers here are extremely uncomfortable. They are rough and ill fitting. They are some good incentives to using the potty.

APRIL 16

Today was the first day that I saw Alexandra play. We were out back in the sun, and she was home from school for a holiday. She and the neighbor girl swung on the clothesline for a while.

Beto had a great time this afternoon. He had a slingshot and he kept trying to hit birds with it. He missed every time. He was really talkative, and I teased him mercilessly. He's fun to tease because he has these pauses as he tries to figure out whether I am serious or not. I kept telling him that if he caught a bird I'd make a pie out of it because that's the kind of food we eat. Once he figured out I was teasing, he would act all put-out and pretend he knew all along I was joking.

When I arrived, Beto was outside the house playing, the baby was locked inside sleeping,[3] Vicente was studying at a friend's house, Alexandra was at school, and Rosa had gone to take care of some business at the bank.

Beto entertained me for about forty-five minutes. I taught him tic-tac-toe. He was full of questions. He wanted to know, for example, if there really were buildings as high as the moon. He asked me about baptisms in the United States; and when I told him that all I remember getting was a silver cup, he was shocked. Here, he said, you get all sorts of things from your godparents.

Marisol tries really hard to get her mother's attention, but she is often put off. Now that she is no longer the youngest, she is supposed to be helpful and she doesn't really want to be. Sometimes I think Rosa is hard on her — giving her very little sympathy — but I imagine she does this as a means of making her more self-sufficient. Marisol is not even four, but already expectations are there for her to help out at home.

MAY 9

Rosa told me today that Beto was a slow developer. Actually her words were that he was "lazy." He didn't walk until he was two and didn't talk well until he was four. She said her family in Cumbe thought there was something wrong with him. She said he still mispronounces a lot of words and he talks too fast. It's as though "someone is standing behind him pushing his back," she said. She said it does no good to hit children when they don't listen or behave because hitting them doesn't make them any less stubborn. I think she tries to shame them out of being "stubborn."

MAY 19

Rosa recognizes her children's contributions to the household, especially Vicente's and Alexandra's childcare, but she wants all of them to do more, and without always being told. She will often tell me in front of them that they are *ociosos* [lazy] when they hesitate to clear the table or help with the baby. She wants her children to put family responsibilities first, or at least a close second to schoolwork. This must be tough sometimes for them, especially Vicente. At fourteen he is so sweet and innocent and I can't imagine him staying that way for too much longer. I saw that the other day when he came home late it wasn't well received. Both subtly, through guilt, and not-so-subtly, such as through overt comments about being lazy, she reinforces the message to them that helping out at home is extremely important. By my standards these kids are so helpful, but by Rosa's standards there is real room for improvement. Could it be that they are more obliging when I'm around?

Rosa told me she set up the children's school schedules so that there is always an older child at home to help.

MAY 20, CUMBE

The grandmother's kitchen in Cumbe is a simple country *choza,* a small adobe hut with a thatched roof so the smoke can find a way to escape. Even though the smoke can get overwhelming sometimes, I spent most of my time in the kitchen. I like the smells of wood and food; I like the busyness of the kitchen, as there's always something going on. I find the sounds of the guinea pigs under foot really comforting. No wonder they call them *cuys:* that's exactly what they do—make "cuy, cuy" sounds all of the time. Some of them are really enormous. Most of all I like being around Rosa's mother.

As I was watching the guinea pigs being killed and cleaned, Alexandra came and sat next to me. It was the first time we chatted at all. She said she didn't like watching them killed and that she only likes to eat the feet. Yet when she was given one she threw it away without eating it, saying the nails on it frightened her. She told me that she learned in school that it was wrong to kill animals because they are "like us." I asked her how they were "like us," but she couldn't answer. I wonder about the contrasts she lives daily between her school life, where smoky kitchens and guinea pig slaughter are looked down on, and her home life, where these very same things are highly valued. I wonder what it must be like to walk to school every day and look at the women who work in offices. They are always so well groomed, with bright red lips and nails and their high heels click-clacking down the street. Then she spends her Sundays in Cumbe, where none of that matters.

Rosa's mother is even more insistent that Alexandra care for Cecilia than is Rosa herself. Whenever Cecilia ended up with Rosa, Grandma would ask, "Where's Alexandra?" Poor kid, she is really not allowed to be a kid in the American sense of limitless (well, almost) play time.

JUNE 8

Taking responsibility for their siblings seems to be an important value that Rosa wants her children to learn. Today when I arrived I saw that Cecilia had a cut on her lip. When I asked what happened, Rosa said, "She fell off the table because of Alexandra."[4] What happened was that Beto and Marisol were playing on the kitchen chairs and Cecilia was crawling around them. A chair tipped over and knocked her down, and she hit her lip on the table leg. Alexandra is to blame because she wasn't watching her properly.

JUNE 13

What a difference there is between Rosa's children and the kids I see at the day-care center [in the market]. The other day I brought them paper and crayons to draw with, but none of the kids knew what to draw. They kept asking me what to draw and when I'd finally say, "Draw a bus," they would respond, "No puedo," I can't. Both Beto and Marisol had little trouble coming up with ideas and at least trying to do them. Rosa tries to encourage these skills and it shows.

Rosa talked about how much the kids love TV. She said if she were to put it on in the morning they would do nothing but watch it all day long.

JUNE 21

Rosa said that even though her children have more than she had as a child she thinks things are more difficult for kids today. She was raised in a small town where everyone knew everyone else. Friends lived all around them. In the city you cannot trust people, and it is harder to live that way.

JULY 20

Rosa was upset about all of her problems trying to register Beto for school. He did not go to *jardín* [similar to kindergarten but not mandatory] because he had the measles when school started and Rosa thought he didn't speak well enough. When she went to register him for first grade, they gave her a hard time, sending her back and forth for different papers. In the end, one of Vicente's teachers took up her case with the priest, so she was able to register Beto.

AUGUST 9

Alexandra's city manners really show in Cumbe. She kept telling Marisol to use a spoon for *mote* [hominy] and cheese — even though everyone else was using their fingers.

AUGUST 25

Rosa talked a little more about corporal punishment today. She said she doesn't like to hit the kids, but once in a while she gets really frustrated with Beto, who, she says, can be a real brat. Sometimes she spanks him. He is the only one who gets hit.

SEPTEMBER 3, CUMBE

Marisol found an old doll among her mother's things in Cumbe and started carrying it around. The kids have so few toys — a few ratty stuffed animals, a ball or two, and some beat-up plastic figures. Even though Marisol had found the doll and was playing intently and lovingly with it, when Cecilia wanted it she was forced to give it to her.

I thought a lot about male/female differences and urban and rural differences. Lala, the cousin who lives in Cumbe, seems to have a lot more freedom to move around town as she pleases than Rosa's girls do in Cuenca. Also the work she does, like tending animals and crops, is less gendered. In Cuenca, Rosa worries about the girls being out on the street so she purposely keeps them in as much as possible; they don't run to the store or go over to play with friends. Lala has much more flexibility and freedom. Alexandra has developed certain "urban" affectations (if that's a fair term) that I don't see in Lala. Lala cares for the animals, eats guinea pigs with gusto, and seems to care little about "manners."

SEPTEMBER 15

Rosa told me that when Alexandra was little Lucho's parents asked if she could live with them and help them in the house and farm.[5] Rosa refused, since she said she believes that siblings need to stay with each other.

OCTOBER 18

Rosa's idea of health and beauty is being fat. She talked today about how when she was young she was "very fat" in a way that can only be interpreted as positive.[6] Alexandra, on the other hand, does not share this view. She told me that she does not want to be fat.

OCTOBER 23

Rosa compared her kids today to those of her sister who lives in Cumbe. Rosa said her nephew was a really tough kid [he was Beto's age] and that he was very independent. In contrast, Rosa said that her children were "soft" because of their urban existence. There had been some talk of Vicente going to live with the grandparents during vacation to help them out, but Lucho did not like the idea. He said that Vicente was weak and he would suffer too much in the countryside. One major difference that I noted is that even though the children are expected to be ready to pitch in at home at any time, Rosa's daily routine is really fashioned around the children's school. In the countryside the children must adjust to the rhythms of the family's activities: milking, tending animals, hauling wood, and agriculture. By the time they are eight or ten, if not younger, children are expected to be steady help.

NOVEMBER 20

We were at Lucho's family's house when we got into a conversation about the differences between girls and boys. Rosa said she thinks girls mature and develop—physically and mentally—faster than boys. Her sister-in-law qualified this by saying, "Only if they are left in peace and not made to work all the time." She said her daughters were not left in peace [I think she was making references to Lucho's parents, who live next door] and therefore they were small. Her boys were small too, she said. The sister-in-law said she thinks kids in the city develop faster because they don't have to work the way the kids in the country do.

In comparison to her country cousins, Alexandra is very squeamish about all the animals running around. As it turns out, Alexandra did not want to come to Cumbe today, but it seems she has little choice in the matter. In fact, Beto has more choice than she since he got to stay home and she didn't. For the first time Alexandra was a little defiant about caring for Cecilia, and Rosa had to ask her to do it several times before she did so reluctantly.

DECEMBER 3

The morning after my good-bye party in Cumbe. Today was a glorious day, weather-wise. Hot, sunny, and not a cloud in the sky. I was exhausted after sleeping badly. Too much *trago* and too many fleas combined for a restless night. I went down to see the cows in the morning and then began the long wait while they figured out when we were going to leave for Cuenca. After a while I went down by the river and took a nap. When I opened my eyes, I was nestled under these tree branches with the blue sky above and these wonderful mountains all around me. I thought about how in very little time I would be very far away. Pretty soon I had four little kids crawling all over me. I couldn't help thinking how ideal that moment was . . . how if my life were a movie that scene would steal the show. Lying in the warm Andean sun, the sweet pungent smell of eucalyptus in the air, the river tinkling by softly, the shade of the tree, and those lovely little rascals all around me. It was completely perfect.

1993

The youngest child, Billy, was born in 1993 just a few days before I arrived at the house, so when I first saw him he was very small. He was wrapped very tightly in swaddling rags to "help make his bones strong." I noticed that the children had paired off even more, with Vicente and Beto spending more time together, since they often spent the afternoons in Cumbe tending the small store. Cecilia and Marisol, who were around five and seven years old at the time, played together constantly. Alexandra, at twelve, was the only one who did not have a sibling with whom she found regular companionship. Indeed, since the birth of Billy she was expected to perform even more household chores, because Rosa was still in bed.

JUNE 9

I can't believe how big the children are now, especially Cecilia. When I last saw her she was barely walking and hardly talking and now she is a laughing, happy kindergartner. Cecilia seems to have taken having a younger sibling in stride, and she spends her time lost in play with

Marisol. The boys were in Cumbe, where they go after school and tend to the store.

JUNE 27

Alexandra told me today how she was there when Billy was born. She sent Marisol and Cecilia to get the doctor and in the meantime Billy was born right on the floor. Alexandra was scared and thought that birthing was "a horrible thing."

JULY 10

Alexandra and I went out to get her glasses today. She had the exam and picked frames, and we'll go back in a few days to pick them up. I must say the eye doctor was really very nice to her, asking her all about school, etc. She really held her own and was quite mature. Afterward I took her to the frozen yogurt shop for a treat. I noticed that both at the eye doctor and even in the yogurt shop Alexandra is afraid to say, "Yes, I would like those." In choosing frames for her glasses I had to read her face and expressions to tell which glasses she really liked. She wouldn't say directly which ones she wanted. I think she feels presumptuous doing so. Even with the yogurt I had to finally say, "Well, let's have raspberry," because whenever I asked her which flavor she wanted she would just smile and say, "Whichever." I know with the glasses she did have a preference, but the ones she liked cost more so she was afraid to say so.

1995

ENTRY I

Beto, who is now about twelve, is quite taken with Rich. He sits by him every chance he gets and wants to talk about sports. His favorite team is the New Jersey Devils—mainly, I think, because he likes their colors. Rich brought some *Sports Illustrated* magazines, and they poured over the pictures. It's hard to believe that Beto is almost in *colegio,* since he is still so small. Vicente is set to graduate in a month or so. Marisol too starts *colegio* soon and she will go where Alexandra is, at an all-girls' school. Vicente and Beto go to a predominantly boys' school. The boys' uniforms look like waiters' outfits. They wear off-white, hip-length jackets with black trim and black pants. All the kids can size each other up on the buses in the morning according to which uniform they wear.

ENTRY 2

Alexandra and I chatted for a while, and she asked questions about what I was doing and why. She's now fourteen years old and seems to be coming into her own. She is more confident than I remember her in the past and seems happier. She told me that she wants to learn English to help her in her career. She is thinking about getting a job in tourism. I promised her that I would give her money to take an English class.

ENTRY 3

I hardly recognized Alexandra at Billy's baptism—she looked so grown up. She had on a black suit jacket with a short skirt and a white blouse. She danced somewhat sedately and I could see that she was trying very hard to look sophisticated. Marisol wore a dress I remember buying Alexandra six years ago. She and Cecilia are still very content to be little girls, and they played with all their cousins. The kids all seemed to have a great time at the baptism, especially since Vicente was in charge of the music and he played a lot of modern music. I noticed the old folks danced to the San Juanitos, but sat down when the *cumbias* or other snappy tunes came on. A song with a refrain that goes "Moscow, Moscow . . ." cleared the chairs of the younger generation, with them all dancing like Cossacks with arms folded across their chests and legs kicking out. Beto dances like he talks, in super-high gear. The girls were completely thrilled to ride with us from Cuenca to Cumbe in our snazzy white rented Hyundai. It was quite a trick to squeeze them all in.

1997

A year before Vicente left Ecuador, when Alexandra was sixteen, she transferred to Vicente's predominantly boys' high school. She made the move because of the better math and science curriculum. While Rosa and Lucho were a bit hesitant to have Alexandra leave the protected environment of the girls' school, Vicente was there to look after her and to chaperone her to school events. When he left, Alexandra's social life evaporated. Her parents no longer allowed her to attend any after-school functions. Because she was so rarely given permission to visit friends or attend parties, she began to lie to get out of the house. When I visited in 1997, Alexandra was angry at her parents for not trusting her and angry at Vicente for leaving. I think Alexandra had come to realize how truly bleak both her professional and marital prospects were. She told me she would rather "die like an animal in the street" than stay with a man she didn't want to be with. Rosa and Lucho were at a loss as to how to deal with her, since she did not seem to respond to guilt, threats of physical punishment, or shaming. While Vicente had his angry moments, he was never as rebellious as Alexandra; and the fact that she is a girl seemed to make their outrage more acute.

ENTRY 1

I had a long talk with Alexandra today as we drove the bus to her house. She said she isn't happy because "there's no reason to be happy" and that she hasn't seen much reason why she should have hopes for her future. She has no dreams for the future since there is so little to be hopeful about. There are few jobs for girls like her, so why should she care about her future? With a dismissive shake of her hand, she said that she simply wants to "live until I die." She has little interest in getting married, saying that men are all abusive and that the majority beat their wives and she wants no part of that. She said if her husband ever beat her she would just get up and go somewhere where he couldn't find her. She also thinks that having children is awful. She remembers her mother giving birth to Billy, and she does not ever want to go through that "horror." Since her parents hinted to me that she is sleeping with boys, I asked her if she was using birth control. She said no, that she didn't need any, but that some of the girls in school have already gotten pregnant. Even if she wanted to get birth control, she's really in a pickle because she has no way to make money to pay for it. She is really completely beholden to her parents for money, and they aren't giving her any.

She has only two friends and she sees them only at school because her parents won't let her out. She is really angry at them because they don't trust or respect her. The kids at school have parties all the time, and she is never allowed to go — even on the weekends. Alexandra says that Vicente was allowed out; and when he wasn't, he just lied so he could go. She is chafing at the double standard and resents her parents for having so little faith in her.

She recognizes the muddle things are in. She wants to leave her parents' house [like every teenager, I imagine — I know that was my fantasy] but doesn't want to marry. For girls those two things almost always go together. A girl does not leave her parents' house unless she is married. Alexandra told me she thinks about just disappearing one day, maybe to Quito, where she'll find any kind of job and take care of herself.

She asked me what it was like for teenagers in America, and I had to tell her: similar and not similar. I do feel that much of what she was saying was reminiscent of the travails of American adolescence, but that there were also differences. She has no illusion of romantic love, which I think is common among American girls, and she also doesn't seem to think things would be great if she could only get away from her family. She knows too well her future holds few prospects.

ENTRY 2

This afternoon Alexandra watched music videos all afternoon on TV. How could she not notice and think about the differences between her circumstances and the glitzy life she sees on TV? That fancy life is completely out of the range of possibility, and she knows it.

ENTRY 3

Alexandra told me the other day that she wanted to take a computer class, which I thought was a really good idea. We went to a place off of the central plaza that Alexandra said kids in school have talked about. The place looked OK to me, and I think she would do well to learn some computer skills. I gave Rosa the money to sign her up for the next class. I told Rosa several times when I handed her the money that this was for Alexandra's class, but I think, much like the money I gave her for that English class, that Alexandra will never see it. Whenever I ask about the English class, they just change the subject, so I know she never took it. I thought about giving Alexandra the money directly, but I don't want to cause more problems.

Interviews: 1999

While the interviews with Alexandra, Beto, and Marisol in 1999 focused on Vicente's transnational migration, what is striking to me is how his migration provided a lens for them to examine other important issues. Vicente migrated because of poverty, which is linked in their minds to the impenetrable social system of Cuenca, something that they discuss with resignation, anger, and sadness. Yet Vicente's migration is also about the intersection of the individual and the family as well as the extent and meaning of family responsibility. Each is unhappy that Vicente

6.2. Alexandra, Beto, Marisol, and Lucho enjoying a barbecue for our "good-bye" dinner in 1999.

is not helping the family more, yet each also rationalizes his need as a young man to enjoy himself or to prepare for his own future. While they don't really blame him for not helping more, they do recognize that their own lives would be easier if he did. Their narratives go beyond Vicente's contributions or lack of contributions to a discussion of their own futures and identities both within the family and in the world.

Alexandra at Eighteen

For Alexandra, Vicente's departure meant that she lost a friend and confidant with whom she could share her teenage concerns as well as her chaperone and escort. Furthermore, Alexandra was suddenly thrust into the role of being the "eldest child," and she is not so sure about taking on that role. Whereas Vicente was at ease taking part in family decisions, Alexandra is far less comfortable doing so. She does not have the same relationship with her parents that Vicente does. Alexandra's narrative shows her struggles with asserting and establishing her position within the family and her thoughts on what constitutes a meaningful life. Vicente, she notes, is working for money; but Alexandra is preparing for a career, an important distinction.

Alexandra's Story: "Time Cures Everything"

Vicente was the oldest, and he would always tell us what to do. He was always very tranquil, so the only time he would really get mad was when we wouldn't listen to him. Sometimes he'd get mad at Mami too, because he wanted money for something or other and she would say no. He'd say, "I have to go here," but we wouldn't have the money.

He was always really concerned about how we did in school. But Marisol and Cecilia are such good students. They would get in fights to see who could get the most perfect scores! Vicente would always ask us if we finished our homework, things like that.

I don't think the family is the same as it was before Vicente left. To have an older brother was always good; there was someone to tell things to. Now I am the oldest, and it's awful. There are so many things that you have to deal with the same as your parents do and Vicente always got along so well with Mami. I don't get along that well with her . . . I mean, we don't get along badly, but I have a really strong personality, and I don't like to talk a lot about things. I am always rather silent. I don't know, I actually think I'm shy. For years everyone thought that I spent all my time walking around angry because I don't talk that much. Sometimes I just don't know what to say so I am quiet, and they think that I am bitter and angry. My face may look like I'm angry, but I'm not. Then what happens is they keep saying I'm angry, and so that really does makes me angry. Mami was never angry with Vicente; they were always happy around one another and they told each other everything. Between the two of them, they knew everything about each other. If Mami had to do something, she told Vicente all about it, and he would say "yes or no," "good or bad," and that would be that. I'm six years younger than Vicente, so I was never included.

When Vicente left, I believe my mother almost died. She spent half of her time just crying. She gets along fine with Papi, but Vicente was everything to her. Now that I have taken Vicente's place [as the eldest], well, in the beginning Mami didn't tell me anything. But lately she has been telling me about things as she used to with Vicente and asking my opinions, but I don't know what to say to her. I don't really know whether one thing is better than another. My parents have lost the person they confided in, the one they depended on. My Papi, he gets along with everyone, but Mami, well, she gets along better now with Beto than with me. Here it's always the case that the mother is closest to one of the sons. Everyone understands that it's always this way, that the mother confides in the oldest son. The first son is almost like a husband to her.

Mami at first confided in Vicente and now it's Beto. Sure, she talks to me, but really we don't get along with one another all that well. I spend more of my time at the university. Before I had both a morning and after-noon schedule, so I really wasn't home much, and they never saw me. In contrast, Beto is always there to talk to, and he's funnier than me—he laughs more and he's always making jokes. Personally, I don't really like to make these kinds of jokes. I think I'm more intellectual, more seri-ous. I like to listen and laugh, of course, but I don't like to make jokes myself. Mami says I just spend all of my time with my books. She says I study too much. But that's what I want to do right now.

Vicente left because there was no money here. Here it is really diffi-cult to have a career—you need money for that. You need money to go to the university. I think he left because he wanted to look for a better life for himself. In the beginning, I thought he went to make things better for all of us. But now, in the end, it didn't turn out that way. It really is for him alone. I think things are plenty difficult for him there.

I think it was a bad idea for him to go because, well, when someone goes to the U.S. they earn money and they can have things when they come here after a while, but they really are nobody as a person. Because in order to feel good you ought to have a career, something for which a person has a goal. So many people go there, they earn money, and when they come back they have money, but they don't know what to do and they don't have anything. But if you study and have a profession, you have something to struggle for, a goal to achieve. I believe at the least they [the migrants] feel frustrated after all of this. It's much better to stay here, study if you can, in order to be someone. You're not going to be anyone if you go there.

The problem is that there are just no opportunities for work here. Before, people with high school diplomas would leave school and they would have work. My father's friends who graduated from high school all found good jobs; they work in a business or something. Now a high school degree gets you nothing. You have to go to the university, and even then who knows if you'll be able to get a good job. Before, you could start at the bottom and work up, but now you can't even get a job at the bottom.

The current crisis is because of the paying of the external debt. At any rate, this is what Jamil [the president] is saying. But there are other things. There are the government officials who have stolen money and other stuff like that. It's all very political.

I have no hope for the future here anymore. I want to keep studying, but I have the idea that I will leave here for someplace else. Right now I'm thinking about Chile. I have a friend who told me that things are really much better there. Doctors there can make a lot of money. Besides, you can go there legally. I'm going to graduate from here, but who knows if I can find work? With what money can I start work? Who's going to accept me into their practice? When you are new [as a doctor] you have to pay to get a place in a practice. The only way to get a place is through relationships, through friendships. So if you have a friend that works at such and such a clinic, they recommend you. It's *palanca*. Up to now, I don't have any *palanca*. This, you see, is the problem. That's why I think I would rather go and work someplace else. So far my family doesn't know I'm thinking about this.

What everyone at school says is: "When there is no more hope left — to the United States!" In order to make it in any career you have to have money. You need money in order to survive — everyone does. There's no better place for that than the United States. There you earn in dollars and "ya," you have what you want. You return with the money, you get a house and a car, and you are set. You could start a business and make your money that way. I think this is the idea of everyone in the university.

Vicente became serious about going to the U.S. after he came to know Señor Bolívar. It was from him that he became enamored of the idea and, geez, from that point on he couldn't be happy. But before that, I don't think he really was that interested. But maybe he just wouldn't tell me. Day to day I think his life there is pretty routine. He gets up, goes to work, talks with his friends, eats something, goes home, and takes care of his clothes for the next day. When he has a day off, I suppose he goes out dancing. He loves to dance and be with his friends. In the last few years [he was in Ecuador] he only hung out with friends from Cumbe, and the majority of them now are in the U.S. So I imagine that they all get together, they drink and enjoy themselves. He never tells my Mami and Papi about the fun that he has. I think he's afraid that they will start worrying and think badly of him.

Sometimes I think his life there is really good and sometimes I think it's not good. Sometimes I think it's good because when I answer the phone he always tells me about when he goes out to have fun, when he goes to parties. And I say to myself, "Wow, he really is having a good time!" But sometimes when he calls Mami he tells her that he is bad, that he doesn't have work, and that he is unhappy. Mami of course starts to cry. So really, I don't know if he's doing well or not. It's so variable. I know that he misses the family, especially Mami. He's living with Bolívar's family and they are very friendly and nice, but nobody can take the place of a mother.

When he first went, he would call and ask about everyone. He'd ask how all of us were doing in school, he'd ask after all of the grandparents, everyone. He would even ask about our uncles. But not anymore. Now he isn't interested in anyone. But I don't blame him. He told me he didn't care to know anymore about anyone other than us. I think what happened is that a friend of Papi's told everyone that Vicente was a drunk. Someone was showing pictures of Vicente at a party looking drunk. This made Papi feel really bad. Then my uncle who lives in Cumbe told Mami that Vicente had gotten married. The next time he called, Mami asked him if he was married and she said she didn't care if he was, but at the very least he needed to tell them. This made Vicente really angry, and he said he doesn't care anymore about any of them. I think people make up these stories out of jealousy and to hurt you. They just can't stand it when someone behaves well and gets along with everyone. Vicente always got along with everyone. The bad thing is that Mami wouldn't tell Vicente exactly who was telling these stories. She said it didn't matter who and that we all knew the truth now. I think she should have told him the truth about who it was so that if he wanted to Vicente could have it out with them.

But I do think he has changed some. Before when he called, Vicente always wanted to be helpful and to listen; but now, instead of talking with me, he asks if Mami is there right away. If I say, "No," he asks for Papi; then if I say, "He's not here either," he just says he'll call back later. And that's it. I don't know why he does this, but it makes me cry. We don't talk like we did before. That's why I think he has changed. He doesn't care to talk to me anymore. When I was in the third year [of high school] we talked about a lot of things. He was older than me, and he could help me out with things. Well, really, we just had a lot more in common than we do now. When he left, he left at a very bad period for me. He left right at the time when it was my turn to enter the "age of the burro." It's a period of misjudgment. This is the age when you do crazy things. You lie to your parents, you go around looking for boyfriends, you go to your first parties, and you really are not thinking well. I was fourteen when he left, and there was no one for me to talk to. I can't talk to Beto because for one thing he is younger than me, granted, only by a year or two, but more because he is a real strange one. If you tell him something, he always gets worked up. But Vicente was always really calm. He had a better nature, a calmer personality. You could tell him anything, and he would tell if it was good or bad. You could count on him.

We all miss Vicente, but we are also disappointed, especially the younger ones. When he was first gone, he sent us such wonderful gifts. Oh my, the first package was filled with so many presents. Everyone was so happy. And now that he's not sending any more, everyone is disappointed. He said he can't send more because he has had a lot of problems there, and I believe him. Sometimes they [the younger children] get angry with him, saying, "Why did he send us stuff before and not anymore?"

My Papi is talking about going to the U.S., but he doesn't want to go. I want him to go so that he can help us with money. We need money for so many things, and we don't have any. I think my Papi, as the head of the family, feels like he should be able to help us more. Sometimes Vicente sends money—$100 or $50. It depends. Mami takes the money right away to pay for school, and because there are so many of us it is all used up just to pay for the tuitions. Before, my father's work was more or less good, but now it is really bad. No one has enough money to pay for taxis, so they just walk past him. If he goes, I will really miss him. Everyone will. But I figure this will pass. Time cures everything.

I'm sure that some day I'll see Vicente again. He'll return, probably, to marry. He has a girlfriend here, but Mami and Papi don't like her. Papi says that her mother is a loose woman and that she'll offer herself to anyone. Therefore, they think that if the mother is this way then the daughter must be too. She's never done anything to lose my respect, though, and if Vicente were to marry her it wouldn't be a problem for me. Vicente was always crying about her. He even had a friend who came and told my mother that she really should accept this girl. I think it was something really serious, you know, for his friend to come and talk with Mami for him. But now they are separated, so I don't know what's happening.

The majority of Vicente's friends from Cumbe are in the U.S. now. Some are legal; most are not. Now even younger ones are starting to go. My cousin is also going and he's the same age as Beto [sixteen], no, even less, fifteen years old, I think. We don't know how much this has cost them. I heard that he has three chances to get across the border, and if he doesn't make it by the third time he loses all the money. I've heard this is what happens to everyone who goes "walking"—they get three chances to cross.[7]

I do think about my future too. Perhaps some day I'll get married but right now, no. Sometimes I think that I lack emotional maturity, because when I first meet someone I really like them, but before too long I get bored and I'm looking elsewhere. Here people marry way too young. Of my friends from my first high school, well, all of them are married and pregnant—some are even pregnant and not married. Actually, the majority are not married. But they are pregnant or have little babies. Sometimes this worries me. I'm the only one who is different. Everyone is marrying but me.

At one point my parents' marriage was really awful. Every morning they would fight. They would tell us to go to the other room and then they would argue. It was partly about the store [in Cumbe], but really I don't always know what they were fighting about. But things are much calmer now. Actually, since we've been in this house things have been much calmer. We are happy where we are living, but who knows how long we can stay here? The house is Carlos's and there have been so many problems. When my uncle Carlos first went, he wanted to buy a bus and have my father drive it. His plan was to leave it in my father's hands to take care of until he returned. Once he saw what happened with the money Mami took, he said that he would never send money here again and that my father would only steal money. Things like that were said. It was really bad because my grandmother went against my mother too. They talked and talked against us [Alexandra started crying here].

Papi thinks Carlos is letting us stay in his house now because his conscience has gotten to him. Since he had the house just recently built and there was no one to take care of it, my father offered to take care of it. We were living very badly in that other house. Papi had to convince Mami to move there because she said that after all that was said about her she couldn't live there. But Papi changed her mind. We're doing well on one hand, but my uncle Miguel doesn't like that we are living there. I don't know why he's still so mad when it wasn't his money in the first place. Just to annoy us he rented the third floor to the taxi cooperative. While he was visiting from New York, whenever Miguel got drunk he would come over and bother us about how we were taking care of the house. Honestly, I just think he is a bad person.

Carlos is different—he's a good person. When this first happened he was really angry, but he always got along well with me. He's not really angry anymore, but he is always hearing untrue things from Miguel. I think Miguel is on his way to the U.S. right now and when he gets there he'll tell Carlos the same stuff—that the house isn't being taken care of, those sorts of things. My uncle Carlos will get angry. It's possible that he will come back in July to get married and that when he gets here he'll be mad and throw us out of the house. We can never be tranquil, because we don't have our own roof! This is what Papa says, and that's why he wants to go to the U.S. He wants his own house where no one can bother us, where no one knows our business.

The big problem for the future is who will take care of Mami and Papi. I really don't know. When they are old, only Billy will be with them. At the very least I know that I am not thinking of being here—there are no possibilities for work. I want to go somewhere else since that's the only way I could help them. So, really, I don't know who'll take care of them. I'm sure if Vicente gets married he won't really be able to help very much. The one hope is that we at least have the house in Cumbe. When they are old, they can go there and live tranquilly. If they don't take that away from them, at the very least they will have someplace to go. Billy will probably stay with them; he's a boy, so he'll have a long time to stay with them. He's only six years old now, so he has at least fifteen more years to live with them. Mami always says, "Billy will take care of me." It's a really big worry though. Mami talks a lot about our school fees and money. Right now she is paying my fees. One time I didn't do very well on a test, and she told me I better do better because I might need to take care of Billy. But really, I have seven or eight years more of school and in the beginning you earn very little. Mami is always talking about dying, so she asks me, "Who's going to take care of Bill?" It really makes you think. I mean, what would happen if she did die soon?

Beto at Sixteen

While Alexandra missed Vicente and the role he played in the family, Beto was far more ambivalent. As boys he and Vicente were often put together by circumstances, but they are very different people. Whereas Vicente is easygoing and calm, Beto has always been moody and temperamental. He can be full of jokes and humor one day and quiet and sullen the next. As young men Vicente and Beto fought more than they confided in one another. Beto was the most difficult to interview, and he really could not elaborate on the issues we talked about. While his interview was shorter than the others, it was emotionally charged. I found him to be both a seasoned cynic and a naive boy at sixteen. Beto feels rejected both by society and by his family, and this is a source of deep anger as well as intense sadness. He cried openly several times during the interview, especially when he recounted how his mother insulted him about his dark skin. He is the darkest-skinned member of a family with an Indian name in a city where light skin and Spanish surnames are valued. While skin color is used to belittle him at home, he is also aware that these differences matter little on the global stage of New York, where simply being Hispanic is cause enough to be discriminated against. He calls the other boys in his school "millionaires," which is no doubt a real exaggeration, since his school has a reputation for serving the poorer classes. The comment reveals how little he is able to differentiate among the "haves," but it also hints at how left out he feels.

Beto's Story: "I'm Proud to Be an Indio-Moreno"

Vicente left mainly because of his friends, because all of his friends are there. When he started going to Cumbe to tend the store, he got in with a bunch of friends there. All of those guys are in the U.S. That's why I think he left. Vicente is the only one who really had friends in Cumbe. The rest of us don't. Those guys from Cumbe all have gone to the U.S. because they don't study. They don't go to school, and they don't have dreams. They don't have anything, so they go.

I think that Vicente works a lot there and he really works hard. He has to work really hard because of the way people there think about Hispanics. They think that we are all . . . like . . . an inferior race. Something like that. It's like they think we are animals. They think we don't have the spirit to work hard, that we are lazy and only good for low work. I've heard everyone who's gone there say this, that they save all the worst jobs for the Hispanics. So most of Vicente's time he is working. He gets up, eats, and goes to work. When he comes home, it's late and the family is already asleep. I think he watches TV and goes to bed. On his days off he goes out with his friends from Cumbe.

I never really got along that well with Vicente. We just don't understand each other. He never really treated me well. I think he didn't because I know all that he has done. You see, my father didn't want Vicente to be seeing this girl in Cumbe, and I would always tell my father what Vicente was doing with her. So Vicente got mad at me. He wasn't as good as Mami thinks he was. When we talk on the phone, Vicente always asks me about his girlfriend in Cumbe, and I always lie. Mami always wants us to tell him only good things, things he wants to hear, so he doesn't feel sad. So I always say something about the girls in Cumbe even if I don't know anything because, really, I don't go there at all.

The truth is that Vicente always promises us stuff but he never comes through. So we can ask him for something and he'll say he'll help, but I don't really expect he will. When he first went, he would send us money, but he doesn't anymore. Well, he does, but only once in a while. And then he only sends $20 or $50. I think he's not sending the money because he's having too good a time. Here you can't amuse yourself the way you can there. He told me he bought a car. I think he's always going out to Queens, and they go out dancing. I think he changed there. When he was here there just wasn't that much to do, and he was tranquil. I hear that they are always having parties and dancing.

I think that if Papi left then everything would really change. First of all, it would change things economically. He would send money home. We would really miss him, but, really, he spends most of his time out of the house anyway. Sometimes he works from 7 A.M. until 11 P.M., and days go by and I don't see him. So it would be all right. I mean, nothing would change that much except Papi would send us the money.

I don't want to go to the U.S.—well, actually, sometimes I do and sometimes I don't. I really think that I want to go when Mami gets mad at me. She gets upset sometimes over how much school costs, and she says that I don't study enough. That's when I feel like I want to go. I think that I would feel freer there, and nobody would be watching over me. Mami has never really understood me; she always got along better with Vicente. Mami always treated Vicente better. I think because of his color, because he is white. She's the same way with Marisol too. She's also white, and Billy too. But not Alexandra, and not me. She's always saying that we are *morenos*,[8] things like that. It makes me feel so bad when she says these things to me [he starts to cry]. That why I never tell her anything really personal. I'll tell her something that happened in school but nothing more personal, because it really hurts when she says those things to me.

Here if someone has dark skin it's an insult, because the whites think *morenos* are inferior to them. The whites are the majority, so they think that. But I think the opposite. I think we *morenos* are superior to them. Look at how much harder things are for us. I am proud that I am an *indio-moreno*. You know, most of the people from here are poor. The ones with money, they come from somewhere else. From Spain and other places. Being poor is the worst thing that there is when others have so much. Most of the students from school aren't thinking about going to the U.S. because, well, because most of them are millionaires. If they went to the U.S., it would be only for vacation to amuse themselves, not to work. The reason I know they are millionaires is by their last name. You tell everything by the last name here. Vásquez, Suárez, Alvarez, these are the names of the rich people. They think that we are Indians. Their names are from Spain, and they are smooth and easy to say. That's how they think. But I have this name and I have to carry it.

I don't want to go to the U.S. because I think that if I stay here and study I could be somebody. In contrast, there I could never be anyone. I would just have a low [status] job. I don't know what I want to study yet, but I want to go to the university. In the future I want to graduate from high school, and the first thing I want to do is buy a car. I was thinking I would go to school [university] in the morning and then work in the afternoon. But the problem right now, though, is there are no jobs.

Marisol at Fourteen

What was most present on Marisol's mind during our interview was the looming possibility that with only two years left in her studies she would have to change high schools. Her parents were finding it increasingly difficult to pay for the tuition of all the children, and something had to give. In the interest of fairness, Rosa and Lucho felt that Cecilia should get a chance at private high school, because she had attended a public elementary school. Since Marisol had attended private school her entire life, the plan was for her to finish her last year in a public school and use her tuition money for Cecilia. Marisol hated this plan and was heartbroken even to think of it.[9] It was decided that Marisol, and not Beto, should make this sacrifice, because she was a much better student and would adapt better. Beto, they worried, would do even more poorly. Marisol wept her way through this interview.

Marisol's Story: "It Wouldn't Be Fair to Ask Vicente for More"

Vicente was the oldest and the head of the family. I really miss him and wonder what happened to him. He always understood me, and we could talk. He would always help me with math homework—no one else will help me as he did. Papi is thinking about going too, but I know he worries about all of us, especially Beto. He needs his father here. I would be really sad if Papi left, worse than when Vicente left because he is the person who gave me life and who shares everything he has with me. I never want to see him go. Papi is good to all of us—he understands all

of us. Sometimes he'll give us a little pocket money because he understands how things are with us. He is fairer than Mami. Sometimes she is
not that fair. But Mami is really the person who is most important in my
life, well, Mami and Papi both. It was just terrible when Vicente left—
I even saw Papi cry.

I never lie to Mami and Papi about where I am going or what I am
doing. If I'm going to a dance, I tell them. That's why I think they always
let me go, because they know I won't lie to them. Papi just made me a
dress for the end-of-school dance this year. I know Beto lies to them and
that makes me feel really bad. They are our parents, and we shouldn't lie
to them. I don't always help out around here as much as I should—none
of us do. Sometimes Mami gets mad at us. We all have to take our turn
to help Mami; because there are so many of us, there is a lot of work.

Since the stories they [the people of Cumbe] told about Vicente, I
don't like going to Cumbe anymore, because everyone there is very rude.
My cousins look at me and ask too many questions like, "Where did you
get your clothes? How much did you pay for this?" Things like that. I
say to them, "Why do you treat us like that? Why do you talk to us that
way?" I think it's because they don't want us there. I don't know why
Papi's family doesn't like us. We don't really get along with his family at
all. They all think that Papi and Mami are too proud. When we go there
they try to give Papi *trago* [alcohol], and when he doesn't drink it they
think he is being proud, that he is being rude. He just doesn't want to
drink, that's all. We get along better with Mami's family, but even there
we have had lots of problems. I'd rather not go to Cumbe at all anymore.

I want to go to the university, but I don't see how that would be possible. Right now they [her parents] want to change my school, but I don't
want them to. I've been in this school since first grade and if I stay until I
graduate I'll get a scholarship to the university [a private university that
is run by the same priest]. But Mami and Papi are talking about moving me to the public high school because of money. Cecilia has been in
a public school her whole life, and they want her to have a chance at a
better, private school. They can't pay for all of us. So I would finish at the
public school. And Billy too because he is the youngest—it's important
that the youngest go to a good school. I thought that Vicente could help,
but he doesn't really anymore. When he first left, he sent us all sorts of
things. He sent us backpacks and $50 for each of us. We bought clothes,
everything that we needed. It was like a miracle.

School costs so much that sometimes Mami gets mad. All our money
goes to school, she says. It costs 140,000 sucres [about $14] to take the

exams and 140,000 to collect our grades. Every few weeks it's another 140,000. And Mami gets upset that school costs so much, and she doesn't want to pay it anymore. She told Vicente not to send presents anymore but just send money so that we can pay for school. But I think he got tired of us asking for money all the time. I feel bad sometimes because Mami gets upset about all the money going to schools. Mami sometimes thinks that we should do something else with the money, some investment like the store. But I think differently; I don't think this money is being badly spent. I want to be a professional to have a good future. It wouldn't be fair to ask Vicente for more — he's a single man and he went there for himself, not to pay for all of us.

A while ago the professors from accounting, secretarial, from the university came to school and talked to us about careers and what we might want to do, and what classes we should take next year to get ready for the university. Because I am a good student, a teacher asked me what I was going to do, and I had to say that I was going to change schools next year. So everyone asked me where I was going to go. When I said to public school, the professor told me that I shouldn't go there. There's another high school in mathematics that is really good, and she told me I should go there if I was going to change schools. Everyone just looked at me. We can't afford to go to that other school either. She made me feel so bad, because she didn't understand the impossible economic situation that I live in. She did not know that what she was saying for me was impossible. It made me feel really bad, and I came home and cried.

Cecilia at Eleven

Back in 1989 Rosa did not want her children to work, since she thought it would distract them from school, which she considered the most important thing. But that changed over the years as it became increasingly difficult for the family to make ends meet. First Vicente, accompanied by Beto, tended the small store in Cumbe in the afternoons for a few years in the early 1990s; and now that the economic situation is so tight, the children must again help out. A few months before we arrived in 1999, Rosa had opened a small store in Cuenca; Cecilia and Marisol take turns minding the store in the mornings while Rosa shops and prepares lunch. Beto takes an occasional turn at the store in the afternoon. While Rosa is not pleased that the girls are working outside of the home, with Lucho earning so little they badly need the income that the store provides.

Cecilia's Story: "Papi and Mami Really Love Us"

Vicente left because, well, because there are so many of us, he left to help us. And now he's helping us, just a little, but he is. I miss him because I think that siblings shouldn't be separated. When I think about where Vicente is, I think that in New York there are lots of tall, tall buildings — in contrast, here there are only one or two. In New York there are big, big streets lined with buildings and lots and lots of cars — in contrast, here there aren't too many. And in New York there is plenty of money, and, in contrast, here we have a shortage. I don't know whether Vicente will ever come back. Sometimes I think he will, and other times I don't. One time he told us he would come at Christmas; and then December came, and nothing was said. So I don't know what to think anymore. I think Vicente has changed there. He used to be nicer, he cared more about us. I don't think he misses us anymore.

Vicente always asks how I am doing in school and if I am helping out Mami. I have to tell him "only sometimes," because all of us could help more. We spend most of the time at the store, and Mami is home alone. Sometimes Marisol helps cook and I have to make the beds. Most days I get up at seven and get dressed and then I wake up Billy to get him ready for school. Then I go and buy bread and then I take Billy to the bus stop. Then after I'm good and warm, because it's not good to do when you first get out of bed, I wash my face and comb my hair. Then around eight A.M. I go to the store. Sometimes Marisol goes with me, sometimes not. I like working at the store. I like making change. At 11 or 11:30 Mami comes to the store, and we go home and eat, change our clothes, and go to school. Sometimes Mami stays home and Papi watches the store. I get home around 6 P.M. from school. After school I change my clothes and watch TV for a little bit, do my homework, and when I feel like playing I play with Billy, because the others are too old and they don't like to play anymore.

My Mami and Papi take care of us. You know, there are kids who don't have parents who look after them. They send us to school. They really love us. If Papi were to leave, we would be really sad. He's always joking around and he helps us. If he were gone, it wouldn't be the same.

7.1. *Vicente at fourteen years old, with Marisol, in 1989.*

7 | *Vicente*

Introduction

Much of the Quitasacas' concern about Vicente in the United States centers on whether he has changed in some fundamental way. They worry that he is no longer the person that he was when he lived at home and question whether he has been corrupted by money and fast times. I know why they are so concerned, because I too have very fond feelings for Vicente and I'd hate to see him change too much. Indeed, I have often thought that I would never have come to know the Quitasacas if it were not for Vicente. I began my research in Cuenca by going door-to-door with an Ecuadorian sociology student conducting surveys. While I found most adults to be fairly polite if not particularly forthcoming, I was always a bit taken aback at how hostile children could be when they answered the door. They would boldly announce that their mothers were not at home and quiz me pointedly about what I was doing there. They offered few answers to my questions concerning when their mothers might return. More often than not, I could see the mother behind the door, so I knew the child was lying to me.[1] I frequently found myself vaguely insulted by being put off in such a rude manner by a child. Later I found out that especially in the city children are indeed taught from an early age that strangers are not to be trusted and that they should divulge as little information to them as possible.

Vicente was quite different. He greeted me at the door very cordially and suggested a good time for me to return. Although I was to learn later that he was fourteen years old, at the time I thought that he was about ten. He was quite small and thin, with a boy's high voice and a child's enthusiastic manner. While I didn't often make an effort to return to a particular address to follow up on a single survey, I did this time simply because Vicente seemed so likable. I was not wrong about him.

Growing up on the margins of Cuencan society was never easy for Vicente; and I noticed back in 1989 that, for all of his apparent confidence at home, he was quite reticent out on the street. When we were at his home, Vicente was always full of conversation and would speak quite confidently about a host of things to his mother and me. But in public situations he would lose his assuredness. Although he had no problems hopping onto city buses or going to the corner store, he would get very uncomfortable around those he categorized as upper-class or "millionaires." At one point he even stopped coming by my house because he had to pass by my middle-class landlady, who had opened a small store in the doorway of my building. Even though I had introduced him to her and told her to let him in whenever he came by, her disdainful looks were enough to keep him from visiting me. Vicente was acutely aware of how he was judged by those who considered themselves socially superior to him, and this was clearly a source of anxiety that plagued him throughout his teenage years.

When Vicente returned to school after summer vacation in 1989, his parents and I began to see some changes in him. He was quieter around the house and sometimes seemed withdrawn. Vicente was anxious to spend more time out with his friends, something that Rosa was not happy about. While he may not have known it at the time, I really sympathized with Vicente during this period. To me he was still a really good kid who was merely becoming interested in socializing more with his friends. This seemed perfectly normal for a teenager. Rosa, however, found this behavior disturbing, in part because she counted on Vicente for so much, but also because it was upsetting when Vicente expressed shame about his family's poverty. Vicente went to school with boys from a variety of economic backgrounds and was probably among the poorest boys there. While his mother always made sure the children had clean clothes and were well fed, there was not much room for extravagances. School officials had few objections to drawing attention to the class differences among the pupils, who were often singled out in the classroom if they fell behind in paying their school fees. Vicente's bad mood in 1989 was fairly short-lived, but his interest in spending time with friends and his shame about the family's poverty were to linger for several more years.

Although as a teenager Vicente made plenty of comments that were hurtful to his mother and occasionally lied to his parents to get out of the house, his parents were never as concerned about him as they were about Alexandra. Vicente was given much more liberty than Alexandra and at certain times (for example, during the years when he went to Cumbe after school to tend the store) was largely unsupervised. Gender, of course, played a very important role in why Alexandra was more highly monitored than Vicente, since the stakes are higher should a girl's honor be compromised; but I think it is more complicated. Personality and birth order also played a role. Vicente was often able to get what he wanted, especially from his mother, because he has always been a cheerful and easygoing young man. Alexandra, in contrast, is quiet and reserved, which her parents interpret as sullenness. Rosa found it hard to say no to Vicente but not so hard to say no to Alexandra. In the end, Rosa had to admit that Vicente had not done all that well in school. He was held back for a year in high school (which is not unusual in Ecuador), and his grades were never very good. Rosa believes that she was too liberal with Vicente, allowing him to go "out in the street" too often; and she vowed to me that she would not make that mistake with the others.

After 1989 Vicente was always very busy doing a variety of things, and our paths crossed only infrequently during my visits. By the end of 1995 he was living on Staten Island. From 1996 to 2000 we spoke a few times a year on the phone; he would tell me about his job and his living conditions. He was always cheerful, and at least to me he minimized any troubles that he was having. I learned more about the difficulties of his adjustment from his mother in 1997 than from Vicente himself. I got a firsthand view of Vicente's life in New York in 1999, when we visited him on Staten Island prior to our trip to Ecuador. Vicente was happy and content with his life and took us around town in his new car. For the first time since 1989, Vicente and I were able to sit down and really talk. I think we were both inordinately pleased to see one another in New York, since it brought a little piece of Ecuador and perhaps the past back to both of us. In the summer of 2000 we met again to put his thoughts on tape.

Field Notes: 1989–1998

1989: Vicente at Fourteen

At fourteen, Vicente was courteous, helpful, and interested in just about everything. He honestly seemed to enjoy helping his mother, and I found him to be gentle and kind to his younger siblings. Vicente had a real curiosity about the United States and asked me countless questions about my life and work. Because I am an anthropologist and broadly interested in all things "cultural," Vicente would repeat for me what he had learned in school or picked up in Cumbe about Ecuadorian history and culture. He often spoke in a surprisingly authoritative tone, which reflected the fact that after two years of high school he was the best-educated person in his family. He was also a good artist and painted numerous pictures for me, mainly of bucolic country scenes. Vicente accompanied me to cultural events now and then, and often I would invite him to go to talks at the university if I thought they would interest him. I enjoyed spending time with Vicente and hearing his ideas, since he was at that wonderful age when grown-up sensibilities are developing but the child's enthusiasm and naiveté have not yet completely disappeared.

MARCH 19

When I showed the pictures from home to Vicente he was full of questions. He wanted to know how skyscrapers were built, what happened to elevators when they stop, and whether there were robots in factories. He was also impressed with the large glasses of cold milk he saw Americans drink in the movies. He wondered why it didn't make you sick.[2] So many people comment on American food. They think that all we eat is canned food because that's what they see on TV.

MARCH 24

In the afternoon we made empanadas together, and Vicente started to tell stories about devils. He told them marvelously, with his voice rising and falling at all the right times. Rosa said that anyone can encounter the devil, and he can take a variety of forms, even that of your best friend. You are most likely to encounter the devil, she said, if you have done something wrong like fight with someone in your family.

APRIL 1

On the spur of the moment I decided to ask Vicente to go to the folklore concert with me. When I got to their house, Rosa was really pleased and said, "What a miracle!" The concert was excellent, and he had a huge grin on his face the whole time. Rosa told him to see me home afterward because he was now an *hombrecito* [little man].

APRIL 5

Vicente talked about wanting to go to college someday, but he said he would do so after his year of compulsory service in the army. However, if he liked the army maybe he'd stay in and make a career of it.[3] He showed me his school notebooks today. The kids really don't have much in the way of schoolbooks here. The teachers lecture, and everything is written in a notebook. He had one school book on civics, but the other subjects like math and English are taught without books.

APRIL 16

Here are some questions that Vicente has asked me.

Why do *gringos* think Ecuador is only a jungle and dress in safari clothes?

Why, if they come from rich countries, do the tourists always look so dirty and ugly?

Is it true that people in the U.S. just throw clothes, furniture, and TVs out onto the street?

Are ice cream cones really large in the U.S.?

Is it true that there are portable TVs that you can carry around with you wherever you go?

What cartoons do we have?

How many TV stations are there?

What fruits do we/don't we have?

What is skiing like?

Doesn't snow and ice hurt the leaves on the trees?

How do you get around in the snow?

How do people know where they are going on those "super-highways"?

Does everyone in the U.S. have a car?

Does everyone eat hamburgers all the time?

APRIL 23

I helped Vicente with his English homework today. He has to memorize some phrases and verbs. His pronunciation is really bad, but he told me that's how his teacher told him to say certain words. If that is true, then I would guess that his teacher doesn't really speak English. Vicente showed me his report card today. From what I could make out, his grades are passing but not really good.

MAY 16

Vicente and several other young men I have met speak with such authority in their voices, even when they clearly do not know what they are talking about. Girls, on the other hand, never speak like that. They are more likely to say "I don't know" if I ask a question that they can't answer. Vicente is not bossy or patronizing, but he does speak with a certain confidence. Rosa really encourages this, and I figure he needs all the confidence he can get, so I don't correct him even when I know he is wrong about something.

MAY 20, CUMBE

We stayed too late in Cumbe, past the time that the regular buses operate. Rosa suggested that we all stay the night, but Vicente and I really wanted to go back to Cuenca. He needs to be in school a little before seven and I had an eight-thirty appointment in the city. Since the regular buses weren't running, we had to walk up to the highway and wait for the long-distance "Viajero" bus. Vicente said that the bus might stop or it might not, you couldn't be sure. While we were waiting for the bus, lots of cars passed along the road; and every time a jeep or Trooper passed, Vicente said, "There goes another millionaire." He explained that they were all returning to Cuenca from their weekend homes in the country. I was getting anxious about whether a bus would come anytime soon, so I started waving down anything that came along. Vicente was really hesitant about me doing that, saying that no one would ever stop. As it turns out, a very nice couple stopped and took us right to our corner in Cuenca. I'm sure this would not have happened if I had not been there. They probably stopped more out of curiosity, wanting to know what that *gringa* was doing on the side of the road, than anything else. Vicente was really pleased with how fast and how cheaply we made it home. He and I both know he alone would never have been offered a ride.

JUNE 5

Sometimes I get the impression that Vicente humors Lucho, almost the way you would expect a father to humor a son. Vicente has more education than his father, and he has spent most of his life in the city. When Lucho was foolishly imitating English words, Vicente just shook his head tolerantly.

SEPTEMBER 3, CUMBE

Vicente, Beto, and their cousin Lala and I took a really long walk up a mountain near Cumbe. Legend has it there are Inca treasures up there, but we didn't find any. We did find some pretty rocks, which Vicente said I should keep as a remembrance of Cumbe. Vicente really seemed like such a city kid in comparison to Lala. She knew all the plants, crops, and people of Cumbe and practically ran up that hill. Vicente and I huffed and puffed after her. The kids talked the whole way about the artifacts and gold that supposedly are on the top of the hill. Lala was the source of all knowledge. Vicente's stylish blue-jean jacket was a stark contrast to Lala's raggedy outfit, but he had none of her country competence.

Later, back at the grandparents' house, Vicente told me that while he likes to come and visit Cumbe, he wouldn't like to live here all the time. He's not used to the life in Cumbe, all of the walking and the hard work.

SEPTEMBER 6

The big news in Cuenca and spreading fast across Ecuador is the appearance of the Virgin of Cajas.[4]

Vicente is really interested in seeing the Virgin, and he and one of his friends from school are going to leave at three this morning to go to Cajas for the scheduled appearance of the Virgin tomorrow. Many people are sleeping there overnight. Vicente is not sure what to believe, but he is going, it seems to me, for the spectacle of it all. He asked if he can take my tape recorder because he wants to tape the messages. When I asked him if he thought this really was the Virgin, he said, "I don't know, but it could be." This led to a long conversation between Rosa and a neighbor about apparitions of the Virgin in general.

SEPTEMBER 8

Vicente's experience at Cajas was disappointing. They had to walk for a painfully long time before they got to the site and by the time they got there they were cold and hungry. Then there were so many people that they couldn't see or hear anything. He said that some people claimed to have seen the clouds part to reveal some special lights, but Vicente and his friend did not even see that. Vicente doesn't know what to think about the whole thing, but he clearly is not going to become a devotee.

OCTOBER 2

I danced with Vicente a couple of times at the baptism, as did my two guests. Vicente was loads of fun at the party, and he was somewhere between the kids, who just had a good time, and his parents, who were worried hosts. He danced and hung out with some boys from Cumbe, but he also acted like the host when his parents were fussing out back. He made sure I was doing all the things I was supposed to do.

NOVEMBER 8

Poor Vicente. He is given so little leeway that he has to fabricate lies to avoid parental pressures. I asked Rosa if they would like to go to Cumbe with me and Susan [a friend from graduate school in town for a few days on her way to do fieldwork in Argentina] one day this weekend since I wasn't able to go with them last weekend. It was just a suggestion. Rosa said yes, but I wasn't sure she really meant it. On Thursday we were all in the park for the festivities for Cuenca's Independence when I mentioned going to Cumbe the next day. She said she couldn't but that Vicente could accompany us. Vicente wasn't present for this discussion. When I asked him later, he told me that he wanted to go to the military parade the next day and it would be better if Rosa went to Cumbe with me. At that point I realized no one wanted to go, so I told them not to worry and that we'd do something else. It was clear to me that no one wanted to say no to me, but no one wanted to go either. Vicente told his parents that he couldn't go to Cumbe on Friday or Saturday because he had a school paper to write on the festivals and parades. On Sunday they asked to see his work, believing that he made up the assignment. Of course, he never wrote a paper. I felt bad that I had started this whole thing. Vicente wanted to be in Cuenca for the festivals, a natural thing for a fourteen-year-old. Rather than understanding this, they pressured him into fulfilling family obligations. I wish they would just have said no to me, since I didn't care that much. Rosa was very disappointed in Vicente for lying and for not putting family first.

NOVEMBER 11

I've noticed for the last month or so that Vicente is acting differently. He is a bit distant and difficult to engage in conversation. School has started after vacations, and Rosa thinks there may be some connection. She said that he used to be very loving but that now he is not. She even had to tell Lucho that Vicente is not helping her the way he is supposed to. The other day she asked him to wash dishes, and he said he didn't want to eat. She told him, "Well, the rest of us are hungry," so he had to wash them anyway. Vicente is really angry at Rosa for going to Lucho with her complaints about him. Rosa thinks that Vicente has changed because of high school and his friends. Although she is giving him some freedom, she really expects him to carry his weight at home.

Rosa's feelings were really hurt when Vicente was mad at her for being "the last parent to pay his school fees." Rosa said this isn't true; but, regardless, it is clear to me that Vicente is sensitive to their poverty and is ashamed of his background.

NOVEMBER 18

Vicente seems better. He is talking again and not so quiet and sad. We went to the store today, and I told him I didn't blame him for wanting to go to the parade. He didn't say anything, but I think we are OK with one another.

DECEMBER 3

Rosa showed up at my door with a big plate of tamales left over from the weekend in Cumbe. She said Vicente chastised her for not making sure that I had something to eat at home.

DECEMBER 12

Vicente couldn't go to the airport because he had school, so we said good-bye the night before. He held out his hand for me to shake and was surprised when I gave him a big hug. People don't hug here, and they always make an effort to control and contain emotions. A mutual pat on the shoulder is considered a warm and affectionate gesture.

1993: Vicente at Eighteen

In 1993 Vicente, who was almost eighteen, went to school in the morning and to Cumbe most afternoons. While he physically still looked very young, he had lost his childlike naiveté. Vicente was awkward around me at that time, seemingly unsure of what to say.

JUNE 11

Vicente looks very much the same as he did before. He's a little taller and broader and his skin looks like that of a teenager, but he hasn't changed all that much. Vicente was very pleased with the camera we brought him. He asked me to send him one a long time ago, but I didn't trust the mail. Gift-giving is a funny thing here. You have to read between the lines because people won't gush, "Oh, I love it! Thanks so much." Gifts are received politely but with little fanfare. I imagine it has to do with several factors. First, material gifts like a camera can never be reciprocated, hence putting the receiver in an awkward position of feeling indebted. While I trust the Quitasacas don't think I'll take advantage of them if they accept my gifts, it must still be uncomfortable for them, an obvious marker of our differences. Second, I think it is deemed uncouth and grasping to be too pleased with a gift. I selfishly would like the gratification of thinking that they *loved* what I brought, but I will have to settle for their sincere, but well-modulated, thank-you.

JUNE 27, FESTIVAL IN CUMBE

Vicente spent the day off with his friends, and we didn't see too much of him. He was playing soccer. He did show up at the school grounds this afternoon when we went to watch the competitions. Vicente seemed almost as grossed out as I was at the competition where they string up a live chicken upside down and men on horseback try to pull its head off.

Vicente is learning to drive, and he very tentatively drove Lucho's taxi back to Cuenca.

JULY 2

I tried to talk to Vicente a bit about the family troubles and his role in them. He repeated to me what Rosa had told me, that is, that if he had to he would leave school and find a job to support the family. I didn't pursue this conversation for too long since Vicente clearly did not want to talk about it.

1995: Vicente at Twenty

I saw little of Vicente in 1995. He worked many afternoons and weekends as a DJ for parties and was spending a lot of time that summer with Bolívar. He was almost twenty years old, in his last year of high school, and was preoccupied with thoughts of going to the United States. When I saw Vicente during these visits it was for short periods at his house and always in the company of the family. He was warm and affectionate to me and my family as well as to his younger siblings.

ENTRY 1

Vicente is a grown-up now. He is taller now, although still short. I don't think he is more than 5 feet 5 inches.

ENTRY 2

Vicente is talking about going to the United States. He doesn't know when or how he'll go, but he is thinking it will be sometime in the next six months.

ENTRY 3

At the baptism Vicente was like a second host, making sure everyone was eating, dancing, and having fun. He was in charge of the music. Vicente clearly loves little Billy, and he held him on and off all evening. Vicente is quite the dancer. He sort of weaves in and out of the crowd on the floor. Vicente looked really nice today. Whenever his father gets dressed in a suit, he looks awkward. The suit is always ill-fitting, and he looks

7.2. *Vicente's last family party was Billy's baptism in 1995. The party was held in their home in Cumbe.*

uncomfortable in it. Vicente, on the other hand, can carry it off. He had on a pair of khaki pants, an off-white shirt, and a tweed sport coat. He looked great. When I mentioned this to Rosa, she told me that Vicente was upset about his clothes and thought that they weren't nice enough. He was impressed with this skinny guy who was at the party. This fellow, according to Rosa, is "rich" because all of his relatives are in New York. Rich and I had been having a secret laugh about him all night because we thought he looked ridiculous. He had these baggy black pants, a shiny black belt and a white shirt, and this loud splashy vest. Around his neck were draped gold chains, and his long hair was rather greasy [this is the fellow who later introduced the family to the *pasadora*]. I made a point of telling Vicente that in fact he looked elegant while that guy looked cheesy. I don't know if he believed me. Vicente was desperate to drive our white rented Hyundai from Cuenca to Cumbe. Since we weren't sure about insurance issues, we didn't let him. Once we got to Cumbe, though, we let him drive the car around there.

The Phone Call: 1995

The phone rang a little after midnight on New Year's Eve. I was almost asleep, so I let the answering machine take the call. The next morning when I listened to the tape, I was greeted by Vicente's voice. He was in Staten Island. He sent his best wishes for the New Year.

New York: May 1999

On our way to Ecuador in 1999, my husband and I stopped to visit Vicente in New York City. We made arrangements for him to meet us at the Ferry Terminal on Staten Island. When we entered the terminal, it was almost empty; but it slowly filled with passengers headed for Manhattan and then, in a flurry of activity, suddenly cleared out when the next ferry arrived and departed. I had been on the Staten Island Ferry innumerable times, but this was the first time I'd actually stepped off the boat onto the island. I wasn't really sure where we had said we would meet Vicente, so we stayed in the central waiting room, which had rows of benches and an unobstructed view of the whole terminal. The ferry terminal was one of those timeless New York places that gives the impression that it has looked more or less the same since at least the 1940s. I had a hard time imagining Vicente, whom I still often think of as fourteen years old, in such a place. Rich and I watched several rounds of passengers come and go and were beginning to think we were going to be stood up when Vicente came bounding into the room. He stopped for a moment to look around and, spotting us, came rushing over. We hadn't seen Vicente since the summer of 1995, and he looked really different. He was now fully an adult at twenty-four years old; and although he was still pretty short, his chest was broad and his shoulders wide. His hair, which had previously been boyishly parted on the side, was now in a brush cut.

For the next several hours Vicente showed us around Staten Island and told us about his life. He had recently bought a sporty black car, which he drove with confidence around town. He had purchased the car a few months earlier after being assaulted in the subway coming home from his job as a busboy in a restaurant. He had been pretty shaken by the incident and no longer felt safe on public transportation late at night. He bought the car for $4,000 from a friend of a friend. Even though he did not have residency papers to stay in the United States, Vicente carried an official driver's license issued by the State of New York. He obtained the license through what he called the Hispanic "mafia" for $1,000. Altogether, the car set him back more than $5,000, preventing him, he told me, from sending much money back home. Cars had always had an allure for Vicente, and his pride in ownership was obvious. Yet the expense of owning that car meant that other obligations had to be put on hold, at least temporarily. His family mentioned the car to me numerous times as the reason why Vicente was not sending money home. Usually they explained that he had to have it for safety reasons. Beto was not so sure, however. Even though Beto wanted a car for himself very badly, he was highly critical of Vicente's choice to buy a car and complained that he used it to go from one party place to another. That car was loaded with symbolic meanings for everyone, and it came to stand for both the best and worst of Vicente's life in the United States.

Despite his financial troubles, Vicente seemed fairly content with his life; but he was still very sentimental about Ecuador and those he had left behind. In fact, we spent a good deal of time at his house watching videos that the family had recently sent him of Alexandra's high school graduation party. He also gave me two cards to hand-carry to Ecuador. One was for his mother and contained $100, and the other was for a girl in Cumbe (but not the one his mother so objected to). Vicente was somewhat coy about who this girl was or what she meant to him, but he was quite anxious that she be given the card. He told us that his father had been talking about coming to New York. Vicente thought it was a terrible idea for his father to come, especially at his age. The work was too hard, he said, and Lucho too stuck in his ways. He said that because of the assault, the time he lost from work because of it, and the expenses of the car he had no money to give his father; nor could he offer him a place to stay at Bolívar's house. Therefore, he said that, if his father came, it would be on his own and that they would live "very apart" from one another.

The house where Vicente lived in Staten Island was in a tree-lined, working-class neighborhood. The houses were mostly in good repair, with chain-link fences enclosing a small grass or concrete yard. Bolívar's house was small although comfortably furnished, but Vicente essentially lived in the living room, storing his meager belongings under a table in the corner. The house had three bedrooms: one for Bolívar and his wife, one for two of their children, and the third occupied by another child and Bolívar's nephew. Vicente said that at one time he and the young man had shared the small third bedroom, but they simply could not get along. Because of the tension between them, late the previous year Vicente had moved in briefly with a friend in Queens. He returned to Bolívar's after the February assault. Since then, he and Bolívar's nephew co-existed with one another, but they did not speak. Vicente claimed that he was comfortable on the couch and that he was not a bother to anyone because he was there so little. He paid the family $50 a week for room and board. While Vicente's living situation seemed less than ideal to me, he found it far preferable to living with friends in an apartment: it was neat and clean, he enjoyed playing with the children and talking with Bolívar and his wife, and he ate well. He considered himself lucky to be part of a family. Most apartments were overcrowded, poorly furnished, cockroach infested, and very pricy.

Interview: August 2000

Vicente and I met again in the summer of 2000. We spent the day together, walking around Brooklyn (where I was staying), having lunch, and talking about his life. Vicente struck me as very different in 2000 than in 1999. He seemed more mature and circumspect this time; and although he now thought his father's arrival would be a good thing for him, he also seemed much more emotionally removed from Ecuador. He was no longer sure at all about whether he would ever return, and if he did he now predicted it would only be to visit. His life in America, while tough and sometimes lonely, was now "normal" in a way it hadn't been just a year earlier (see Constable 1999). I was surprised when I saw him how much he now looked like Rosa's brothers did back in 1989. His face had gotten fleshy, and he had put on a little weight. Vicente was none too happy about his girth and made a number of disparaging comments about how he needed to get in better shape. We spent a great day together, laughing, recalling the past, and talking about his future.

At the time of the interview, Vicente's life was in some flux, especially his relationship with Bolívar. Vicente paints a very different picture of Bolívar than did Lucho and Rosa, who likened him to a parent figure. Vicente, in contrast, explains that he and Bolívar became friends in Cuenca because Bolívar was interested not in being a father to him but in reliving the life of a carefree youth. Over the years, he has been a devoted friend to Vicente, making his life in the United States as comfortable as it could reasonably be. Vicente knows this and is thankful. Their relationship had recently soured, however, because of some troubles with Vicente's car. His car, which was insured in Bolívar's name, had been totaled in a crash. Although Vicente claimed the accident was not his fault, Bolívar lost his insurance coverage and was having trouble getting reinsured. He was angry at Vicente; and even though they lived in the same house, they had not spoken much since the accident.

When we spoke, Vicente was making plans to move out, perhaps to live with some friends in Queens. He was also thinking of leaving his job as a drink waiter in an Italian restaurant in Staten Island to work in landscaping in the suburbs of New York. He has lots of friends from Cumbe in Ossining who do this type of work. Landscaping is physically exhausting and very lucrative, but it is only seasonal. Vicente was worried that if he left his job in the restaurant to work in landscaping in the spring he would find himself unemployed come winter. He thought that if his father did come and ended up in landscaping he would join him so that they could be together. This, of course, is quite a change from 1999, when he was displeased with the thought that his father would migrate. I wondered if his estrangement from Bolívar contributed to his growing desire for companionship.

Although he does not talk about it here, at the time Vicente was dating a Salvadoran girl of fifteen. He said that they were not serious at all and that they just went to movies or to the park on his days off. He met

her through a friend at work. He seemed well aware of the problems
(both legal and emotional) of dating a girl so young and mentioned several times that it was not a serious relationship. The girl lived with her
mother and younger sister, and Vicente said that they often went out as
a group. He almost seemed surprised himself that her mother approved
of their relationship when even he thought that he was too old for the
girl. His comments during the interview about his own strict upbringing
may reflect his unease about the freedom this girl seemed to have.

Roger Rouse (1992) argues that one of the changes for rural Mexicans
when they migrate to the United States is that they undergo transformations in relation to class as they move from working their own lands
to being members of a proletariat or working class, subject to a distinct
work-discipline. The transformation to proletarian labor requires that
the workers' time be organized to provide consistent and dependable
labor. This includes even the workers' free time to some extent, as they
must always be aware that they have to arrive at work the following
day rested and prepared to work. Fulfillment, Rouse argues, does not
come from independence but rather from earning and spending well. To
be sure, it is not hard work per se that distinguishes proletarian labor
from independent labor, but rather the ways in which it disciplines the
workers both on and off the job toward producing and consuming in
the capitalist marketplace. For Vicente the case is somewhat different
than it is for rural Mexicans, in that he comes from an urban setting that
never held many possibilities outside of the proletarian sector. Nonetheless the work discipline of the United States has been transformative.
In his interview Vicente explicitly describes how his days are organized
around work, not family. Indeed, his co-workers have become "family,"
and even on his days off he is careful to keep in mind that he must be
prepared for work the next day. In fact, he has become so accustomed
to the work-discipline in New York that he questions whether he could
readjust to life in Cuenca should he return. The irony, of course, is that
Vicente, like most migrants from Cuenca, has as one of his goals to open a
small business one day and be done completely with working for others.

Vicente's conversation, both on and off the tape, reflects his multicul-
tural experiences in New York and the ambiguities of his shifting emotions about his ethnic and national identity. Early on he told me (and he
repeated on tape) that he is not "such a follower" of Ecuador anymore.
By this he means that his social life is not centered on Ecuadorians any
longer, he does not seek out news from Ecuador as much as he had done
previously, and he is not as emotionally bound to Ecuador. While he had

in fact attended a celebration of Ecuadorian independence in Queens just the day before we met, he had taken his Salvadoran girlfriend, and he said he hadn't stayed all that long. Before that he had not gotten together with Ecuadorians in quite a while. While Vicente may have felt less connected to Ecuador, he invariably saw himself linked, for better or worse, with the broader Hispanic (to use his term) community. For example, when speaking about money Vicente consistently used the word "peso" instead of "dollar." He told me that he pays fifty pesos for room and board at Bolívar's. When I asked him for clarification on this, since pesos are not the Ecuadorian currency, he laughed and said that's what "we" call it. The "we" in this case refers to his co-workers at the restaurant, who come from elsewhere in Latin America but primarily from Mexico and Colombia.

Furthermore, while Vicente generally uses the term *paisano* (countryman) to refer to his friends from Cumbe who are in New York, at one point—to make a contrast to the youths who assaulted him on the subway—he also calls his co-workers *paisanos*. He points out that he spends up to fifteen hours a day with his (mainly Hispanic) co-workers and that they are like a family because they have to help each other to succeed. Finally, Vicente explains his disappointments with Hispanics, but he does so always using the term "we." "We don't help each other," he bemoans, as he describes how Hispanics can make things difficult for other Hispanics.[5]

While in the narrative that follows Vicente seems sure of himself as a person, his life at this point was in fact very uncertain. His father might come in the upcoming year or he might not. Vicente was thinking of moving in with friends in Queens, but that hadn't really been decided yet. The next summer might see him doing landscaping upstate or still working in the restaurant. He might save money, buy land, marry, and move back to Ecuador or he might spend the rest of his life in New York. He was like a river, he said: who could tell where he would end up?

Vicente's Story: "My Life Is a River"

I left Ecuador because other countries offer so much more economically. That was the first thing. I left for money, because there is no money to be made in Ecuador as there is in this country. I left to help the family because we are not a family of high resources, we are a family of low resources. We all leave to help out the family and to look for our futures.

This is the goal that everyone has, to be able to do something for yourself and for the future. In our country they don't let us. The government there, well, each one leaves us poorer than the one before. Therefore, if you want to look for good opportunities, you have to leave your own country behind.

There's work in Ecuador, but it is really only for the people, well . . . the people who have more resources. They get good jobs. But the people without those capacities, there is nothing. They just don't even give you a chance if you are not one of them. They don't give you any opportunities. And with the economy the way it is, with prices rising and with the presidents changing all the time, the government is falling apart. Because of this the jobs are scarce. They cut people from jobs all over. They might give you work for a month or two months; after that they cut you. It's very hard for a person to find a stable job.

I really didn't have a hard time finding work here because I already knew people here. Bolívar found me my job. Of course, for others that arrive here *a la aventura* [under riskier conditions] it is much more difficult. They have to find an apartment and work. For me, it wasn't difficult at all. I took two days of rest and then started work as a busboy in a restaurant.

When I first left, I felt really sad. There's a lot to think about. First, you leave the family behind you, and you just don't know what is waiting for you in the other country. Second, you never know if you are going to arrive or not. You have to deal with immigration and you could get sent back. Third, the money that you borrow . . . you worry whether you can pay it back and when. All of these troubles you think about while you are on the road. This is what you think about when you leave your country. I was lucky: everything went really smoothly. I didn't have to wait long in Quito. The longer you wait there, the more money it costs. I'm not sure why sometimes it goes quickly and other times it doesn't. I think it depends on who is working at the airport or something like that. But I went right away. Thank God, everything went really well, and I left Quito in one day.

I had one problem on a stop that the plane made in Venezuela. When they stopped to look at my passport, they didn't want to let me go because they said that my passport wasn't the original, that it was fake. They made me wait for quite a while, but in the end they let me get on the plane. They [the airline employees] called my name, well, the name on my passport, and they let me go because the plane couldn't take off if it was missing a person—and that person was me! [He laughs.] My ticket was "complete," which meant that in Venezuela they weren't even supposed to stop me since I was going through to New York. That's why the plane couldn't take off without me, because I had a "complete" ticket all the way to New York. They asked me all kinds of questions, and I answered them normally. They asked me how I got the passport, things like that. I just kept saying that the person on the passport was me and if they really didn't believe me they could just send me back. I told them I wasn't afraid. I told them I was just going for a visit to New York and on the way back I would bring them souvenirs. But really, I never want to go that way again.

It cost $8,000 to the *pasadora* to come here, and then I owed Bolívar another $1,000 in interest. It took about two and a half years to pay him back.[6] And then it's been one thing or another. That's why I've only been able to send a little bit back to the family. It took more than two years to pay the loan and then I had the problems with the car, which was very expensive. Because of all of that it's really hard to send money back.

The thing that is hardest for me here is the language. I understand some and I want to learn more, but it's really hard for me. If you don't speak English it's really hard to get a good job. I took English classes a while ago. It was on Saturdays for five hours. Every Saturday I would leave Staten Island for Manhattan, where the classes were, and then back again to Staten Island. But I didn't really learn much. The English always stayed behind me on the ferry! I've bought some books that I read and sometimes I read the newspaper too. The words I don't know I look up in the dictionary. For me, it is really difficult. I might try to learn three or four words, but in the end only one stays with me. I'm always listening, but I don't think I have much of a capacity for English.

The other thing that's hard here is the life, the working all the time. It's hard here to find well-paid, stable work. But little by little it gets better. There are some people who have really good jobs. They work their eight hours and they get benefits, social security, medical. I work sometimes fifteen hours a day, and sometimes I get paid very little and I have no benefits, no sick days, nothing. In some jobs you need to have the right papers to work, but in restaurants you don't. I have a social security number, but, well, it's not really mine.

I think about going back to Ecuador. I think that maybe I wouldn't really like it there now. I think that I may be too used to life here. I could go for a visit of two or three months but then I would want to come back. I'm really used to the rhythm of life here. I get up, go to work, on my days off I go out here and there doing what I want to do. In Ecuador, well, it's all different. Perhaps one day I'll start a business there, but I really don't know.

I'm not so sure if I'll marry an Ecuadorian. No one knows really. Perhaps tomorrow I'll meet a *paisana* here or even someone else. There are lots of Cuencan women here. But, you know, the ones that come, well, they really change when they get here. I don't really like how they change. Their characters change, and they only care about having a boyfriend who makes a lot of money. It's all about material things.

I don't think that I have really, really changed. I've always been a person who tries not to talk badly of others, who tries to get along with everyone, and that hasn't changed. Well, maybe I've changed in some ways. I'm not a real follower [*muy seguido*] of my country anymore. Before, I was really a follower, but now I would not call myself that. I don't think that much about Ecuador as some others do. Maybe because I'm out here in Staten Island. Here I am with people from all over. At work it is pure Hispanics, but not ones from Ecuador. They are all from Mexico, Colombia, Guatemala, El Salvador. So I don't talk about Ecuador as much as the others. I don't call Ecuador as I did before. I used to call every two weeks without fail. Now I'll call maybe once a month or so. You know, it's because time is so short and there's so much to do. On my days off I go out, and before I know it it's time to go home and the next day I work. But I still miss a lot of things from Ecuador. Mostly, I miss the family. I miss having my father and mother close by. It's the sentimental things of a person's life that I miss. I think about the girlfriends I had and didn't have. [He laughs.] But, you know, you have to move on and struggle and with the passage of time you begin to forget. Now I don't think about these things as I did before. Before yes, now, no. As the years pass, this life becomes normal.

My life here is like that of all young men. I have two days a week off from work to rest, sometimes less. The rest of the time I work—fourteen or fifteen hours a day. The days that I work I start at noon, so in the morning I get up and go for a walk or a run; I might do some cleaning in the house, listen to some music. And then I head out for work. I won't get home until 2 A.M. or so.

I work in a really big Italian restaurant. It's new: it's only been open about seven months. We can serve something like 150 people. There are three separate dining rooms. It's a very expensive place—it has only the best wines, it has a cigar list, cigarette list, it has a really big bar too. It's a place for people with lots of money. Most of them are Italian. They consume a lot, they spend a lot. The atmosphere is perfect. Most of us who work there started together, and we are like a family. Before this one opened, I was in another restaurant and I had lots of problems there. There were lots of fights between the people who worked there. But since we've all started at this new place it's been different. [This new restaurant is owned by the same people as the old one he worked at.] We are the ones who opened this place, so we have a special bond. So now it's the ones who start new who have to watch out for us old guys, those of us who opened it. We all stick together, so no one says anything to us if we're late or something. But every new guy who comes has to go through the same things. They give him a hard time. They make him clean tables again and again, things like that until, well, until one day he decides to leave. If he stays, then they begin to leave him alone after a while. They give him one month like this, when he is treated really badly. If he stays and can endure it, he is one of us. There are lots of people who can't endure it and they leave.

I don't really do this. I like to help people. It's mainly the Mexicans who do this. I think they are jealous. I think they are worried that the new guys are going to come and take their places. But I don't worry about this. Everyone is fine with me. I try to explain how things work until they get used to it. I never like to yell at them about what they are doing or tell them what is bad or good. Sometimes they [the other workers] just annoy someone because he is a good worker. I don't like that, and I try to stop them. That's just not right to me. When I arrive every day, I say hello to everyone. If someone has done something that I don't like or if they were acting rude, I just say hello and nothing more. This is my way of castigating them, "the rule of ice" [the cold shoulder]. So everyone knows if I help someone I am doing it with good intentions, not to cause him trouble. The others, well, they just don't have any patience to help anyone.

My feeling is that if you do good things now, later on you will harvest good fruits. If you do bad things, you will also get bad things. So I try to be helpful to everyone. I think about my family, my brothers and sisters, and I think that if I were a bad person here, if I were someone who said rude things, did bad things, the ones who come after you, well, they would have to clean up after this. Perhaps I would never pay the price, but the rest who come after me, my brothers and sisters or perhaps even my children, are going to pay one day, no? I want to be a good person for me and for them. This is the way I think about it, the way I am. I don't want to change that. I've grown used to being able to work with anyone.

The restaurant has to be like a family, we spend so many hours all together. If we were fighting, that would be a lot of hours spent without talking and having conversations. It would be really awful. At work you have to give a hand to others, and they do the same for someone else. That's how we have to help each other. If we work together, we can get people in and out faster and we can get more people seated and eating. And that's more money for all of us. That's why we ought not to be fighting. That's how my restaurant is.

Most of my friends are from the restaurant. Some are younger than me and they have more free time, and some have families they go home to every night. Sometimes on Fridays if we've had a good night we'll go out after work. We go to a bar, have a few drinks; sometimes we play pool. We spend a few hours like this, but we don't do it all the time, maybe just once a month or so. Most of them have wives and kids. There are no Ecuadorians around here, so I see them only occasionally on Sundays. Most of them live in Ossining. Then when we meet we play volleyball or soccer and drink beer. I have to be careful because I can't drink too much, though, or the next day I feel bad. Those guys like beer too much. When we get together we talk a lot about Ecuador. We talk about Cumbe, we recall this girl or that one, the fiestas we went to back when we were there. It's nice to sit around and talk about our memories with *paisanos*. Of course, with the guys at work it's completely different — we talk about what we are going to do.

The most important thing to have here [in the United States] is your health. If you are strong and healthy, then you can work. Thank God, I have my health. That's the most important thing because if you can't work, well, then things are impossible. The way I think about it is, if you don't have your health, you can't reach any of your other goals.

The person I miss the most in Ecuador is my girlfriend. She's going to graduate from high school this year and then maybe go to the university. But, you know, as time passes you begin to forget about people. One more year and I don't think I'll be thinking about her anymore. Each year I think about her less and less. In the beginning it was really terrible, but it's not so bad anymore. I miss my friends from my high school. We would always go out every Saturday afternoon and play some sport out in the fresh air. Then we'd go back to someone's house and have a meal with their family. Sundays too. It's the same where my grandparents live [in Cumbe]. On Saturdays and Sundays we got together, played sports, and ate at a different person's house. I really miss being able to leave on the weekends to the country where the air is fresh, as it is in Ecuador.

Here I don't have this—I can't visit the family on the weekends. There my time was free, but here I always have to think about work, either that day or the following day. My time is never free. And I miss the festivals there, in Cuenca and in Cumbe. I miss the parades and the fireworks, things like that. We would always do things together as a family.

I like to remember back to my childhood. They say that to remember is to relive, and that's true. We moved to Cuenca when I was about five. My parents were tailors when we first came to Cuenca, gosh, about twenty years or so ago. We lived from the time I was in kindergarten until fourth grade in Cuenca and then returned to Cumbe for a while, for a year or so. We would still go to school in Cuenca, and it was too hard to take transportation to school. So we moved back to the city. Most of my life I lived in the city. When I was young we lived in the center of town, on Luis Cordero. This was a neighborhood where I had lots of friends. Every apartment nearby had someone. We moved there when I was ten years old or so. On Friday afternoons we would play soccer in the patio, all of us together. Saturday or Sundays we'd all go to a big park in Miraflores [a neighborhood] up the hill from where we were renting. I'd go up there with all my friends; we'd go on bicycles. Well, my friends had bicycles anyway, but not all of them. Some had money, some didn't. They'd let me borrow their bikes. We did childish pranks [*travesuras*]— lit firecrackers, threw airplanes around, things like that. We'd play lots of games, especially soccer, running here and there with the ball. It was a really nice time in my life and one I like to think about. With the other kids in the neighborhood every weekend we'd go to a dance or a party. When it was New Year's we'd do a *muñeca* together; everyone would get together to do it.[7] It was really nice. The same thing for Carnaval. We'd all get together and play. We'd get all wet and all dirty with the flour. These were the festivals we had, and I like to remember them. This was my young life.

Life got more difficult later. When you leave childhood and become a young person, things are more difficult. You leave behind the bicycles, the ball, all the toys, and you start thinking about girls. You start looking for girlfriends, first one and then the other. This was from about sixteen years old or so. You spend a lot of time looking in the mirror and think about having the best clothes, best shoes and hair, to make a good impression on the girls. It's a difficult time if you don't have much—if you don't have the means to buy nice clothes and to go out. At school we stopped talking about games and started talking about parties, about girls and which school they went to. It's all about girls. It's the time of first love, and the first love is one that you can't control. This is the time when you don't listen to the advice of your mother. Sometimes you get really rebellious, you get angry at your family. You say, "Why do you yell at me when I am almost an adult? I want to have a life!" Things like that. I didn't realize it until I got here that they [his parents] were right. I don't think the parents here are so strict. I thank them now, because if they hadn't been like that, I would be married now with a family. The majority of their advice is worthwhile. It's good to listen to your parents some because you shouldn't be so free. If you are too free you'd be a parent by now, with who knows how many kids. A worse headache.

It's good on the one hand that Ecuadorian parents are so strict. On the other hand it's bad for us because we think they are harming us. "They are always controlling me, they don't give me permission to do anything." But I think it's good and I say it should be 50 percent/50 percent. I mean, 50 percent of the time the parents should give their permission, and 50 percent of the time they shouldn't. It's bad to let them go out all the time. My parents were really strict, and I think it was both good and bad. They were strict 80 percent of the time, when 50 percent is good. They never let me go to friends' houses or to dances at night. I used to get really mad at them. Sometimes I would lie so that I could go where I wanted to, and this is bad. Your best friend that you have is your parents, and you should be able to tell them anything because they have more experience than you. You should be like two friends with your father and be able to talk about your girlfriends. If I talked about girlfriends, they'd have killed me! So I was quiet about it. That's how I got by.

Years ago there were lots of problems at home. When I was about fifteen or sixteen years old, there were big fights between my parents. This was a really bad time. The problem is that my father is very macho. You know, almost all Latin American men are macho. He wanted to have his wife in the house, and he didn't want her to leave and do the things she wanted to do. He was also really jealous if another man so much as looked at Mami. It's really bad to think this way. But I don't think at the time he realized how bad this was. You know, he had his own history. His parents had their own way of bringing him up. When he was younger, he was a real womanizer. But once he married my mother, he had to respect her, and he didn't always do that. They would fight about it. But I think these are mainly things of the past. Little by little he changed, because as the years pass you can't be the same as when you were young. It was bad years ago; there were lots of problems, lots of fights and shouting, but you have to endure it. He used to be really macho and really angry, but he's really not anymore. As I grew and the others too, Alexandra and Beto, he realized he couldn't be that way. Life goes around, and you have to change. That's the life of the old man there.

When I lived there, we were all still really young; but now we are all growing up and we all have our different ways of thinking, our different friends. Sometimes I wanted to be the controller, to control my brothers and sisters. But there's no way. I wanted to control Alexandra and Beto, the people they were seeing, things like that. Now I don't know if that was good. But we still all get along now. When I call, I talk to everyone. Beto always tells me about my girlfriend there. Alexandra's the same. She tells me about the things that are happening in the university. Cecilia and Marisol too. We haven't changed for one another. When we talk on the phone, we get along really well. Sometimes they grumble about one thing or another in a letter, and I tell them to do this or that because they have to think about how Mami would feel about that. But really, I haven't noticed any real differences between us. Who knows, perhaps when we are together again I'll say something else!

My future plans are that I want to do something. First, I need to think about having a home. Here I would need more papers to do something like that, so I am thinking it will be in Ecuador. I was thinking about working this whole next year just to buy something there. After I have this, then maybe I'll go there and look for a wife. And then return here again. But now we will be two. Right now I'm still young and I know with two of us we'd be able to do more. It wouldn't be just me. It's not my goal to have a child right away. What I mean is, if I marry I don't want to have kids right away. If she likes it, we'll stay here, but if she doesn't like it we can work two or three years more and we can go back there and live a stable life. I'm thinking of starting a business, a clothing boutique or something like that. But first I want to buy a piece of land. Right now I have to pay back the debts I have. Most recently I bought a car, and other things have happened. [He's referring to the problems with Bolívar about insurance and the other car.] So I'm still behind, but I'm beginning to rise up. Perhaps by next year I'll be able to send everything I earn there so I can buy the land. This is my goal. When I have a bit more, I'll go there and see how things are, see if my future is there. If not, well, no one knows.

I have to save money first. I owed money on the other car when it crashed and now this one cost me $3,800. So right now with what I owe Bolívar I have only $200 in the bank, and I can't touch that or they'll close my account. Really, I'm broke. That's what I told the family. I am completely broke. I've had to spend money all over the place, and now I have nothing.

I have to have a car because of where I work. Two years ago I was robbed when I left work. I was in the subway around 12:30 A.M. with three or four *paisanos* [here he means people from work] in the car with me. They all got out at one stop, leaving me there by myself, when three black guys got on. They were boys really. I was sitting there reading a magazine and I didn't think they were going to come after me. I didn't have any money. Well, I did, but not that much, $20 or $30. I was the only one in the car, so they came up to me and asked for my money and they wouldn't leave me be. I don't know if I thought I was a superman or something, but I guess because they were so young, I mean they were big but still just kids, fourteen or fifteen years old—I didn't think they'd do anything. Then they assaulted me. They beat me up pretty bad. They left me with a swollen eye and, well, it was awful. At the next stop the doors opened, but no one came on; they went to another car when they saw these guys beating me up. No one wanted problems, I guess. Luckily, at the next stop when the doors opened I got out, and they stayed on. In the end, they didn't even rob me. My wallet was really well hidden inside my jacket. They beat me up because they thought I didn't have anything. Here if you don't have money, they beat you up; and if you do have money, they beat you up anyway. You can get beaten up for both those things. They said that they were beating me up so that the next time I would carry money. This is life in New York at night. I went into a bar outside the station and asked for some ice, and I called a taxi to take me home. After that I bought a means of transportation. I work really long hours, and it's hard to get a bus at that time. It was really serious: they kicked me, and both my eyes and ear were really swollen. I couldn't work for a while.

Here you don't know if people are American-American or if they come from somewhere else . . . Italy, Austria, who knows. Everyone is mixed up. You don't really know where someone is from and whether they are a true American. But mostly I have had good experiences with Americans. They treat you well for the most part. So, for example, in the grocery store they don't treat you badly if you are a Hispanic. If you need a cart or if you are waiting in the lines they are usually polite and they don't see that you are a Hispanic and treat you badly. But other people, no. Among Hispanics, for example, it's not like that. We don't like each other. I don't know why, but we won't help each other. It's almost as though we hate each other. So, for example, at work if an American gives you a job, he'll help you, he'll explain everything. But Hispanics, they won't. It's the same thing if you are out—the Americans never say anything to you. For example, at the beach. If you have the volume on your music up, the other Hispanics will come and see if you are drinking and they'll call the police. It's Hispanics that do this to each other. Americans never bother you. I've never really had the opportunity to work with Americans, but I encounter them at the beach—everywhere. Americans are fine. Once I got lost out on Long Island and they explained really well to me which way to go. But if I stopped to ask a Hispanic, he wouldn't help me that way. It's like the same thing that happens at work. Among us there is no helping.

My father is still thinking of coming, perhaps this winter. He'll come *por el camino* [another way of saying *andando por la pampa*]—and if nothing happens, he'll cross. He's going to borrow the money from someone. He might live with me, he might not. We'll have to see how things go. I would be glad if he came. I'll have someone close to me. The bad side is he might try to control me too. But really I don't think so. I think he's realized I'm not so young anymore. I think we'll get along fine. We'll be friends and talk about and comment about things to one another. It bothers me that Mami will be left alone, but it's the economy that is sending him. He can still do something—he is not that old yet. He can do something for himself, no? And for the young ones. Everyone has to do what he has to do.

It's the job of the eldest to take care of things in the house, to take care of the brothers and sisters. You have to see that they are well taken care of, perhaps give them a bottle, change diapers, everything. Sometimes you have to wash their clothes, things like that. Whatever you can do to help your mother. Here they expect more economic help. Especially if you are single, you should help your family. You can send money or things from here. Things they need but don't have. I'm always thinking about them [his siblings] and my parents.

Sometimes I get sad here, but not as much as I did before. Maybe once a month or so I get really sad. Usually when I listen to music from home. It makes me think of the old times. Sometimes if something happens at work, if ugly, coarse words pass between me and someone else, then I'll come home and I'll feel like—well, I'll ask myself why I ever came here. Then I'll make myself sad. But by the next day I forget, and it all passes. Once in a while I'll remember lots of things. Sometimes I get mad because we are taken advantage of at work. But then again, I think they have the right to take advantage of you, it's business. If they don't watch their business, who will? They have the right to cheat us. But then again, I think that I don't deserve to be taken advantage of like that. I'm conscientious, I don't deserve that. But that's the way it is. I go home somewhat bitter and listen to music, and it passes. There's really no one I can tell my problems to, only Bolívar's wife. But even then I don't know her that well, and I don't want to tell her too much. She's not my family, you know? Therefore I don't have too much faith to tell her my problems. I'd rather wait until I see my uncle Patricio—he's family.

I have known Bolívar since Ecuador and, well, he was a lot like me when he was younger. He was really young when he came to the United States. And he went right to work. He never had his youth, as I did in Ecuador. He never had the time in high school when you see girls and go to parties. He came here very young and worked right away. When he came to Ecuador he was older than us [about ten years older than Vicente]; but I introduced him to my friends and to some girls, and he would go to parties with us. He would take us to some of the best clubs in town to dance because he had money, no? He got married really young, at eighteen years old or so, and they had kids right away. The Señora is only twenty-seven or twenty-eight years old. What he told me was that he had never had a youth like the one he lived with me in Ecuador.

Bolívar was my great friend there. We'd talk about all of our problems. I never thought it would end up where it did, but he really gave me a hand. I am here and in his house. He's a good person, but with what just happened, I don't know. We need to talk about things and straighten things out. There are words that we need to say, but we don't. We are old friends, friends of many years. But he doesn't want to talk to me, so what can we do? Since the crash we have hardly spoken—just this week we said hello. He has problems with his insurance now, and it's caused him pain. He has a right to be mad. He has a right. But we should talk about it. I know that insurance is a real problem and that his record is damaged now. And in this country this is a serious thing. I know last week he did some paperwork about it. I had to pay a fine. It cost me $800, and this is why I am broke. But little by little I'll get out of it.

The thing that I most worry about is my legal status here. To get legal papers here is the most difficult thing, and it's the thing I most want. If you have legal status you have many more options to support yourself. Until now I am like a river, going, going, but I don't know where I'm going to end up. If you have residency you have a place to end up. If you like it here you can stay, you can look for the means to stay. You can look for a good job or even invest in a business. This is the most difficult thing, not having legal status. It causes me a lot of anxiety. They say there is going to be an amnesty, but we'll see. I worry now and then that I'll be picked up by immigration and thrown out. I heard that if you have a driver's license it can save you a little, but I don't know. At work sometimes they talk about whether immigration could come one day and catch us all. They say it could happen.

I imagine when my parents get older they'll go back to the house in Cumbe. Someone will have to be there to take care of them. Maybe it will be me or one of the others. But I think it will be me. I should take care of them. I'm never going to leave them without help. I'll either live there or send them money from here. But we'll have to see what happens. Sometimes when you get married you no longer have the same ideas you had before. You have to take into account the ideas of your wife. You change sometimes. But, actually, I don't think anyone will change me. Mami hasn't really changed over the years either. She's still really sentimental and sad. I think she's sad because of all the things that have happened in her life, all the bad things. But I tell her, "You have to be tough." Because she is like that she has gotten sick. I try not to get too involved in the problems with relatives and the family. I just like to treat people the same and not carry bad feelings from years past. I want to live for right now, not the past.

8.1. *The Quitasaca family without Vicente and Lucho, August 2000.*

8 | *Lives and Stories*

This book has been most concerned with telling the story of transnational migration as it is understood by one Ecuadorian family. Along the way I hope that I have given the reader some sense of the underlying dynamics that create not only the circumstances that make migration seemingly inevitable but also those that give life texture, nuance, and meaning. Ecuador is a nation severely challenged economically, and Cuenca a city firmly entrenched in a patriarchal tradition. The Quitasacas are constrained by these conditions and suffer considerably because of them, but they do not represent "fixed attributes" (Buechler and Buechler 1996). Indeed, what the points of view presented here show is how cultural meanings are artfully reworked by individuals and families at different points in time. To be sure, the lives presented here have been changed dramatically by transnational migration; but the direction of those changes defies easy summaries. In the end, I hope that this book is not just an account of transnational migration but also a story about poverty, social inequality, resilience, unending toil, and, always, dogged perseverance.

The Quitasacas are unlikely heroes in this human drama. They are obscure, unimportant people who have their share of flaws. I have shown here that they fight, conspire, and gossip, while at the same time they are extremely hard workers, very generous, and unfailingly thoughtful. But, like all of us, they are more than the sum of their good and bad characteristics. Indeed, explaining the complexity of human lives and how an anthropologist comes to understand them has been a central concern in writing this book. Sometimes I have looked for structural explanations, as in the failing economy; sometimes globally or locally constructed cultural ones, such as the juxtaposition of identity images; and sometimes I have speculated on the nature of intrafamilial dynamics. Always, I have been concerned with exploring the ways in which power dynamics and the pressures of competing interests—on the level of the state, community, or family—influence individual lives. Indeed, I am not unaware of how power dynamics that are taken for granted affected the production of this book. This multisited ethnography is predicated on the assumption that I, as a middle-class North American, can move easily between Ecuador and New York. The Quitasacas, positioned structurally very differently than I am, do not enjoy this luxury.

While the subtitle of this book says that it is a "story" about transnational migration, in reality multiple interconnected stories are presented here. Sometimes these stories cover the same ground, but often they do not. This became the driving force behind the organization of this book: my aim was to show the subtlety of differences as the interpersonal intersects with the structural and ideological. Rosa and Beto, for example, interpret Vicente's migration very differently because of the different affective relationships they have with him, which are partly constructed from the larger models of gender, family, and class that are broadly shared by poor Cuencanos. I have tried to show how these cultural ideologies can shape some of the thoughts and behaviors of the Quitasacas; but my focus has been on the ways in which these ideologies are interconnected and how family members rework and reposition them as they move through time. The Quitasacas are like the rest of us, created from a complex of influences that range from the completely idiosyncratic to the blatantly stereotypical. Emotions and interpersonal relationships are culturally coded and framed just as surely as religion and ritual are—yet that does not negate the fact that they are felt and experienced deeply and very personally.

My use of the word "story" to describe this book should not be interpreted as meaning that what is written here is "fiction." Like the Spanish word *historia,* which translates to both "story" and "history," to me it implies that what is told is understood to be "true," but with the biases that perspective invariably lends. I like the word "story" because I think we all use stories to make sense of our life experiences and our feelings about those experiences (see Wikan 2000). Moreover, stories give meaning and order to individual experience at the same time that they generate sentiments in others. As Linda Garro and Cheryl Mattingly point out, "stories are intended to be evocative and provocative" (Garro and Mattingly 2000:11).

The Quitasacas are in fact the unlikely protagonists in this book precisely because of their ordinariness. To be sure, this is not the story of ordinary people doing extraordinary things, but rather of ordinary people trying as hard as they can simply to live good lives. In that respect, I hope the reader is moved by their story. Most of us are more ordinary than not. One of my "provocative" goals has been to make real the lived experiences of the Quitasacas so that they emerge in their complexity as people battered by structural violence but also struggling with love, tested by constraints and commitments, and facing an uncertain future. This was what the Quitasacas themselves told me they wanted the reader to know. The Quitasacas wanted me to write this book because they think that others, especially North Americans, ought to know about their lives. They know they are invisible or dismissed as unimportant, both in Cuenca and in New York City. They also know that this invisibility helps to disguise the exploitation they experience.

The field notes sections highlight the ordinariness of the Quitasacas as they move through their everyday lives but also, I hope, reveal some of the truths about the anthropological process. My goal was for readers to recognize and appreciate the processual nature of fieldwork and how understanding builds over time as small and sometimes seemingly insignificant actions or words are layered one upon the other. In an age when satellite television beams North American sit-coms to Ecuador and Brazilian soap operas to Grand Rapids, Michigan, what constitutes "culture" often appears less distinct, less bounded, and less obvious than it might have before. Indeed, after I concluded my first interviews with rural-to-urban migrants in 1989, I was "disappointed" that I hadn't come up with anything more exciting and perhaps exotic. Despite the "colorful" differences in clothing or food choices, families, I learned, migrated to the city to find a better job, get a better education for their children, and save for a house and a car—not much different from what I could hear from middle-class Americans making the opposite journey from city to suburb.

What I hope I have been able to show the reader here is that the real work of doing anthropology today is very often about finding and analyzing patterns in details that may seem quite common and perhaps even mundane. So, for example, I have shown the ways in which the tensions between rural and urban lifestyles are revealed in the devil stories Rosa tells the children and in seemingly insignificant moments, such as when eight-year-old Alexandra makes a passing comment that she doesn't like to eat guinea pig or that ladies use spoons. On the surface "global culture" often appears to be homogenizing differences; while that impression is often true, it does not tell the whole story by any means. The members of the Quitasaca household have "invested" in or rejected aspects of "global culture" in different ways at different times for different reasons.

While the field notes from 1989 focus primarily on the ordinary and everyday, Vicente's transnational migration can only be termed an extraordinary event. Not only are discussions of his migration and its aftermath highly emotionally charged, but they opened the door for the family members to talk to me about their lives in new ways. It was a defining moment in the family history, one that altered their perspectives on themselves and on one another. Family relationships were laid bare after Vicente left, as his sudden removal from the home revealed just what roles he had played in the family—son, confidant, chaperone, tutor, cultural broker, and beloved, although sometimes resented, older brother. Vicente stopped being someone who was integrated into the everyday and became, for better or worse, the embodiment of the family's dreams, desires, and hopes. The fact that he did not fulfill those dreams weighs heavily upon everyone. Because of his lack of success, his father has had to migrate, his mother is quite literally worried sick, and his siblings question the strength of familial bonds in the face of both temptations and challenges. The Quitasacas are repositioning the line between irrational hope and reasonable expectations as their vision of Vicente's experiences in the United States (and what that would do for their life in Cuenca) fades in order to make way for reality.

Alexandra has turned Vicente's lack of obvious success into a rationale that justifies her different choice: to "be somebody" by focusing on a "career" and not just a job. Personal identity, she seems to be saying, cannot be found in simply making money, which is what she thinks transnational migration is all about. Beto vacillates between blaming Vicente for having too much fun and blaming structural conditions that not only forced him to leave but marginalized him once he got to the United States. Beto poignantly tells us how skin color and ethnicity are used at home and in school to create dichotomies (*blanco/moreno,* Spanish/Indian) that always seem to find him on the marginalized side; but he also tells us that, as he understands it, race cuts a much wider swath in the United States, where subtleties are erased and "Hispanics" are universally scorned. Beto is in some ways the most politicized Quitasaca and identifies himself as a *moreno* (in the home), an Ecuadorian *indio* (in Cuenca), and a "Hispanic" (on the world stage) in order to subvert the power that accrues to those who would call him these names. I'm not sure that he has been successful yet at really subverting the power of racial discourses; if he had been, I doubt he would still be so hurt when he discusses them.

Vicente's own experiences in New York with race, ethnicity, and identity are less clear-cut than Beto's descriptions of being Hispanic might imply. Over time Vicente has found that he is "not such a follower of Ecuador anymore"; and while he frequently romanticizes his past in Cuenca, he cannot entirely envision a future there. He is similar to other transnational migrants described in the anthropological literature who become ambivalent about returning to their "home" countries (see Constable 1999). New York, for better or worse, has become "normal" for Vicente; and he often talks about Ecuador as though it were in caricature — on the one hand, it is the happy and bucolic land of his youth; and on the other, the place that caused him great pain and forced him into a kind of exile. One thing is for sure: Vicente does not believe he can go back to Cuenca until he makes enough money to set himself up independently in business. By then, he's not sure that he will want to. Vicente seems equally ambivalent about his Hispanic identity in the United States. He does identify himself as a "Hispanic," which he contrasts with "American." Most of his time is spent with people he calls Hispanic — co-workers from Colombia, El Salvador, and Mexico — although he expresses little real solidarity with other Hispanics. Competition over limited resources (or the perception that they are limited) leads, he tells us, to suspicion and distrust. While he perceives that other Hispanics often give him a harder time than "Americans," his moments of greatest regret in New York have come from the knowledge that he is exploited by the system that is, in fact, "American." He speaks of this pain as personal, however, and not, as Beto does, as a member of an ethnic group. He knows that he is perceived by others as Hispanic and he identifies himself as such — he is just unsure right now what that really means to him.

Vicente is less ambivalent about the question of what kind of person he is. Much of the literature on transnationalism discusses the ways in which individual migrants experience increased feelings of a fragmentation of the self as they struggle to come to terms with conflicting notions about their national, ethnic, or class identity (see Friedman 1994; Constable 1999). While discussions of the "self" are complex and there are multiple perspectives on how to think about studies of the "self" in anthropology, for Vicente the issue is not that complicated. Indeed, while he does question the strength of his attachment to being a Hispanic or an Ecuadorian (as do most of us when faced with monolithic labels), and while he wonders if he was always an obedient son or a helpful brother, he is remarkably sure about who he is as a person. His basic character — which so concerns his family back home — is, he assured me, very much as it always was.[1] Indeed, he told me that he tries in all that he does to be a good person and to be conscientious and responsible. He did not pass the buck when it came to his parents or gloss over his role in creating problems for Bolívar. He makes few excuses for himself and knows he ought to do better when it comes to saving money; but he is proud of the fact that despite the hardships of his life in the United States from time to time he has never taken advantage of others. Vicente is circumspect about his nationality and ethnic affiliation, but he does not experience any real dissonance of the self because he questions these categories — certainly no more than I do when thinking about being an "American" or an "Anglo."

Similarly, Vicente's migration reveals the Quitasacas' very complex and ambivalent understandings of the systems of stratification in which they operate. Because of their own agency in relation to their structural position, the Quitasacas cannot be viewed solely as victims of global economic processes — nor, as the elites of their own country would have it, as unwitting and indiscriminating consumers of "global culture." Yet the nature of their relationship to the cultures of power is not easy to disentangle. Granted, I have tried to make the point in this book that they live in a world (both in Ecuador and in New York) that consistently marginalizes them and limits opportunity and that the processes of local and global capitalism are key to the institutionalization of this marginalization. This does not mean, however, that the Quitasacas passively accept all that they are told they ought to. Their discussions of both Cuenca and New York are circumspect, and they are somewhat astute observers of the power of class and ethnicity to limit the opportunity of "people like them."

I have watched this sensibility develop and mature over the years as the dreams they had when the family was young have been battered and left unfulfilled. As the field notes here document, the Quitasacas have been assiduously trying for years to succeed within the system in Cuenca; they worked hard at low-paying jobs, they dressed in western clothing, and the children went to school. But this made little difference in the face of a shrinking economy. Now, of course, they know that migration to the United States is no panacea either. While they believe that the

United States can offer greater economic possibilities (why else would Lucho have gone?), they also know that they are leaving one system of exploitation for another. Hispanics, as both Rosa and Beto point out, especially undocumented ones, are treated like dogs. They are hoping that one system of exploitation will simply pay much better than another. Unfortunately, Lucho may have missed the boat on that one too: Ecuador's decision in 1999 to adopt the U.S. dollar as the national currency means that "earning in dollars" no longer has the exchange rate advantages it had previously.

While discussing his undocumented status in the United States, Vicente explained that he was troubled that he could not really plan for his future since his legal status was so dubious. Legal residency, he told me, would give him many more options. Without it, his life was like a river, moving and flowing, but with no clear indication of where it was going. The image he evoked reminded me of the lives of his parents and his siblings in Ecuador as well. Despite high hopes in the late 1980s that they would succeed in the city if they worked hard on the job and at school, they have not managed to prosper. In the end, their hard work mattered less than they thought it would: they found that economic and social conditions prevented them from ever getting ahead. While none of us can predict with certainty where life will take us, the inability to control opportunities is much greater for the marginalized, both in New York and in Ecuador.

In describing their feelings about living in a hierarchical social system, both Vicente and Beto made a comment that is useful in thinking about class in a very general sense. They did not say that it is awful to be poor (Vicente in fact romanticizes his poor childhood); they said that it is awful to be poor "when others have so much." I often repeat this statement in the classroom to help my students come to terms with the ways in which hierarchy operates on the level of the lived experience. In the introductory anthropology classes that I teach, I try to introduce students to the construction and consequences of social inequalities. For the most part, students accept the critiques I make about the impact of Spanish colonialism on Latin America (it's long ago and far away); and they are becoming increasingly willing to listening to critiques of the impact of nineteenth- and twentieth-century North American capitalist expansion on Latin American economies—this is still one degree removed from their daily experiences. Yet, when I turn to looking at poverty within the United States, I frequently find students less willing to consider its multiple implications. The popular perception continues to be that the United States is a land of abundance and equal opportunity and that poverty is either short-lived or self-inflicted. The chronically poor in the United States do not suffer from real deprivation, students have often told me, but rather from poor choices. Vicente's comment, simple as it is, helps me to explain to students the relative nature of poverty. The painful and sometimes debilitating effects of poverty are not solely caused by absolute deprivation but—in circumstances of abundance— by relative deprivation, discrimination, and exploitation. In this way the Quitasacas' story becomes the story of many others.

Finally, one of the more implicit points of this book is to reaffirm the importance of long-term relationships to the ethnographic process. The twelve years that this ethnographic study covers represent a period of rapid change in Cuenca, as the pace of both transnationalism and global- ization continued to quicken, but also a significant time in the life-cycle of a family. For example, in this period Rosa stopped dressing like a *chola* Cuencana; her children fought with her to achieve greater free- dom; and the family started depending on remittances from the United States. Moreover, in these years the family has grown, matured, and aged. Lucho is very different today than he was twelve years ago. Middle age and failed expectations have rounded out his belly and softened his demeanor. His focus today is less on assuring that his children are being raised properly and more on providing for his declining years. Alexan- dra has grown from a little girl into a surly teenager and then a dedicated college student. She challenged her parents a great deal along the way, often making them angry and occasionally bringing them face-to-face with their worst fears about modern life. And, finally, Vicente's trans- national migration marks his own coming of age as well as the family's most obvious and most ambivalent confrontation with globalization. I imagine that the next ten years will bring a host of new challenges.

Of course, like all true stories, this one does not really have an ending. While satisfying fictional stories usually end with some sort of resolu- tion, stories about living people cannot be summed up neatly. Although each of the central chapters in this book ends with the narratives col- lected in 1999, too much has happened in the intervening time for me to leave the story there. Indeed, concluding with the edited tapes of 1999 is an arbitrary cutting-off point, one that may suit the writing process (albeit clumsily) but does not do justice to real life. Because the events of 2000 and 2001 were so far from routine for the Quitasaca family, and because they demonstrate in a very dramatic fashion the themes of insecurity and resilience, I have chosen to continue this story for just a bit longer.

Fall 2000–Winter 2001

I spent the better part of election day 2000 walking the neighborhoods of Kalamazoo in an election-day "get out the vote" campaign. Little did any of us know then what an unforgettable day that would become for so many people. For me it was unforgettable for more than the bizarre presidential vote outcome that left us without a clear victor. It was also the day that I first became aware that something was very wrong in Ecuador. When I got home in the evening, my husband told me that Vicente had called. Right away I was concerned, since he rarely calls me. Rich wasn't sure why he had called, but he understood something about Rosa being ill. When I called Vicente back, I was relieved to hear from the tone of his voice in the first words he uttered that it did not appear to be an emergency. But what he told me made little sense. Rosa had apparently been ill for quite some time and then had suddenly taken a turn for the worse. The doctors were not altogether sure what was the matter. Vicente understood that it had to do with her stomach or her bone marrow. Clearly, he had little idea of what was going on with his mother, but at least it did not seem urgent. Vicente also told me during that phone call that Lucho was no longer in Ecuador. He had arrived in New York the month before and was living in Queens, trying to patch together odd jobs. Vicente said he was doing fine. I was shocked to learn this; even though Lucho had said for so long that he was going to migrate, I just never thought he would.

When I called Ecuador a few days later, I was not altogether relieved by what Marisol and Alexandra were able to tell me. In her usual tremulous voice, Marisol told me how her mother had grown progressively weaker over the past six months and that she had fainted a couple of times at the store. Rosa's legs were swollen and ached terribly. She was not able to walk or even stand. They reported to me that she had been in and out of the clinic over the past couple of months and that she had just had surgery on her kidneys. The doctors were not sure what exactly was wrong with them, but their diagnosis was that she had "tumors on the ganglia of her kidneys," whatever that meant. But the doctors could not rule out leukemia, lymphoma, or cancer. My first reaction was annoyance at the doctors that they could not do a better job of diagnosing her problem. I also worried that in order to save money they had gone to an inexpensive doctor. In my experience, the good doctors in Ecuador are quite good, while the rest are woefully undertrained. But, Alexandra assured me, they had gone to one of the better clinics in town, and Rosa was improving after the surgery.

The girls were understandably very upset. Not only had they been watching their mother decline for the last few months, but with Lucho gone they were put in the position of making all of the household, financial, and medical decisions. They said they spoke to Lucho quite often; but he was not able to send money yet, and the medical bills were beginning to mount. On top of their justifiable concern for Rosa's well-being was the worry about how they could pay for more tests or surgeries should they become necessary. I was impressed with how well Alexandra seemed to understand the medical procedures that her mother had endured. She sounded competent and informed.

I called Ecuador in early January 2001 just to see how things were going. Only Rosa was home, and she spoke to me from her bed. Her voice was thin and weak. She told me that she had just gotten a blood transfusion the day before and that she was doing much better. She seemed to know very little about what was wrong with her—something to do with her kidneys, she said. We talked a little about Lucho. She said that he was terribly unhappy in New York. He missed his family, he didn't care for the cold weather, and so far he didn't have a good job. Rosa wasn't sure what he was doing or even where he was living. We chatted a bit about my daughter and her children and then we said good-bye. After I hung up the phone, I wondered about the possible psycho-social component in Rosa's condition. She was always "sad and sentimental," as Vicente put it, and I considered the possibility that her condition was partly exacerbated by the worry and sadness of having both her son and husband in the United States. Over the years I had listened to the wives of migrants complain many times of a vague and indeterminate unease called *pena,* which they suffered because of the loneliness, stress, and worry about their missing loved ones (see Pribilsky 2001). How much did the social stress of Lucho's migration contribute to her illness, I asked myself? While there is never a good answer to questions like that, and I never questioned the depths of her suffering or the "reality" of her pain, a few days later I was to learn just how serious her physical condition was.

January 9, 2001

On January 9 I received an email from Alexandra and Marisol:

Dear Anita,

   Greetings from Ecuador to you, Richard, and Isabel and we hope you have a happy New Year. We are here, Marisol and Alexandra, in a cybercafé because we must tell you about Mami's illness. I don't know how to say it, but we are all scared and really desperate. A few days ago you called the house and Mami told you something, but really she does not know about her illness. We don't want to tell her because we don't know how she'll react—you see, her condition is critical. My hope is that you can help us because as things are going now we aren't getting anywhere. I never thought I would say this, but Mami is slowly dying right in front of us.

   It is almost a year since she hasn't felt well and has had trouble walking. We've been to many doctors who have diagnosed varicose veins. The veins in her legs are enlarged and the blood is stationary. They prescribed aspirin to improve her circulation. She started taking this and she deteriorated little by little until September, when she was at the point where she couldn't walk or even talk. Luckily we went to a clinic where they were able to help us because Papi was no longer with us. You must understand that we are alone in this because no one else in the family understands what's going on.

   We went to various specialists. A hematologist diagnosed "Medullary Dysplasia," probably produced by the aspirin, and she stabilized some. We were happy, but just a few days later she fell into convulsions and since then we have lived a veritable odyssey until today. She needs blood all the time, as her blood is deficient in red blood cells and leucocytes. Then they thought she had non-Hodgkin's lymphoma, which as far as I understand is a malignant cancer. For about a month she would get a transfusion and be better and then she was worse again. Finally they did an examination of her antinuclear antibodies and they diagnosed Lupus Erythematosus.

   Today we went to the clinic with Mami again because now she has an inflammation around the heart called pericarditis and she suddenly lacks blood to the heart and has tremendous pains with tachycardia. Her body trembles terribly. We give her pills, which controls this some, but nothing is really helping. We are going to the clinic every 15 days for more blood. I found out that there is a lupus specialist, but now I don't have faith in anyone. Today she left the clinic and she is worse. The family is crying all the time and they are always asking me if she is going to die. They don't understand the medical terms that the doctors are telling me about, and what is happening to my mother.

Cecilia is the one who is suffering the most, and Beto is crying right in front of Mami; Billy so far really doesn't understand what is happening. Papi knows that Mami is sick, but he does not know really how sick she is. If he knew he would be calling all the time and desperate to come home, but as he said, if he came home there would be no money and things would be worse. I don't know if it's good to keep my father in the dark like this, but every time I try to tell Vicente he just starts crying and he never lets me talk with the sincerity that I need to.

For now, only we, Alexandra and Marisol, really know what is going on. Can you help us? We are so anxious and each day that passes is worse for the family and Mami grows more desperate since she doesn't know what is happening. They say she won't recover if they tell her what is the matter.

Please excuse me for this enormous letter, but I don't have anyone else of confidence to tell this to. Thank you for answering this letter.

Alexandra and Marisol

After I received this email from Alexandra, I was deeply saddened and worried. I didn't know much about lupus but I knew that it was serious. When I did some research on the Internet to learn more about the disease, I didn't like what I read. Lupus is an inherited disease of the auto-immune system, which means essentially that the body's immune system starts to attack its own healthy cells. The disease is life-long, unpredictable, and characterized by periodic flare-ups. The course and severity of the illness vary among patients, but it often affects multiple organ systems. Most commonly lupus can strike the kidneys, heart, joints, central nervous system, intestines, eyes, and skin. It is a painful and debilitating disease.

Lupus must be closely managed throughout the patient's life. If a flare-up goes untreated for a while, the inflammation to blood vessels and organs can create permanent damage. There is no cure for lupus, only the ability to manage symptoms. The most common drugs used in the management of lupus, however, especially corticosteroids, carry significant risks. Corticosteroids, which are used to suppress the inflammatory process, have been linked to gastrointestinal problems, high blood pressure, bone loss, and other complications. It seems this is one of those conditions where, if the disease doesn't kill you, the treatment might.

What scared me most about what I read about lupus was the importance of early diagnosis and the need for continual and ongoing treatment. I knew Rosa was at a disadvantage, since it took months to get a diagnosis and her kidneys might already be permanently compromised. The question was: how badly? From what I read she seemed to have a serious, rather than mild, form of lupus, which meant continual monitoring of her condition. A physician friend whom I consulted reported that complete kidney failure was always a possibility, in which case dialysis might be necessary. While people live for years on dialysis in the United States, I wondered, if this should happen, how Rosa could possibly pay for it but also whether it was really safe. I read that infections following kidney failure are a common form of death for North American lupus patients, so I imagined the risks in Ecuador would be even greater. Moreover, I knew that it would be difficult for Rosa to pay for continual care and medications that she would need to keep the disease in check. I feared that as soon as she felt better she would stop treatment to save money, thus putting herself at risk. In addition to the medicines, lupus patients are encouraged to eat plenty of green leafy vegetables and soy products and to stay out of the sun. Again, I thought that Rosa had gotten the short end of the stick. There was little possibility that she could consistently afford such a diet; nor would it be easy to stay out of the equatorial sun. Because of the altitude, Cuenca can get quite chilly; and without indoor heating sometimes the only way to warm oneself up is to find a sunny spot to sit in. Would Rosa never be able to sit in the sun again? I read some testimonials on the Web to the physical and emotional toll that lupus takes even in the United States, where we can presume that patients get relatively good medical care. In the best of circumstances, this is a very difficult illness to live with. Rosa's circumstances are far from ideal.

Alexandra and Marisol were almost hysterical with grief and anxiety when I called Ecuador soon after receiving the email. As soon as the girls heard my voice on the phone, they each in turn broke into heart-breaking sobs. So much had been bottled up for so long. They felt that they had to hide their anxiety from Rosa lest it make her more ill, and they had not been able to tell either Lucho or Vicente all that had happened and what it meant. Even at home they tried to disguise their anxiety in order not to scare Cecilia and Billy. I spoke first to Marisol, who could not stop crying, and then to Alexandra, who was only marginally better. Rosa was sleeping, and they did not disturb her. Alexandra wanted me to call Lucho, whom she hadn't heard from in a few weeks, to let him know what was going on and how serious things were. She asked me to urge Lucho to come home. Both girls were clearly exhausted from worry and concern and the responsibility of caring for their mother on their own.

That evening when I talked with Lucho he sounded like his usual chipper self. He was doing well, working a few days a week in the back of a store, moving stock. When spring came, he would change to land-scaping. He asked about my family, and we exchanged pleasantries for a few minutes. When I told him why I was calling, Lucho's voice changed immediately. He had no idea of the severity of Rosa's condition and had never heard of lupus. Indeed, he thought, much as I had, that Rosa was on the mend. When I told him that there was no cure for lupus and that she would never be the same physically even if everything went as well as could be expected, he was devastated. Over and over he repeated, "What terrible luck, and me so far away. I didn't know when I left that my Señora would fall so ill . . . What should I do? What should I do?" He asked me if she could die, and I told him that it certainly was possible but that there was treatment that could help. I reported that Alexandra wanted him to come home and that, if he wanted to, I would help him pay for the ticket. Lucho, however, did not think that going home made any sense, and I couldn't blame him. He reasoned that if Rosa would need medical attention for the long term, the only way he could pay for that was to stay in New York. If he went back, he'd be even more useless to them. I agreed with him, but I felt that I had to deliver Alexandra's message.

Using all the *palanca* I could muster, I forwarded Alexandra's email to Lourdes, a friend in Cuenca who is well connected to the medical community there. My hope was that she could assist them in finding a good doctor. That seemed to me to be the only hope. She had acted as an intermediary for me previously, calling Alexandra and then emailing me to let me know what was happening.

January 10, 2001–February 20, 2001

The emails that Lourdes sent to me reveal the vital role she played. On January 10 she wrote:

This afternoon I will consult with two doctors, a cardiologist and a pathologist, about Rosa's condition. If she is able to get new treatment, that is good. Right now the good news is that we know what she has, the bad news is that she has lupus. It is useful to know that you can help financially. I will also try to talk with —— of the Archdiocese who works with migrants and their families to see if they can help.

On January 17 she reported:

On Friday I took Rosa and her daughter to a rheumatologist who wanted to know about her case. He works closely with Dr. G——, the most important doctor treating lupus. He confirmed the diagnosis of lupus and said that she should make an appointment with Dr. G—— since she will need long-term treatment. Rosa is very deteriorated and she looks very sick. She looks ancient and it is not because of her age. Today I talked with Alexandra to find out if she had gone to see Dr. G——. She told me not yet and I told her not to waste any time in going and that you would help financially. She told me that the doctor is very expensive for someone with scarce resources. I sure hope she follows through. Maybe you should call her.

On January 29 I received an email from Lourdes:

Saturday night I received a phone call from Alexandra. She told me that she had the first appointment with Dr. G——, the expert in rheumatology who is the person who should treat her, according to all the doctors I spoke with. He confirmed as well the diagnosis of lupus and he explained in detail to Alexandra the course of treatment and he asked for blood samples. Rosa must go to the clinic again one day this week for a blood transfusion. Her [previous] doctor said that she has to come at least one day a week for transfusions, but the rheumatologist has another view and he wants to start a new treatment immediately. What a shame that Alexandra didn't take her to him more quickly. She did promise to take Rosa there today and she asked me to advise you of what is happening. I hope all goes well. If she starts the treatment with the rheumatologist there is hope—so the doctor says.

On February 20 Lourdes wrote:

I talked for a long time to Alexandra and finally we know all there is
to know about Rosa's condition. She has the right medications now,
but she may need one or two more blood transfusions. Your money
arrived just in time, thankfully, and it paid for the hospital stay,
biopsies, etc. She does not have leukemia, cancer, or anything else,
just lupus. Now she must convalesce and live with lupus. They don't
have any more money though. Every 20 days it costs $50 for
medicine and every 10 days it is 10 dollars for the doctor. I don't
know if you can send some more money to help with the treatment.
They are very thankful for what you have sent, and it has helped a
lot. The youngest now needs medicines for the rheumatic fever that
he has. The father has not called in two weeks, and he hasn't sent
money. Alexandra wanted to know if you could call him and find out
what's happening. Rosa seems depressed, but she is doing better and
Alexandra is happy that things are improving.

Fall 2002

Under the treatment of the rheumatologist, Rosa's condition appears
to have stabilized. Like most lupus patients, however, she is in delicate
health and has periodic flare-ups that occasionally put her back in the
hospital. The financial costs of her illness are very high, and there is
little reason to think that they won't remain so. Lucho and I have spoken
many times over the past year since Rosa was diagnosed, but I'm not
sure that he really understands the chronic nature of her condition. He
seems surprised every time Rosa suffers a flare-up. He does not like to
hear that these will happen to her for the rest of her life. Someday one
will probably kill her.

The effects of Rosa's condition have reverberated throughout the
family. During her mother's crisis, Alexandra fell hopelessly behind in
her schoolwork and failed her exams. She will have to repeat a year of
medical school. Little Billy just barely passed into the third grade. While
his mother was deathly ill, no one noticed that Billy had a strep infection.
His sore throat was considered minor, given the urgency of Rosa's condition. Left untreated, however, strep infections can progress to rheumatic fever or as in Billy's case to a "pre–rheumatic fever" infection. He

they no longer knew what to do, they turned to me for advice and assistance. Never before have I been called upon to play such a prominent role in the immediate well-being of the family, and I am deeply grateful that I was able to help. The fact that they found a good doctor in Cuenca via Kalamazoo, Michigan, reinforces what I wrote in the early chapters of this book concerning the workings of the class system and the importance of knowing people.

In the end, Lucho's migration and Rosa's illness provide the final irony to their lifelong story of the vicissitudes of trying to get ahead. Over the years, so many of their plans for economic betterment have failed, even in the face of dedicated hard work. Migration to the United States represented for Lucho his last, best chance for them to have a little something to call their own. His plan, remember, was to go for only a few years—long enough to pay off his debt and save some money to buy a house. They would no longer have to rent from questionable strangers or depend on the capricious kindness of relatives. Now, of course, this will all be much more difficult and will no doubt take a good deal more time. Most painful of all is the truth that—given the cost of her health care—Lucho may never be able to save enough money to go home while his wife is still alive.

missed weeks and weeks of school, and for a while they worried that he too would be held back.

Vicente has moved out of Bolívar's house and is living on Long Island. He is working in construction; while he is making better money than he did in the restaurant, he also has more expenses living on his own. He is sending more money home to help with the medical bills, which means his own plans may have to be postponed indefinitely. The last time we spoke, Vicente complained about his job, noting that while the pay is good the work is very hard. A bit sheepishly, he told me that he has never worked so hard before; but things are so expensive that he is having trouble saving. Renting a room costs almost $800 a month, he complained, and coffee and a donut can run almost $4. How, he wonders, is he going to save money doing this? He told me he is lonely and is thinking about getting married. He has no particular girlfriend in mind—he just thinks that the state of marriage sounds increasingly appealing.

Lucho is living in Ossining, New York, and spent the summer of 2001 working in construction, laying concrete foundations. The money was good, and he has been able to pay back much of his debt and send money home to Rosa. Since the fall, however, and especially since the terrorist attacks of September 11, things have slowed considerably. Even day-work has been hard to find. He told me with chagrin that he is taking an unwelcome "vacation." The last time we spoke, Lucho tried hard to disguise his frustrations under a veneer of cheerfulness. Rosa had just gotten out of the hospital following a flare-up, he was unemployed, and he missed his family terribly. He was on the verge of tears as he told me again how he thought his life was one of endless suffering and unbearable loneliness. We laughed about his bad luck, only because there was nothing else to do. Soon after he arrived in the United States, the economy was officially declared in a recession and his wife was diagnosed with a serious illness. Then September 11 happened. How, he wonders, is he ever to get ahead and save enough money to "buy a little something" and return home?

A Final Irony

When I starting writing this book in the summer of 2000, I could never have known the turn of events that would take place over the course of the next year and a half. While I might have been able to predict that Lucho would one day come to the United States, I was nevertheless very surprised when I heard the news. I still cannot picture him walking the streets of New York. There is really no way that I could ever have foreseen what happened to Rosa. While she had been feeling increasingly weak and tired over the years, I presumed it was part of the normal aging process, combined with her worry and sadness about Vicente's departure and the structural violence of their lives. It did not occur to me as I watched her deteriorate steadily over the years that something far more serious was lurking in her slowly thinning body. These events, coming when they did, informed this manuscript in ways that are obvious to me but also in ways that I may never fully realize. There were several weeks when I stopped writing altogether because I was just too upset.

Over the past year I have talked more with Lucho than with any of the other Quitasacas, and what emerges is a picture of transnational migration that is fundamentally different from that experienced by Vicente. Vicente came to the United States during the height of the economic boom of the 1990s, a young man seeking to make his fortune and see the world. He has worked hard over the years but also taken time to enjoy himself. Living on Staten Island, he was somewhat removed from the center of the Ecuadorian migrant population in New York; and he identifies himself as a Hispanic as easily as he does as an Ecuadorian. His vision of the future is unclear; and while he longs to visit Ecuador, he makes no assertions that he will return to Cuenca to live. Lucho can think o nothing else. Lucho has lived and worked with other Cuencanos sin his arrival in the United States. While they provide companionship has little else in the way of a social life. He calls home to Ecuador e ten days or so; and when he is not working, he is at home wor Every day of unemployment adds one more day to the length of t must stay in the United States. Eventually Lucho may find mor about living in New York, but I think it unlikely.

Lucho's migration and Rosa's life-threatening illness have tered the course of the family's history and each member's that will continue to unfold as the years go by. Alexandra see now how truly indispensable she is to her family: no have navigated the medical system, including understan nology and procedures as she has. Her mother needs her never did before. Moreover, these events have also alt ship to the family. I feel even more deeply connected previously, since we weathered this latest family c Vicente and Lucho gone, the two eldest girls were f or death decisions under conditions of real finan

8.2. *Lucho, in New York, pays his respects to the "Virgin of Cisne," the patron saint of the poor in the southern Ecuadorian highlands.*

missed weeks and weeks of school, and for a while they worried that he too would be held back.

Vicente has moved out of Bolívar's house and is living on Long Island. He is working in construction; while he is making better money than he did in the restaurant, he also has more expenses living on his own. He is sending more money home to help with the medical bills, which means his own plans may have to be postponed indefinitely. The last time we spoke, Vicente complained about his job, noting that while the pay is good the work is very hard. A bit sheepishly, he told me that he has never worked so hard before; but things are so expensive that he is having trouble saving. Renting a room costs almost $800 a month, he complained, and coffee and a donut can run almost $4. How, he wonders, is he going to save money doing this? He told me he is lonely and is thinking about getting married. He has no particular girlfriend in mind—he just thinks that the state of marriage sounds increasingly appealing.

Lucho is living in Ossining, New York, and spent the summer of 2001 working in construction, laying concrete foundations. The money was good, and he has been able to pay back much of his debt and send money home to Rosa. Since the fall, however, and especially since the terrorist attacks of September 11, things have slowed considerably. Even day-work has been hard to find. He told me with chagrin that he is taking an unwelcome "vacation." The last time we spoke, Lucho tried hard to disguise his frustrations under a veneer of cheerfulness. Rosa had just gotten out of the hospital following a flare-up, he was unemployed, and he missed his family terribly. He was on the verge of tears as he told me again how he thought his life was one of endless suffering and unbearable loneliness. We laughed about his bad luck, only because there was nothing else to do. Soon after he arrived in the United States, the economy was officially declared in a recession and his wife was diagnosed with a serious illness. Then September 11 happened. How, he wonders, is he ever to get ahead and save enough money to "buy a little something" and return home?

A Final Irony

When I starting writing this book in the summer of 2000, I could never have known the turn of events that would take place over the course of the next year and a half. While I might have been able to predict that Lucho would one day come to the United States, I was nevertheless very

8.2. Lucho, in New York, pays his respects to the "Virgin of Cisne," the patron saint of the poor in the southern Ecuadorian highlands.

surprised when I heard the news. I still cannot picture him walking the streets of New York. There is really no way that I could ever have foreseen what happened to Rosa. While she had been feeling increasingly weak and tired over the years, I presumed it was part of the normal aging process, combined with her worry and sadness about Vicente's departure and the structural violence of their lives. It did not occur to me as I watched her deteriorate steadily over the years that something far more serious was lurking in her slowly thinning body. These events, coming when they did, informed this manuscript in ways that are obvious to me but also in ways that I may never fully realize. There were several weeks when I stopped writing altogether because I was just too upset.

Over the past year I have talked more with Lucho than with any of the other Quitasacas, and what emerges is a picture of transnational migration that is fundamentally different from that experienced by Vicente. Vicente came to the United States during the height of the economic boom of the 1990s, a young man seeking to make his fortune and see the world. He has worked hard over the years but also taken time to enjoy himself. Living on Staten Island, he was somewhat removed from the center of the Ecuadorian migrant population in New York; and he identifies himself as a Hispanic as easily as he does as an Ecuadorian. His vision of the future is unclear; and while he longs to visit Ecuador, he makes no assertions that he will return to Cuenca to live. Lucho can think of nothing else. Lucho has lived and worked with other Cuencanos since his arrival in the United States. While they provide companionship, he has little else in the way of a social life. He calls home to Ecuador every ten days or so; and when he is not working, he is at home worrying. Every day of unemployment adds one more day to the length of time he must stay in the United States. Eventually Lucho may find more to like about living in New York, but I think it unlikely.

Lucho's migration and Rosa's life-threatening illness have forever altered the course of the family's history and each member's life in ways that will continue to unfold as the years go by. Alexandra must surely see now how truly indispensable she is to her family: no one else could have navigated the medical system, including understanding the terminology and procedures as she has. Her mother needs her now in ways she never did before. Moreover, these events have also altered my relationship to the family. I feel even more deeply connected to them than I did previously, since we weathered this latest family crisis together. With Vicente and Lucho gone, the two eldest girls were faced with making life or death decisions under conditions of real financial constraint. When they no longer knew what to do, they turned to me for advice and assistance. Never before have I been called upon to play such a prominent role in the immediate well-being of the family, and I am deeply grateful that I was able to help. The fact that they found a good doctor in Cuenca via Kalamazoo, Michigan, reinforces what I wrote in the early chapters of this book concerning the workings of the class system and the importance of knowing people.

In the end, Lucho's migration and Rosa's illness provide the final irony to their lifelong story of the vicissitudes of trying to get ahead. Over the years, so many of their plans for economic betterment have failed, even in the face of dedicated hard work. Migration to the United States represented for Lucho his last, best chance for them to have a little something to call their own. His plan, remember, was to go for only a few years— long enough to pay off his debt and save some money to buy a house. They would no longer have to rent from questionable strangers or depend on the capricious kindness of relatives. Now, of course, this will all be much more difficult and will no doubt take a good deal more time. Most painful of all is the truth that—given the cost of her health care— Lucho may never be able to save enough money to go home while his wife is still alive.

Notes

2. Transnational Migration

1. In this region of Ecuador use of the term *cholo* (masculine) is most often a derogatory comment to insult a male who aspires to be more than he is. It is often said as an insult to rural or Indian men who try to be cosmopolitan but clearly can't really pull it off. In Cuenca, *chola* (feminine) is a much more positive designation—but it is not without controversy and contradiction (see Weismantel 2001). A *cholo boy* in local humor indicates someone (usually of the popular classes, either rural or urban) who admires and emulates all things North American—especially consumer goods. *Iony* is a more recent term, which, according to Jason Pribilsky (2001), describes returned migrants who have adopted North American attitudes and customs. The term derives from the New York tourism slogan of the 1980s, "I ♥ New York!"

2. See Belote and Belote (1984) for a discussion of the processes of "transculturation" in Saraguro during this period. The authors discuss the process of shifting identities as well as the resurgence of indigenous identity at the same time.

3. The *chola* (female) of Azuay typically has her hair plaited in two long braids and wears a wide gathered skirt embroidered at the bottom, a woven "Panama hat," and an embroidered shawl and blouse. The *cholo* (male), increasingly rare today, is identified by his *poncho* and felt hat. Although many rural women still dress in the traditional style (or a modified version of it), very few men who aren't grandfathers are openly identifiable as *cholos*. The use of the term *chola* in a romantic sense seems to be unique to Cuenca (Weismantel 2001). Elsewhere in Ecuador *cholo(a)* is considered an insult, because it highlights a lack of cosmopolitan orientation. Whereas the word *cholo* (male) can be considered an insult, implying that the person is an Indian who has taken on Hispanic cultural characteristic and is not fooling anyone (Brownrigg 1972), a *chola* (female) in

Cuenca is a cultural symbol of traditionalism of the highest order. The city's anthem is called the *Chola Cuencana,* and a statue of a *chola* graces the western entrance to the city from the Pan American Highway.

4. Enrique Serrano wrote that the 30,000 emigrants from the region were responsible for $120 million in investments as early as 1990 (Serrano 1991:177).

5. Jason Pribilsky, an anthropologist studying transnational migration outside of Cuenca, reports exactly the opposite. He notes that transnational families are investing heavily in education, sometimes sending their children to live with relatives in Cuenca in order to attend better schools (Pribilsky 2001).

6. Susan Hamilton (2000) in a review of "urban legends" argues that the telling of such stories ultimately says more about those telling the stories than about those they are supposedly about. These myths serve the needs of those telling them by reifying differences and therefore justifying particular actions or positions in relation to the groups being discussed (see also Perlman 1976).

3. Family Matters

1. See Taussig (1980) and Crain (1991) for more analysis of the connections between capitalism and devil stories in South America. Both authors argue, much as I do here, that tales of the devil become ways to explain and talk about the inequities of capitalist expansion.

2. Since the mid-1980s, with the publication of *Weapons of the Weak: Everyday Forms of Peasant Resistance* by James Scott, anthropologists and others have been very concerned with looking at the ways in which marginalized peoples are not just victims of oppressive conditions but also manipulate and negotiate within them. While I agree in theory that it is important to see the poor and oppressed as having a degree of agency in their lives, I also join other authors who worry that we may therefore neglect to realize the levels of oppression under which some people live (see Abu-Lughod 1990).

3. These changes are influenced by multiple factors, including the aging of the household members, shifting responsibilities as children grow, and also changing social conditions. Indeed, children, especially adolescents, are often real agents of change within their homes as they challenge their parents to adopt to shifting social conditions (see Caputo 1995).

4. While there is not really space here for a full exploration of the shifts and changes in gender ideologies between rural and urban settings, much has been written about the connections between the kinds of patriarchal behavior described for Lucho and urbanization, wage labor, and capitalism (see Ferguson and Folbre 1981; Nash and Fernandez-Kelly 1983; A. Scott 1986; Weismantel 1997).

5. See Stolen (1991) for a very different interpretation of domestic violence in Ecuador.

4. Rosa

1. I put the term "typical" in quotation marks to emphasize the real meaninglessness of this word. As Lynn Meisch points out (1998), the *pollera* itself is a style made popular during the colonial period; moreover, the fashions of the *chola* Cuencana (the traditional peasant woman from this region) shift over time and space. Blouses, shawls, sweaters, and even *pollera* styles and fabrics reflect current fashion preferences. For example, in 1989 the paisley sweater that Rosa wore was very fashionable among *cholas,* and *polleras* were usually made of red, orange, or blue wools with machine-embroidered flowers on the borders. In 1999 darker fabrics with a velvety look were popular for the *polleras.*

2. See Foster (1982) for more on envy illness.

3. There is considerable discussion in the anthropological literature about the importance of godparentage (*compadrazgo)* in Latin America and the various forms it can take. Mintz and Wolf (1950) pointed out that *compadrazgo* could be either symmetrical, meaning that godparents are chosen from the same social class as the initiate, or asymmetrical, which usually involves choosing someone of higher social status. They argued that verticality was often associated with upwardly mobile urbanites, while Ingham (1974) found the opposite. I saw little discernible pattern in Cuenca, and there was a great deal of flexibility in individual families. As a rule, however, Rosa's family selected godparents asymmetrically. Sometimes these godparents have been very disappointing to the family; but at other times, as in the case of Vicente's godfather, Bolívar, it has paid off in ways they could never have predicted.

4. There is a well-documented association between urban living and reduced fertility rates for women globally (Chant 1999), in Ecuador (Scrimshaw 1975), and in Cuenca (Borrero and Ugalde 1995). Rosa's concern about the size of her family clearly reflects an urbanized view of the ideal number of children.

5. See Allen (1988) and Weismantel (1988) on the importance of food, and lots of it, in Andean social relations. To give me less than far too much would have been a serious breach of etiquette.

6. This is not an unfounded fear, as many men from Ecuador have married women in the United States to get permanent residency status. While Rosa could not have known this in 1989, her brother Carlos was to do exactly this years later. He married a Puerto Rican woman and got his citizenship papers, then they divorced. In 2000 Vicente told me that Carlos had married a woman from Cuenca and that they were living in New York.

7. Women in Ecuador, especially rural women, traditionally stay in bed for forty days after the birth of a child. This period, known as the *dieta,* is one of rest for mother and infant. Most of the women I worked with could afford neither the time in bed nor the expense of the special diet required of the *dieta.* Most women were lucky if they were able to stay in bed for a week or two.

Dietas may be more likely to occur in rural areas, where female kin are nearby and willing to help with the new mother's domestic responsibilities.

8. In Ecuador illnesses are often thought to be linked to imbalances between hot and cold. Hot and cold can be thermal conditions, but they are also purely conceptual (see McKee 1987). Childbirth is considered a "hot" condition, for example, so that it must be treated with foods, like chicken, that are considered cooling. Sudden exposure to cold is almost always problematic, but even more so when the body is in a heated condition. The shock of the sudden change can be debilitating (see Foster 1987 for more expansive treatment).

9. Nancy Scheper-Hughes (1992) argues that in conditions of extreme poverty such as those that she witnessed in northeast Brazil mothers often withhold affection from infants until they have some indication that the children will in fact live. While I do not think that conditions in Cuenca were at this desperate stage, I do think that it is possible that in 1993 Rosa was not sure that Billy would survive. She was depressed herself; and Billy was small, lethargic, and bottle fed, all of which was distressing to her. But survive he did, and now he is very well loved indeed.

10. Cooperatives are common throughout Ecuador for a variety of jobs, including driving a taxi or bus. Individuals must purchase a place in a taxi cooperative, and their taxis then carry that cooperative's logo. Taxi drivers are only allowed to park and wait for passengers in the cooperative's assigned pickup places (although they can drive around as much as they wish). Cooperatives attempt to protect their members' livelihood by limiting membership and therefore the numbers of taxis on the street as well as working with other cooperatives to designate zones of service. Cooperatives by their nature are run by their members, and decisions are ideally voted on by the majority. Things had gotten so bad in 1999, however, that Lucho believed that he would never be able to sell his place in the cooperative because no one had the money to buy it, and it was not worth much in any case since no one was really earning a lot.

5. Lucho

1. See Pribilsky (2001) for a discussion of the effects of transnational migration from Ecuador on children.

2. I interpreted the joking relationships I had with many men in Ecuador during my first field stay similarly to the way in which A. R. Radcliffe-Brown discusses joking relationships in Africa (Radcliffe-Brown 1952). In particular, he argues that people who are in ambiguous relationships to each other, such as a son-in-law and a mother-in-law, often maintain joking relationships to ease the potential tensions that the ambiguity could create.

3. Ecuadorians at this social class level very often ask to be "pardoned" when

they serve food to someone that they perceive may be of a higher social status. They are asking pardon for the simplicity of the food or the potential unacceptability of it. This is a recognition that the person being served may be unaccustomed to such food. I found that as the years went by and families became more comfortable with me, they asked for pardon less and less.

4. Notice Lucho's use of "Señor" when referring to Bolívar. He uses this term to highlight the respect he has for Bolívar and to acknowledge the debts that they owe him.

5. Lucho is referring to something Alexandra talks about more explicitly in Chapter 6. That is, according to Alexandra, Rosa has always favored the boys in the family and paid less attention to the girls. Alexandra gives a cultural explanation, saying that this is how it often is in Ecuador. See also Chapter 2 for a discussion of male/female relations.

6. Lucho may have gotten this idea because Spain was offering 30,000 work visas to Ecuadorians in the late 1990s. The United States, however, was not (*Tiempos del Mundo*, February 11, 1999).

7. During the financial and banking crisis in 1998–1999, President Jamil Mahuad had savings accounts frozen for a period, and many people lost a good deal of money in the confusion that ensued over bank records. The government froze dollar accounts to prevent massive disinvestment from Ecuadorian banks, which would cause further stagnation of the economy.

6. The Children

1. This is a fairly common pattern noted decades ago in the Harvard studies conducted by Whiting and Whiting (1975). Their cross-cultural studies on child-rearing indicated that in situations of economic scarcity parents count on their children to help with household responsibilities and cannot "afford" to promote independent children who will not contribute to the household maintenance (Whiting and Whiting 1975; Hendrix 1985).

2. *Wawa* (meaning baby) is a Quichua word that has entered into common Spanish in Ecuador. Quichua is a native language of Ecuador spoken by several indigenous groups (see Harrison 1989). Rosa does not speak Quichua; nor do her parents.

3. It is not at all unusual for mothers to lock their very small children in the house when the mother has to go out and cannot take the children with her. McKee (1997:21) mentions one mother who tied her children's ankles to the bed to keep them out of harm's way. While this might seem shocking to middle-class Americans, poor Ecuadorian women often see this as the best of bad options. If there is no one to watch a child, as is often the case in urban environments, it is considered safer for the child to be in a controlled environment than to roam free and possibly wander off or be harmed in some way. One of

my informants locked her three-year-old in the bedroom every morning while she cleaned houses. Although she was unhappy with this arrangement, she felt there was nothing she could do about it: her employer did not want the child in the house, and she could not afford to pay someone to watch her. A neighbor had a key and kept a begrudging eye on the girl.

4. Consider the devil story at the beginning of Chapter 3. I think it is very important to Rosa that her children have a well-developed sense of responsibility for one another, and she reinforces this notion in multiple ways.

5. This type of child fostering is more common in rural areas. A family member who has no children or an older couple living alone may be "given" a relative's child to raise, to provide company and help around the house (see Weismantel 1995). Rosa told me that this practice was more common a generation or two ago than it is now.

6. The idea that being thin is more beautiful than being fat is a very modern one. In most poor societies being fat is an indication of a certain degree of wealth (or at the very least the absence of want) and is considered healthy and beautiful. Indeed, standards of thinness seem to increase with economic wealth.

7. I tried to get Alexandra to elaborate on this, but she really couldn't. I think this is a bit of folklore: individuals probably have as many tries to cross the border as they have money to pay a *coyote*.

8. *Moreno* is a reference to dark skin. An individual can self-identify as a *moreno* as a means of establishing racial pride (as Beto does here); or the word can simply be used as a means of identifying shades of skin. In other words, it is not implicitly an insult. When used in anger, however, as Beto describes, *moreno* is meant to be a putdown. I have on occasion heard Rosa make mention of the different skin tones of her children, with Vicente, Marisol, and Billy being lighter than Alexandra, Beto, and Cecilia. While I only noticed these differences when they were pointed out to me, in Cuenca they are very important in establishing social potential. Rosa assumes (probably rightly) that the lighter-skinned children will be better accepted in Cuencan society than the darker ones. She may see her lighter skin color as one of the few advantages she has over other poor Cuencanos, even though it has never resulted in any real material gain for her.

9. In the end, this did not happen: Cecilia did well enough on an examination to enroll in one of the better public schools in town.

7. Vicente

1. While the children's lies were meant simply to get rid of me, I found that it was not uncommon for people occasionally to lie to me over small things that to me hardly seemed to matter. Hirschkind (1988) discusses the greater

significance of lying in a rural community in the nearby province of Cañar, where, she argues, it is a legacy of the hacienda system and serves as a means of better positioning individuals in relation to scarce resources. In urban Cuenca I found that my informants resorted to lying when they were afraid that the truth might be uncomfortable. For the most part I found that people lied about insignificant things, usually in an attempt to please me.

2. In keeping with concerns about maintaining a hot/cold balance, Andean Ecuadorians do not usually drink beverages right out of the refrigerator, particularly if the person is too warm. The shock of the cold in the warm body is thought to induce illness. As I have discussed earlier, while the hot/cold dichotomy is usually not considered "thermal" in that foods are classified according to qualities that are not based on temperature, there is a thermal element to concerns about hot and cold. In particular, sudden exposure to cold through immersion in liquids or by drinking them is thought to "shock" the soul from the body—leading to illness.

3. Vicente never entered the military but instead paid the requisite fine to release himself from service. This seems to be an increasingly popular option for boys in urban schools.

4. Cajas is a very large and mostly undeveloped National Park about 30 kilometers west of Cuenca at a higher altitude. It is known for its ecological diversity and its stunning lakes. I found Cajas to be wind-swept and stark. Earlier that year, Patricia Talbot (a young girl from a very well-to-do family in Cuenca) was supposedly visited by the Virgin Mary, who said that she would appear in a grotto in Cajas and send forth messages. Busloads of pilgrims from all over the country were making the trek to Cajas at the appointed times to see the appearances of the Virgin, who spoke through Patricia. National TV news covered these events, and I once saw two news anchors debating whether the way the sun's rays emanated from the clouds during the pilgrimages indicated something divine. The whole phenomenon of the "Virgin of Cajas" became a media circus and spawned much debate as to the authenticity of the apparitions. Exposés about Patricia Talbot appeared in the local newspapers, chronicling her family life and her fledgling modeling career. Some wondered why a rich girl and not a poor one would be singled out by the Virgin; others mentioned her emotional instability after her parents' recent divorce. Locally, scholars and intellectuals discussed the fact that the more conservative leaders of the Catholic Church embraced Patricia because the messages she delivered from the Virgin were very conservative and therefore much to their liking. The messages—warning of the dangers of modern life, scorning materialism, and advocating humility, faith, and devotion—were espoused by the Catholic Church orthodoxy, which found itself threatened from within by more liberal clerics and from without by the increasing spread of evangelical Protestantism.

5. I use the term "Hispanic" here rather than "Latino" because that is the term Vicente uses. See Oboler (1999) for a discussion of the historical and politi-

cal significance of the terms "Hispanic" and "Latino" in relation to transnational migration.

6. Bolívar had to borrow the money himself, so the interest was not profit that he made but went to the person who loaned him the money.

7. On New Year's Eve in many places in Ecuador they celebrate Año Viejo (the old year) by making effigies of wood and paper, parading them around town and then setting fire to them. The effigies are often meant to satirize political events and persons or to recall newsworthy people and events of the year. I was in Guayaquil for the preparations for Año Viejo in 1988 and saw the building of magnificent caricatures of Ecuadorian politicians, as well as one of the American president and vice-president, George Bush, Sr., and Dan Quayle.

8. Lives and Stories

1. I borrow from Paul Ricoeur here in using the term "character" to mean "consistent dispositions" by which a "person or community recognizes itself" (Ricoeur 1992 : 121). "Character" conceived in this way contrasts with much of the discussion in anthropology about the "mutable" self, since the emphasis is on the consistencies that a person recognizes in himself or herself, not the relational nature of personal identity. I do not disagree with discussions about the situational nature of the self and can apply such an understanding to much of what Vicente says. Rather, I consider character to be a part of self-identity, not an explanation of it. In other words, character composes a part of the self that is perceived to be relatively consistent across situations. The consistent "part" can be nestled within a variable and relational self with little concern for contradiction.

References

Abu-Lughod, Lila

1990   "The Romance of Resistance: Tracing Transformations of Power through Bedouin Women." In *Beyond the Second Sex: New Directions in the Anthropology of Gender,* edited by Peggy Reeves Sanday and Ruth Gallagher Goodenough, 311–337. Philadelphia: University of Pennsylvania Press.

Aguilar, Orejuela Rodrigo, ed.

1998   *Cuenca de los Andes.* Cuenca, Ecuador: Ilustre Municipalidad de Cuenca, Casa de la Cultura Ecuatoriana, Núcleo del Azuay.

Allen, Catherine

1988   *The Hold Life Has: Coca and Cultural Identity in an Andean Community.* Washington, D.C.: Smithsonian Institution Press.

Anderson, Jeanine

1978   "The Middle Class Woman in Family and Community: Lima, Peru." Ph.D. diss., Cornell University.

Anderson, Joan B.

1997   "Ecuador." In *The Political Economy of Latin America in the Postwar Period,* edited by Laura Randall, 232–274. Austin: University of Texas Press.

Apolo, Manuel Espinosa

1995   *Los mestizos ecuatorianos y las señas de identidad cultural.* 2d ed. Quito: Tramasocial Editorial.

Appadurai, Arjun

1991   "Global Ethnoscapes: Notes and Queries for a Transnational Anthropology." In *Recapturing Anthropology: Working in the Present,* edited by Richard G. Fox, 191–210. Santa Fe: School of American Research.

1996   *Modernity at Large: Cultural Dimensions of Globalization.* Minneapolis: University of Minnesota Press.

Astudillo, Jaime, and Claudio Cordero E.
1990   *Huayrapamushcas en USA.* Quito: Editorial el Conejo.

Babb, Florence
1989   *Between Field and Cooking Pot: The Political Economy of Market Women in Peru.* Austin: University of Texas Press.

Baudrillard, Jean
1988   *Jean Baudrillard: Selected Writings.* Edited by Mark Poster. Stanford: Stanford University Press.

Becker, Mark
1992   "Nationalism and Pluri-Nationalism in a Multi-Ethnic State: Indigenous Organizations in Ecuador." Paper presented at the Mid-America Conference on History, September, Lawrence, Kansas.

Belote, Linda Smith, and Jim Belote
1984   "Drain from the Bottom: Individual Ethnic Identity Change in Southern Ecuador." *Social Forces* 63 (1): 24–50.

Benería, Lourdes, and Martha Roldán
1987   *The Crossroads of Class and Gender: Industrial Homework, Subcontracting, and Household Dynamics in Mexico City.* Chicago: University of Chicago Press.

Bernard, Carmen
1985   "The Many Faces of Manuel: Illness and Fate in the Andes." *History and Anthropology* 2: 145–152.

Bocco, Arnaldo, M.
1990   "Ecuador: The State, Public Policy and Capital Accumulation, 1970–83." In *The State and Capital Accumulation in Latin America,* edited by Christine Anglade and Carlos Fortin, 88–104. Pittsburgh: University of Pittsburgh Press.

Bordo, Susan
1993   *Unbearable Weight: Feminism, Western Culture and the Body.* Berkeley, Calif.: University of California Press.

Borrero, Ana Luz Vega
1991   "Las migraciones y recursos humanos: Situación reciente y tendencias." In *Cuenca y su futuro,* 93–171. Cuenca, Ecuador: CORDES.

Borrero, Ana Luz Vega, and Silvia Vega Ugalde
1995   *Mujer y migración: Alcance de un fenómeno nacional y regional.* Quito: Abya-Yala.

Boyd, Monica
1989   "Family and Personal Networks in International Migration: Recent Developments and New Agendas." *International Migration Review* 23 (3): 638–670.

Brownrigg, Leslie Ann
1972   "The Nobles of Cuenca: The Agrarian Elite of Southern Ecuador." Ph.D. diss., Columbia University.

Bruner, Edward M.

1986   "Ethnography as Narrative." In *The Anthropology of Experience*, edited by Victor W. Turner and Edward M. Bruner, 139–155. Urbana: University of Illinois Press.

Brusco, Elizabeth E.

1995   *The Reformation of Machismo: Evangelical Conversion and Gender in Colombia*. Austin: University of Texas Press.

Brysk, Alison

2000   *From Tribal Village to Global Village: Indian Rights and International Relations in Latin America*. Stanford: Stanford University Press.

Buechler, Hans, and Judith-Maria Buechler

1996   *The World of Sofía Velásquez: The Autobiography of a Bolivian Market Vendor*. New York: Columbia University Press.

Butler, Barbara Yale

1981   "Indigenous Ethnic Identity and Ethnic Identity Change in the Ecuadoran Sierra." Ph.D. diss., University of Rochester.

Caputo, Virginia

1995   "Anthropology's Silent Others: A Consideration of Some Conceptual and Methodological Issues for the Study of Youth and Children's Culture." In *Youth Cultures*, edited by Verit Amit-Talai and Helen Wulff, 19–42. London: Routledge.

Carpio, Patricio Benalcázar

1992   *Entre pueblos y metrópolis: La migración internacional en comunidades austro-andinas en al Ecuador*. Quito: Ediciones Abya-Yala.

Chant, Sylvia

1999   "Population, Migration, Employment and Gender." In *Latin America Transformed; Globalization and Modernity*, edited by Robert N. Gwynne and Cristobal Kay, 226–269. London: Arnold Publishers.

Chavez, Leo R.

1998   *Shadowed Lives: Undocumented Immigrants in American Society*. 2d ed. Fort Worth: Harcourt Brace.

Clifford, James

1986   "On Ethnographic Allegory." In *Writing Culture: The Poetics and Politics of Ethnography*, edited by James Clifford and George E. Marcus, 98–120. Berkeley: University of California Press.

Colloredo-Mansfield, Rudi

1999   *The Native Leisure Class: Consumption and Cultural Creativity in the Andes*. Chicago: University of Chicago Press.

Conroy, Mary, Robert D. Hess, Hiroshi Azuma, and Keiko Kashiwagi

1980   "Maternal Strategies for Regulating Children's Behavior: Japanese and American Families." *Journal of Cross-Cultural Psychology* 11 (2): 153–172.

Constable, Nicole

1999   "At Home But Not at Home: Filipina Narratives of Ambivalent Returns." *Current Anthropology* 14 (2): 203–228.

Crain, Mary

1990   "The Social Construction of National Identity in Highland Ecuador."
        Anthropological Quarterly 63 (1): 43–59.

1991   "Poetics and Politics in the Ecuadorian Andes: Women's Narratives of
        Death and Devil Possession." *American Ethnologist* 18: 67–87.

Crandon-Malamud, Libbet

1991   *From the Fat of Our Souls: Social Change, Political Process, and Medical Plural-
        ism in Bolivia.* Berkeley: University of California Press.

Deere, Carmen Diana

1995   "What Difference Does Gender Make? Rethinking Peasant Studies."
        Feminist Economics 1 (1): 53–72.

Díaz Barriga, Miguel

2000   "The Domestic/Public in Mexico City: Notes on Theory, Social Move-
        ments and the Essentialization of Everyday Life." In *Gender Matters: Re-
        reading Michelle Z. Rosaldo,* edited by Alejandro Lugo and Bill Maurer,
        116–143. Ann Arbor: University of Michigan Press.

Ehlers, Tracy Bachrach

1991   "Debunking Marianismo: Economic Vulnerability and Survival Strate-
        gies among Guatemalan Wives." *Ethnology* 10 (1): 1–16.

Estrella, Eduardo

1978   *Medicina aborigen: La práctica médica aborigen de la Sierra Ecuatoriana.*
        Quito: Editorial Epoca.

Featherstone, Mike

1995   *Undoing Culture: Globalization, Postmodernism and Identity.* London: Sage.

Ferguson, Ann, and Nancy Folbre

1981   "The Unhappy Marriage of Patriarchy and Capitalism." In *Women and
        Revolution: A Discussion of the Unhappy Marriage of Marxism and Feminism,*
        edited by Lydia Sargent, 313–338. Boston: South End Press.

Finerman, Ruthbeth

1987   "Inside Out: Women's World View and Family Health in an Ecuador-
        ian Indian Community." *Social Science and Medicine* 25: 1157–1162.

1989   "The Burden of Responsibility: Duty, Depression and *Nervios* in
        Andean Ecuador." *Health Care for Women International* 10 (23): 141–157.

Folbre, Nancy

1986   "Cleaning House: New Perspectives on Household and Economic De-
        velopment." *Journal of Economic Development* 22: 5–40.

Foster, George M.

1982   "The Anatomy of Envy: A Study of Symbolic Behavior." *Current An-
        thropology* 13: 165–202.

1987   "On the Origins of Humoral Medicine in Latin America." *Medical An-
        thropology Quarterly* 1 (4): 355–393.

Friedman, Jonathan

1994   *Cultural Identity and Global Processes.* London: Sage.

García Canclini, Néstor

1993   *Transforming Modernity: Popular Culture in Mexico.* Austin: University of Texas Press.

Garro, Linda C., and Cheryl Mattingly

2000   "Narrative and Construct and Construction." In *Narrative and the Cultural Construction of Illness and Healing,* edited by Cheryl Mattingly and Linda C. Garro, 1–49. Berkeley: University of California Press.

Gelles, Paul, and Gabriela Martínez Escobar, trans.

1996   *Andean Lives: Gregorio Condori Mamani and Asunta Quispe Huamán.* Ed. Ricardo Valderrama Fernández and Carmen Escalante Gutiérrez. Austin: University of Texas Press.

Georges, Eugenia

1992   "Gender, Class and Migration in the Dominican Republic: Women's Experiences in a Transnational Community." In *Towards a Transnational Perspective on Migration,* edited by Nina Glick Schiller, Linda Basch, and Cristina Blanc-Szanton, 81–100. Annals of the New York Academy of Sciences, vol. 645. New York: New York Academy of Sciences.

Gill, Lesley

1993   " 'Proper Women' and City Pleasures: Gender, Class and Contested Meanings in La Paz." *American Ethnologist* 20 (1): 72–88.

Glass-Coffin, Bonnie

1998   *The Gift of Life: Female Spirituality and Healing in Northeast Peru.* Albuquerque: University of New Mexico Press.

Grasmuck, Sherri, and Patricia Pessar

1991   *Between Two Islands: Dominican International Migration.* Berkeley: University of California Press.

Gupta, Akhil, and James Ferguson

1997a   "Beyond Culture: Space, Identity and the Politics of Difference." In *Culture, Power, Place,* edited by Akhil Gupta and James Ferguson, 33–51. Durham, N.C.: Duke University Press.

1997b   "Culture, Power, Place: Ethnography at the End of an Era." In *Culture, Power, Place,* edited by Akhil Gupta and James Ferguson, 1–29. Durham, N.C.: Duke University Press.

Gutmann, Matthew C.

1996   *The Meanings of Macho: Being a Man in Mexico.* Berkeley: University of California Press.

2000   "A (Short) Cultural History of Mexican Machos." In *Gender Matters: Rereading Michelle Z. Rosaldo,* edited by Alejandro Lugo and Bill Maurer, 160–184. Ann Arbor: University of Michigan Press.

Hamilton, Sarah

1998   *The Two-Headed Household.* Pittsburgh: University of Pittsburgh Press.

Hamilton, Susan

2000   "Seeking Higher Ground: Housing Replacement Strategies of Families Displaced by the Yacyret '87 Project in Posadas, Argentina." Ph.D. diss., Syracuse University.

Handelsman, Michael
2000   *Culture and Customs of Ecuador.* Westport, Conn.: Greenwood Press.

Harkness, Sara, and Charles M. Super
1983   "The Cultural Construction of Child Development: A Framework for the Socialization of Affect." *Ethos* 11 (4): 221–231.

Harrison, Regina
1989   *Signs, Songs and Memory in the Andes: Translating Quechua Language and Culture.* Austin: University of Texas Press.

Harvey, Penelope
1998   "Afterword." *Journal of Latin American Anthropology* 3 (2): 168–180.

Hebdige, Dick
1994   "After the Masses." In *Culture/Power/History: A Reader in Contemporary Social History,* edited by Nicholas Dirks, Geoff Eley, and Sherry Ortner, 222–235. Princeton, N.J.: Princeton University Press.

Hendrix, Lewellyn
1985   "Economy and Child Training Re-examined." *Ethos* 13 (3): 246–261.

Hirschkind, Lynn
1980   "On Conforming in Cuenca." Ph.D. diss., University of Wisconsin.
1988   "La mentira y la estructura social." *Universidad Verdad: Revista de la Pontificia Universidad Católica del Ecuador* (Cuenca) 2: 57–83.

Hondagneu-Sotelo, Pierrette
1994   *Gendered Transitions: Mexican Experiences with Immigration.* Berkeley: University of California Press.

Hondagneu-Sotelo, Pierrette, and Michael A. Messner
1994   "Gender Displays and Men's Power: The 'New Man' and the Mexican Immigrant Man." In *Theorizing Masculinities,* edited by Harry Brod and Michael Kaufman, 200–218. London: Sage.

Honig, Alice, and J. Ronald Lally
1973   "Assessing Teacher Behavior with Infants in Day Care." Paper presented at the American Educational Research Association, New Orleans.

Hurtado, Osvaldo
2002   *Deuda y desarrollo en el Ecuador contemporáneo.* Quito: Editorial Planeta.

Ingham, John M.
1974   "The Asymmetrical Implications of Godparenthood in Tlayacapan, Morelos." In *Contemporary Cultures and Societies in Latin America,* edited by Dwight Heath, 395–405. New York: Random House.

Isbell, Billie Jean
1978   *To Defend Ourselves: Ecology and Ritual in an Andean Village.* Austin: University of Texas Press.

Jameson, Frederic
1984   "Postmodernism and the Cultural Logic of Late Capitalism." *New Left Review* 146: 53–92.
1998   "Notes on Globalization as a Philosophical Issue." In *The Cultures of Globalization,* edited by Frederic Jameson and Masao Miyoshi, 54–77. Durham, N.C.: Duke University Press.
Jokisch, Brad D.
1997   "From Labor Circulation to International Migration: The Case of South Central Ecuador." *Yearbook, Conference of Latin Americanist Geographers* 23: 63–75.
Kearney, Michael
1986   "From the Invisible Hand to the Visible Feet: Anthropological Studies of Migration and Development." *Annual Review of Anthropology* 15: 331–361.
1996   *Reconceptualizing the Peasantry.* Boulder, Colo.: Westview Press.
Kyle, David Jane
1995   "The Transnational Peasant: The Social Construction of International Economic Migration and Transcommunities from the Ecuadorian Andes." Ph.D. diss., Johns Hopkins University.
Larme, Anne C.
1998   "Environment, Vulnerability and Gender in Andean Ethnomedicine." *Social Science and Medicine* 47 (8): 1005–1015.
Larrea, Carlos
1998   "Structural Adjustment, Income Distribution and Employment in Ecuador." In *Poverty, Economic Reform and Income Distribution in Latin America,* edited by Albert Berry, 179–204. Boulder, Colo.: Lynne Reiner.
Leeds, Anthony
1971   "The Concept of the 'Culture of Poverty': Conceptual, Logical and Empirical Problems with Perspectives from Brazil and Peru." In *The Culture of Poverty: A Critique,* edited by Eleanor Burke Leacock, 226–284. New York: Simon and Schuster.
Levine, Robert A.
1974   "Parental Goals: A Cross-Cultural View." *Teachers College Record* 76 (2): 226–239.
1980   "Anthropology and Child Development." *New Directions for Child Development* 8: 71–86.
Levine, Sarah
1993   *Dolor y Alegría: Women and Social Change in Urban Mexico.* Madison: University of Wisconsin Press.
Lewis, Oscar
1959   *Five Families: Mexican Case Studies in the Culture of Poverty.* New York: Basic Books.

1961 *The Children of Sánchez: Autobiography of a Mexican Family.* New York: Random House.

Lomnitz, Claudio

1994 "Decadence in Times of Globalization." *Cultural Anthropology* 9 (2): 257–267.

Lugo, Alejandro

2000 "Destabilizing the Masculine, Refocusing 'Gender': Men and the Aura of Authority in Michelle Z. Rosaldo's Work." In *Gender Matters: Rereading Michelle Z. Rosaldo,* edited by Alejandro Lugo and Bill Maurer, 54–88. Ann Arbor: University of Michigan Press.

Malo, Claudio

1991 "Peso y presencia de Cuenca en la historia del Ecuador." In *Cuenca y su futuro,* 19–93. Cuenca, Ecuador: CORDES.

Mangin, William

1974 "Latin American Squatter Settlements: A Problem and a Solution." In *Contemporary Cultures and Societies of Latin America,* edited by Dwight B. Heath, 340–365. 2d ed. New York: Random House.

Marcus, George E.

1998 *Ethnography through Thick and Thin.* Princeton, N.J.: Princeton University Press.

Marcus, George E., and Dick Cushman

1982 "Ethnographies as Texts." *Annual Review of Anthropology* 11: 25–69.

Massey, Douglas

1987 *Return to Aztlan: The Social Process of International Migration from Western Mexico.* Berkeley: University of California Press.

Maurer, Bill

2000 "Sexualities and Separate Spheres: Gender, Sexual Identity, and Work in Dominica and Beyond." In *Gender Matters: Rereading Michelle Z. Rosaldo,* edited by Alejandro Lugo and Bill Maurer, 90–115. Ann Arbor: University of Michigan Press.

McCarthy Brown, Karen

1991 *Mama Lola: A Voodoo Priestess in Brooklyn.* Berkeley: University of California Press.

McKee, Lauris

1980 "Ideals and Actualities: The Socialization of Gender-Appropriate Behavior in an Ecuadorian Village." Ph.D. diss., Cornell University.

1987 "Ethnomedical Treatments of Children's Diarrheal Illnesses in the Highlands of Ecuador." *Social Science and Medicine* 25: 1147–1155.

1997 "Women's Work in Rural Ecuador: Multiple Resource Strategy and the Gender Division of Labor." In *Women and Economic Change: Andean Perspectives,* edited by Ann Miles and Hans Buechler, 13–30. Society for Latin American Anthropology Publication Series, vol. 14. Washington, D.C.: American Anthropological Association.

1999 "Men's Rights/Women's Wrongs: Domestic Violence in Ecuador." In *To Have and to Hit,* edited by Dorothy Ayers Counts, Judith K. Brown, and Jacquelyn C. Campbell, 168–186. Urbana: University of Illinois Press.

Meisch, Lynn

1992 " 'We Will Not Dance on the Tomb of Our Grandparents': Five Hundred Years of Resistance in Ecuador." *Latin American Anthropology Review* 4 (2): 55–74.

1998 "Azuay Province." In *Costume and Identity in Highland Ecuador,* edited by Ann P. Rowe, 254–262. Seattle: University of Washington Press.

Melhuus, Marit

1997 "Exploring the Work of a Compassionate Ethnographer: The Case of Oscar Lewis." *Social Anthropology* 5 (1): 35–54.

Middleton, DeWight

1981 "Ecuadorian Transformations: An Urban View." In *Cultural Transformations and Ethnicity in Modern Ecuador,* edited by Norman Whitten Jr., 211–232. Urbana: University of Illinois Press.

Miles, Ann

1994 "Helping Out at Home: Gender Socialization, Moral Development, and Devil Stories in Cuenca, Ecuador." *Ethos* 22 (2): 132–157.

1997 "The High Cost of Leaving: Illegal Emigration from Cuenca, Ecuador, and Family Separation." In *Women and Economic Change: Andean Perspectives,* edited by Ann Miles and Hans C. Buechler, 55–74. Society for Latin American Anthropology Publication Series, vol. 14. Washington, D.C.: American Anthropological Association.

2000 "Poor Adolescent Girls and Social Transformations in Cuenca, Ecuador." *Ethos* 28 (1): 54–74.

Mills, Marybeth

1999 *Thai Women in the Global Labor Force: Consuming Desires, Contested Selves.* New Brunswick, N.J.: Rutgers University Press.

Mintz, Sidney W., and Eric R. Wolf

1950 "An Analysis of Ritual Co-Parenthood (*Compadrazgo*)." *Southwestern Journal of Anthropology* 6 (4): 341–368.

Moser, Caroline

1987 "The Experience of Poor Women in Guayaquil." In *Sociology of Developing Societies,* edited by Eduardo Archetti, Patricia Cammack, and Brian Roberts, 305–320. New York: Monthly Review Press.

Naranjo, Marcelo F.

1981 "Political Dependency, Ethnicity and Cultural Transformations in Manta." In *Cultural Transformations and Ethnicity in Modern Ecuador,* edited by Norman Whitten Jr., 95–120. Urbana: University of Illinois Press.

Nash, June, and M. P. Fernandez-Kelly

1983   *Women, Men and the International Division of Labor.* Albany: State University of New York Press.

Oboler, Suzanne

1999   "Racializing Latinos in the United States: Towards a New Research Paradigm." In *Identities on the Move: Transnational Processes in North America and the Caribbean Basin,* edited by Liliana R. Goldin, 45–67. Albany: Institute for Mesoamerican Studies, State University of New York at Albany.

Ong, Aihwa

1999   *Flexible Citizenship: The Cultural Logic of Transnationality.* Durham, N.C.: Duke University Press.

Oths, Kathryn S.

1999   "*Debilidad:* A Biocultural Assessment of an Embodied Andean Illness." *Medical Anthropology Quarterly* 13 (3): 286–315.

Palomeque, Silvia

1990   *Cuenca en el siglo XIX: La articulación de una región.* Quito: Abya-Yala.

Perlman, Janice

1976   *The Myth of Marginality.* Berkeley: University of California Press.

Pessar, Patricia R.

1982   "The Role of Households in International Migration and the Case of U.S. Bound Migration from the Dominican Republic." *International Migration Review* 16 (2): 342–364.

Pitkin, Kathryn, and Ritha Bedoya

1997   "Women's Multiple Roles in Economic Development: Constraints and Adaptation." *Latin American Perspectives* 95 (24): 34–49.

Pribilsky, Jason

2001   " 'Nervios' and 'Modern' Childhood: Migration and Shifting Contexts of Child Life in the Ecuadorian Andes." *Childhood: A Journal of Global Research* 8 (2): 251–273.

2002   "Living the *Chulla Vida.*" In *Personal Encounters in Anthropology: An Introductory Reader,* edited by Linda Walford and April Seivert, 174–179. London: Mayfield.

Radcliffe-Brown, A. R.

1952   *Structure and Function in Primitive Society.* New York: Macmillan.

Rahier, Jean Muteba

1998   "Blackness, the Racial/Spatial Order, Migrations and Miss Ecuador 1995–96." *American Anthropologist* 100 (2): 421–430.

Reid, Barbara, and Jaan Valsiner

1986   "Consistency, Praise and Love: Folk Theories of American Parents." *Ethos* 14 (3): 282–305.

Ricoeur, Paul

1992   *Oneself as Another.* Chicago: University of Chicago Press.

Rogers, Mark
1998   "Spectacular Bodies: Folklorization and the Politics of Identity in
         Ecuadorian Beauty Pageants." *Journal of Latin American Anthropology* 3
         (2): 54–85.
Rosaldo, Michelle Z.
1974   "Women, Culture and Society: A Theoretical Overview." In *Woman,
         Culture and Society,* edited by Michelle Rosaldo and Louise Lamphere,
         17–42. Stanford: Stanford University Press.
Roseberry, William
1989   *Anthropologies and Histories: Essays in Culture, History and Political Econ-
         omy.* New Brunswick, N.J.: Rutgers University Press.
Rothstein, Frances
1983   "Men and Women in Family Economy: An Analysis of the Relation-
         ship between the Sexes in Three Peasant Communities." *Anthropologi-
         cal Quarterly* 56 (1): 1–23.
Rouse, Roger
1992   "Making Sense of Settlement: Class Transformation, Cultural Struggle
         and Transnationalism among Mexican Migrants in the United States."
         In *Towards a Transnational Perspective on Migration: Race, Ethnicity, and
         Nationalism Reconsidered,* edited by Nina Glick Schiller, Linda Basch,
         and Cristina Blanc-Szanton, 25–51. Annals of the New York Academy
         of Sciences, vol. 645. New York: New York Academy of Sciences.
Rowe, William, and Vivian Shelling
1991   *Memory and Modernity: Popular Culture in Latin America.* London: Verso.
Salomon, Frank
1981   "Killing the Yumbo: A Ritual Drama of Northern Quito." In *Cultural
         Transformations and Ethnicity in Modern Ecuador,* edited by Norman Whit-
         ten, Jr., 162–208. Urbana: University of Illinois Press.
Sánchez-Parga, José
1997   *Antropo-lógicas andinas.* Quito: Abya-Yala.
Scheper-Hughes, Nancy
1992   *Death without Weeping: The Violence of Everyday Life in Brazil.* Berkeley:
         University of California Press.
Schiller, Nina Glick, Linda Basch, and Cristina Blanc-Szanton
1992   "Transnationalism: A New Analytic Framework for Understanding
         Migration." In *Towards a Transnational Perspective on Migration: Race, Class,
         Ethnicity, and Nationalism Reconsidered,* edited by Nina Glick Schiller,
         Linda Basch, and Cristina Blanc-Szanton, 1–24. Annals of the New
         York Academy of Sciences, vol. 645. New York: New York Academy
         of Sciences.
Scott, Alison MacEwen
1986   "Women in Latin America: Stereotypes and Social Science." *Bulletin
         of Latin American Research* 5 (2): 21–27.

Scott, James C.

1985   *Weapons of the Weak: Everyday Forms of Peasant Resistance*. New Haven: Yale University Press.

Scott, Joan

1986   "Gender: A Useful Category of Analysis." *American Historical Review* 91 (5): 1053–1075.

Scrimshaw, Susan C.

1975   "Families in Cities: A Study of Changing Values, Fertility and Socio-economic Status among Urban In-Migrants." In *Population and Social Organization,* edited by Moni Nag, 309–330. The Hague: Mouton.

Serrano, Enrique

1991   "Situación actual de la economía del Azuay y perspectivas." In *Cuenca y su futuro,* 173–203. Cuenca: CORDES.

Silverblatt, Irene

1987   *Moon, Sun and Witches.* Princeton: Princeton University Press.

Sinha, Sudha

1985   "Maternal Strategies for Regulating Children's Behavior." *Journal of Cross-Cultural Psychology* 16 (1): 27–40.

Skar, Sarah Lund

1994   *Lives Together—Worlds Apart: Quechua Colonization in Jungle and City.* Oslo: Scandinavian University Press.

Stark, Louisa R.

1981   "Folk Models of Stratification and Ethnicity in the Highlands of Northern Ecuador." In *Cultural Transformations and Ethnicity in Modern Ecuador,* edited by Norman E. Whitten Jr., 387–401. Urbana: University of Illinois Press.

Stephen, Lynn

1991   *Zapotec Women.* Austin: University of Texas Press.

Stevens, Evelyn P.

1973   "*Marianismo:* The Other Face of Machismo in Latin America." In *Female and Male in Latin America,* edited by Ann Pescatello, 89–101. Pittsburgh: University of Pittsburgh Press.

Stolen, Kristi Anne

1987   *A media voz: Relaciones de género en la Sierra Ecuatoriana.* Quito: CEPLAES.

1991   "Gender, Sexuality and Violence in Ecuador." *Ethnos* 56 (1–2): 82–100.

Striffler, Steve

2002   *In the Shadows of State and Capital: The United Fruit Company, Popular Struggle, and Agrarian Restructuring in Ecuador, 1990–1995.* Durham, N.C.: Duke University Press.

Stutzman, Ronald

1981   "*El Mestizaje:* An All-Inclusive Ideology of Exclusion." In *Cultural Trans-*

formations and Ethnicity in Modern Ecuador, edited by Norman E. Whitten, Jr., 45–94. Urbana: University of Illinois Press.

Taussig, Michael T.

1980 *The Devil and Commodity Fetishism in South America.* Chapel Hill: University of North Carolina Press.

Tomlinson, John

1991 *Cultural Imperialism: A Critical Introduction.* Baltimore: Johns Hopkins University Press.

Tousignant, Michel

1989 "Sadness, Depression and Social Reciprocity in Highland Ecuador." *Social Science and Medicine* 28 (9): 899–904.

United States Department of Justice

1996 *Statistical Handbook of the Immigration and Naturalization Service.* Washington, D.C.: Government Printing Service.

Weismantel, Mary J.

1988 *Food, Gender, and Poverty in the Ecuadorian Andes.* Pittsburgh: University of Pennsylvania Press.

1995 "Making Kin: Kinship Theory and Zumbaguan Adoptions." *American Ethnologist* 22 (4): 685–709.

1997 "Time, Work-Discipline and Beans: Indigenous Self-Determination in the Northern Andes." In *Women and Economic Change: Andean Perspectives,* edited by Ann Miles and Hans C. Buechler, 31–54. Society for Latin American Anthropology Publication Series, vol. 14. Washington, D.C.: American Anthropological Association.

2001 *Cholas and Pishtacos: Stories of Race and Sex in the Andes.* Chicago: University of Chicago Press.

Weiss, Wendy

1988 "The Structure of, and Contradictions in, Male Authority in Urban Households in Quito, Ecuador." Michigan State Women in Development Series, Working Paper #163, March.

1990 "Challenge to Authority: Bakhtin and Ethnographic Description." *Cultural Anthropology* 5 (4): 414–430.

1997 "Debt and Devaluation: The Burden on Ecuador's Popular Class." *Latin American Perspectives* 24 (4): 9–33.

Whiting, Beatrice B., and John W. M. Whiting

1975 *Children of Six Cultures: A Psycho-Cultural Analysis.* Cambridge, Mass.: Harvard University Press.

Whitten, E. Norman, Jr.

1981 "Introduction." In *Cultural Transformations and Ethnicity in Modern Ecuador,* edited by Norman E. Whitten, 1–41. Urbana: University of Illinois Press.

Wikan, Unni

2000 "With Life in One's Lap: The Story of an Eye/I (or Two)." In *Narra-*

tive and the Cultural Construction of Illness and Healing, edited by Cheryl Mattingly and Linda C. Garro, 212–235. Berkeley: University of California Press.

Wolf, Diana L.

1990   "Daughters, Decisions and Domination: An Empirical and Conceptual Critique of Household Strategies." *Development and Change* 21: 43–74.

Index